# UNDERSTANDING
# ARABS

## FIFTH EDITION

*A Contemporary Guide to Arab Society*

Margaret K. Nydell

D0097200

INTERCULTURAL PRESS
*an imprint of Nicholas Brealey Publishing*

Boston • London

First published by Nicholas Brealey Publishing in 2012, updated in 2014.

20 Park Plaza, Suite 610          3-5 Spafield Street, Clerkenwell
Boston, MA 02116, USA          London, EC1R 4QB, UK
Tel: + 617-523-3801          Tel: +44 (0)20 7239 0360
Fax: + 617-523-3708          Fax: +44 (0)20 7239 0370
www.nicholasbrealey.com

Printed in the United States of America
16   15   14      3   4   5

ISBN: 978-0-98395-580-1

**Library of Congress Cataloging-in-Publication Data**
Nydell, Margaret K.
  Understanding Arabs : A Contemporary Huide to Arab Society /
Margaret K. Nydell. — 5th ed.
    p. cm.
  Includes bibliographical references.
  ISBN 978-0-98395-580-1 (pbk.)
 1. Arabs. I. Title.
  DS36.77.N93 2012
  909'.04927--dc23
                     2011044169

with her special linguistic expertise to offer today's students insights they are obliged to critically consider before study or research abroad. The accessible presentation succeeds in humanizing as it reveals both the difficult issues and the abiding values that govern peoples' experiences. Nydell reminds us that in the Middle East and North Africa there will be much more to grasp as continued rapid change alters those lives daily."

—Terrence M. Potter, Visiting Associate Professor,
   Georgetown University

"This latest edition of *Understanding Arabs* is a great introduction to the Arab world for both the general public and college students who wish to expand their knowledge of the region. Nydell's book is of tremendous use in the classroom, as it engages the cultural, linguistic, religious and political diversity of the Arab peoples and the Arab lands."

—Douja Mariem Mamelouk, Assistant Professor, French and
   Arabic Literatures, University of Tennessee, Knoxville.

Praise for Previous Editions of
*Understanding Arabs*

"For fifteen years, Margaret Nydell's *Understanding Arabs* has been used by countless Americans preparing to work or live in the Arab world. It is a unique source; there is nothing like it. Written with wit as well as seriousness, it provides a sound cultural appreciation and basic data on the region . . . Her personal message of the tragic events of September 11 should be required reading by all who make decisions or write commentary on the Arab world.

—Max L. Gross, Joint Military Intelligence College

"Middle East specialists have long relied on their worn copies of *Understanding Arabs* for insights about Arab social behavior . . . A whole generation of U.S. diplomats were introduced to the subject by Dr. Nydell in the 1970s and 1980s. In this concise and practical guide, she shares her wealth of scholarly and real-world experience, and she does so without the psycho-babble that too often dominates the other surveys of the subject.

—Ambassador David L. Mack, Vice President, Middle East Institute

# BRIEF CONTENTS

# CONTENTS

# A Message from the Author

I wrote the first edition of *Understanding Arabs* in the 1980s to provide background and context for increasing cultural awareness between Westerners and Arabs. Since then, the world has been bombarded with conflicting images of Arab culture, from planes flying into the World Trade Center, to Arabs crying in grief over the actions of their extremist counterparts; from the self-immolation of a twenty-seven-year-old Tunisian street vendor that launched the "Arab Spring," to the joyous faces of Tunisians voting in the October 2011 open election for the Constituent Assembly. The highs and lows of human nature apply to Arabs as they apply to all other cultures. Still, it is no wonder that Westerners (Americans and Europeans) don't know what to believe when it comes to Arabs. These contradictory images involve one of the most ancient, complex, and interesting cultures in the world.

Arabs are the people in some eighteen countries who speak the Arabic language. The term *Arab* does not mean that they have the same ethnic (Arabian) origin. Rather, *Arab* is a cultural and political term, and Arabs are not all alike—they speak different dialects of the language and there are regional differences in customs and appearance. Contrary to the widespread belief, not all Arabs are Muslim. Muslims make up 95 percent of Arabs, while 5 percent are Christians, mainly in Lebanon, Egypt, Jordan, and Syria. A few thousand Jews live in Arab countries, principally in Morocco, and also in Tunisia, Egypt, and Syria. Muslims are spread throughout the world, and only 20 percent of them are Arabs (see the Preface).

The Arabs have always been in the news because of the strategic location of the region, linking Europe, Africa, and Asia. Oil resources in many countries have led to their geopolitical prominence. Now they dominate the news because of the people, who have impressed the world with their brave calls for freedom of thought, governance, and human rights. 2011 and 2012 saw anti-government demonstrations in most Arab countries, calling for Islamist or democratic rule and the end of their authoritarian systems, some of which have been in place for thirty years or more. This movement, this "Arab Spring," was led by ordinary common people from the younger generation, age thirty and under. Their activities enhanced the image of Arabs worldwide.

## ❋ THE ARAB SPRING

The year 2011 opened with stunning news from the Middle East: the overthrows of the governments of Tunisia and Egypt—Tunisia in a month and Egypt after seventeen days. Such uprisings were an unprecedented event in the Arab world. New ways of thinking and new aspirations have been developing, with communication among the demonstrators greatly facilitated through the electronic social media such as Facebook and Twitter. Wael Ghoneim, who instigated the Egyptian opposition, said, "The revolution started on Facebook." (1) It would have occurred anyway, as previous revolutions have, but not as quickly and not with such a large number of protesters.

The Arab people have become so energized and hopeful that they continue bravely making demands despite sometimes brutal government reprisals. Regardless of the final outcomes, the people want change. The Arab Spring rebellions occurred seemingly all at once; this was a social and political problem just waiting to boil over. It was a watershed event, and the surface stability imposed by repressive governments will never be the same.

The first uprising was in Tunisia, spurred by a seemingly routine (but highly significant) event. A poor street vendor in Tunisia was abused by a police officer and, in his despair, set himself on fire in front of a police station. This shocked the people and pushed them to indignant action, with very fast results: the president, Ben Ali, departed the country after just a month.

In Egypt, a longstanding resistance had been forming too, enabled by communication through Facebook in particular. Action was initiated after a young man was beaten to death by police. Again, it was one symbolic action that brought forth the latent outrage. The Egyptians massed in a downtown square every day and relentlessly called for the end of the Mubarak regime until they had success. Their demand was granted after seventeen days. Now it remains for both Tunisia and Egypt to work out their future governing systems. In each country, there is concern about Islamists in the government, as well as the presence of figures from the old regimes. Egypt's government was overtly Islamist, with the military a constant presence.

Resistance and demands for political and economic reform, for a time, caught on virtually everywhere in the Arab world. The ideas took on a depth and momentum that propelled the demonstrators to face violence and overcome fear of their despotic regimes.

In Bahrain, the Shia majority (70 percent) rebelled against the Sunni government headed by a hereditary Emir. This rebellion was decisively crushed when the government arrested demonstrators en masse, largely through intervention of the Saudi army (Saudi Arabia also contains its own restive Shia).

A rebellion in Yemen was met with harsh reprisals. The president, Ali Abdullah Saleh, left the country, then returned, then left again in early 2012 for medical care. In February, a new president, Abed Rabbo Mansour Hadi, was sworn in. The new government is not entirely in control. Islamists oppose the government with violent attacks and suicide bombings. There is a strong secessionist movement in the south.

Libya is in a real state of flux. President Qaddhafi was killed in October 2011, and much readjustment is coming. Libya has formed a government and officials try to mediate among different factions of the opposition. Early on, the Eastern part broke away and formed its own state. This is a natural division; Libya was three entities until united by Italy after World War I. Unity was promoted by President Qaddhafi and most Libyans want this to continue. Potentially, however, a civil war looms.

Finally, Syria has experienced much turmoil and many civilian deaths, as the highly centralized Assad regime continues to imprison and kill large numbers of the demonstrators, with no end in sight. More than 150,000 were killed by early 2014. Entire cities have been besieged and chaos reigns. To date, international sanctions and statements of condemnation have had no effect. Nine million Syrians have been displaced from their homes.

In other countries, including Morocco, Algeria, and Jordan, spontaneous demands made by demonstrators have led to promises of reform by governments. Lebanon has had demonstrations, but its government is relatively open and so far has absorbed dissent. In the wealthy Arabian Peninsula (Saudi Arabia and the Arabian Gulf states), the rulers, with the exception of Bahrain, have confronted demands, but so far, they have been able to buy off or placate the people with stipends and promised economic growth, as well as more elected positions in the government.

As methods of governing change, Islamism has become dominant, although many people would prefer secular, democratic rule. Some fear that an Islamic state would eventually become repressive, thus replacing one authoritarian government with another. But the majority of voters elected Islamists in Tunisia and Morocco, as well as Egypt.

The Arab Spring has been effective, as the people aspire to create more representative governments. All leaders have promised economic reform to ensure higher employment and more equitable distribution of wealth. The demands will not go away. None of the regional governments can complacently stay as they were before this call to transform their societies. The protesters have taken attention in the media from the constant news about terrorism in the Arab world. This is certainly a time of transition.

## ❁ Terrorism

Equally as newsworthy as the Arab Spring—and the source of much misunderstanding between Westerners and Arabs—is terrorism. We have just passed the tenth anniversary of the attacks on September 11, 2001, the worst terrorist attack in American history. This event changed the public mindset in the United States, and all Americans know where they were when they first heard the news of planes crashing into the Pentagon and the World Trade Center. I was in Washington, D.C., and in the late morning that day I walked from the Georgetown University campus and crossed the Key Bridge into Virginia. I found many buildings evacuated, public transportation stopped, and all roads going past the Pentagon blocked off. I finally found a taxi, and the driver assured me that he would help me get home to Crystal City by skirting around the Pentagon area and going far into the Virginia suburbs. He did so, using small residential streets, until I was close enough to walk home. It took over an hour. He was Pakistani and Muslim. He was near tears. (I was crying openly.) He did not want to take any money. He said he was going to do this all day as a public service. I gave him money anyway and told him that if he didn't want to take it, he could donate it to charity.

The September 11 terrorist attacks left Americans and millions of others around the world bewildered as well as shocked and angry. As the smoke cleared following the September 11 terrorist attacks, a Saudi Arab, Osama Bin Laden, became identified as the chief perpetrator, commanding a network called Al-Qaeda (pronounced al-KAH-e-da, not al-KAY-da), which was previously unknown to the general public. Its known members and accomplices were mostly Arabs and all Muslims.

People all over the world asked why. The media, impelled as always to provide instant answers, came up with a variety of theories of varying degrees of merit. Some of them were based on popular misconceptions about Muslims, notably:

- ❋ This is a religion- and culture-based clash: the "clash of civilizations" theory. The Bin Laden group and others like it are characterized as representative of the thinking of the majority of Muslims.
- ❋ The attackers (and others who "hate America") are envious of the American way of life. They want to change American values and eliminate American freedoms.
- ❋ These particular attackers were motivated by visions of rewards in Paradise because for them this was a Jihad (a so-called Holy War) against infidels.

All of these explanations are incorrect. They do not conform to the facts. They confuse the motives of this particular terrorist group with the prevailing discontent in the Islamic world. But the Al Qaeda group did not come out of nothing; it is an aberrant, cult-like faction that grew out of the Middle East milieu.* This and other terrorist acts are rooted in *political* grievances, expressing anger at American actions and policies through terrorist violence.

---

*Al Qaeda arose from a puritanical version of Islam, Wahhabism (also called *Salafism*), which is followed officially only in Saudi Arabia. It is also the prevailing interpretation of Islam among the Taliban in Afghanistan. This version of Islam forbids, for example, theaters and churches. It forbids the marking of graves. No alcohol or pork products may be imported. Publications are censored. Government-appointed officials enforce the law that requires all commercial establishments to close during prayer time. Wahhabis require women to cover their faces. This puritanical Islam is not practiced elsewhere.

Statements such as "They hate American freedom" and "They want to destroy America" do not satisfy for long; they are impossibly vague. As time passes, we have identified reasons that make more sense. We must dig deeper, because unless the terrorists are all crazy or all evil, there must be more accurate reasons. If the statements listed here were true, they would lead us to despair, then to defiance, and ultimately back to despair.

Resentments against the United States in particular have grown out of a context with which few Americans are familiar. The resentments are not primarily against American wealth and power as such. Rather, many people in the Middle East are profoundly angry at how they *perceive* America using its wealth and power when dealing with other countries and regions.

Perceptions become realities to people who hold them, and people who lack cross-cultural experience can easily misunderstand the attitudes and behaviors they confront. Americans are notoriously ill-informed about the Middle East. In turn, the average Middle Eastern individual actually knows very little about Western (American and European) societies. Each side has enormous misconceptions about the other.

Language is a huge barrier. If we accept the premise that all people express themselves more accurately and candidly in their own language, then we should be skeptical about statements being reported from conversations with foreigners, filtered through English or other languages. Unfortunately, too many of our Middle East experts and reporters do not speak the local languages (imagine an expert on the U.S. who did not speak English). Thus they have severely limited access to information, and they may gravitate toward people with whom they can communicate easily, people who sometimes misrepresent the thinking of the general populace.

There are many arguments that can be made on both sides, but one thing is certain: the language barrier accounts for much of the misunderstanding. In the forty years I have been listening to political discussions in Arabic, among Arabs who were talking to one another and not to me, I have never heard resentment expressed about anything American except for foreign policy. Middle Easterners in general care only about American activities that negatively affect their own lives. Consider the following explanations offered by the terrorist leaders and others we have associated with terrorist movements. We must not ignore what they are saying; we must try to understand their statements, recognizing that this does not require agreeing with them:

- ❁ Bin Laden, 2001: "They violate our land and occupy it and steal the Muslims' possessions, and when faced with resistance, they call it terrorism. . . . What America is tasting now is something insignificant compared with what we have tasted for scores of years. Our nation has been tasting this humiliation and this degradation for more than eighty years."†(2)
- ❁ Muhammad Omar, former leader of the Taliban: "America has created the evil that is attacking it . . . the United States should step back and review its policy." (3)
- ❁ Ayatollah Sayyed Ali Khamanei, religious leader in Iran: "We are neither with you nor with the terrorists. . . . They [America] expect the entire world to help them because their interests demand it. Do they ever care about others' interests? These are the characteristics that make America so hated in the world."

   None of these statements express threats that any group or faction is setting out to conquer the United States, force it to change its society, or impose its own ways of thinking on us. The September 11, 2001, attacks were not aimed at targets like the Statue of Liberty, a cathedral, or a packed baseball stadium, but at structures that symbolize U.S. economic and military power.

   How do Americans respond to this kind of criticism? Righteous indignation is natural but not very productive over time. We need to examine the anti-American statements and try to understand the context out of which they come. It is not appeasement to search for knowledge we do not currently have. How can terrorist acts be prevented from happening again if the *real reasons* for the acts are left undiscovered—or worse, ignored? In my opinion one of the most tragic aspects of this trauma has been that thousands of victims and families are left damaged or bereaved, and they do not know why this happened to them. Perhaps this book can help.

   I offer here some salient points that I believe must be considered as the world's people decide how as nations they will cope with very real

---

†Few Americans who hear this know what happened in the 1920s (see Chapter 12).

terrorist threats. My purpose is to list what I believe to be objective facts rather than to interject recommendations or to suggest specific solutions.

- ❈  Mainstream Muslims do not approve of terrorist acts. In fact they are horrified. The decision to engage in terrorism is the response of fanatic, misguided cult-mentality groups. Terrorism is in no way supported by the doctrines of the Islamic religion, which has always placed emphasis on human relationships and social justice. (There is much material on this topic, some of it available on the Internet.)
- ❈  Al-Qaeda group members in the 9/11 incident disguised themselves as immigrants to the U.S. who wanted to share in the bounties of the West, thus taking advantage of the good reputation Middle Eastern immigrants have earned. As a group, the immigrants to the U.S. are known to be industrious and family-centered. The terrorists had an entirely different agenda and betrayed these people.
- ❈  Mainstream Muslims do not want to change Western (or other non-Muslim) cultures. Many Muslims do not want some Western values to enter their own societies, but so long as their own lives are not affected, Muslims (and Middle Easterners in general) are not concerned with how Westerners and others structure their own lives. The vast majority do not resent Western prosperity and freedom; in fact, millions of them immigrate to the West because they admire many of the social values and want to participate in Western society. They want their children to grow up free and with the possibility of prosperity.
- ❈  We must not allow a cult or extremist subgroup to represent an entire religion. The bombing of abortion clinics is not justified by mainstream Christian faith. Sectarian violence in Ireland does not represent mainstream Protestantism or Catholicism.
- ❈  Muslims, Arabs, and other Middle Easterners do not blame Americans as individuals. Their assumption, right or wrong, is that the people of the United States cannot be held personally responsible because they are generally unaware of their government's activities abroad. Americans are known in other nations

as being uninformed about their country's foreign policies. (Less obvious to Middle Easterners is the fact that many Americans, at least prior to 9/11, also didn't care.) Unlike the terrorists' sympathizers, most Middle Easterners have genuinely grieved for innocent lives lost in any violent warlike act. They are like people everywhere.

❊ The 9/11 attack was not a real Jihad. The term *Jihad*, as used in mainstream Islam, is misunderstood. In fact, its primary meaning is not "Holy War," although that has become its meaning in Western languages. Most pertinent here, a true Jihad must be a response to an overt attack or threat made by non-Muslims toward the Muslim community. *Muslims may not initiate a Jihad.* The terrorists have interpreted Western, and most recently U.S., political and military power in the Middle East as an attack on their people.

❊ The terrorists are trying to promote enmity between Islam and Christianity. They are misusing the term *Jihad* just as they misuse terms like *Crusade, infidel,* and *unbeliever.* The term *Jihad* has become politicized and is constantly being invoked and misused for *political purposes.* During the war between Iraq and Iran, for example, each declared a Jihad against the other.

❊ The Qur'an and other Muslim sacred scriptures, like those of other religions, are long, complex, and open to wide-ranging interpretations. Emphasis on details such as presumed rewards in Paradise for people who die in a Jihad are, frankly, irrelevant and insulting to most educated Muslims. Muslims are not religiously motivated in any way to harm or kill non-Muslims. As with any body of sacred scripture, a selective choice of quotes can "prove" anything, including completely opposite ideas.

❊ Focusing on Islamic terrorists is too narrow a goal. It will not end the threat. These terrorists are short-term enemies, current targets against whom the United States wages war. But even if the groups are eliminated, *the root causes of resentment will continue to exist.* The U.S. must reverse the negative perceptions about itself, and this cannot be done by force. No security is effective enough to prevent an attack by a person who is willing to commit suicide. Long-term strategic thinking is needed.

Sweeping statements that are frightening but do not suggest a remedy are not a solution. What use is a statement such as "Terrorism threatens all humanity"(4)? If American leaders blindly declare that the terrorists hate Americans for their freedom and democracy, where does it lead? It does not help in framing an appropriate response. If the United States and the Western world continue to ignore accusations, especially those they do not fully understand, they do so at their own peril. What brings forth statements that America is "morally corrupt and hypocritical"?(5) Why is America accused of "supporting state-sponsored terrorism"?(6) These are the types of statements that must be thoughtfully considered.

This book is intended to shed light on the causes of anti-Western terrorism, especially anti-Americanism, as a first step in addressing the problem. But this book is decidedly not about politics or U.S. policy; it is about understanding. I hope it will contribute to policies that help keep our country safe.

## ❊ LOOKING TO THE FUTURE

There is much hope for the future. Despite political problems, Arabs as a whole like America and Americans, and Westerners in general. They continue to immigrate to the U.S., Canada, Australia, and Europe. They admire orderly Western societies and want to benefit from political freedom and better economic opportunities. They want to escape despotic governments (and now there is finally hope of change).

We sometimes read outrageous statements made about each other's culture, invariably by ignorant people or those with a political or religious agenda. Unfortunately, these get into the news, especially on the Internet. They do a lot of damage, because many people assume that such characterizations represent everyone in the other culture.

But this is balanced by the great mass of ordinary, well-intentioned people who are open to new ideas. I have lived among Arabs in the Middle East for four decades now and I have seen the goodwill and curiosity of those I meet. On the whole, they are nice people, in many ways not all that different from us.

An Arab saying is "Seek knowledge" (Utlub al-'ilm), and another is "Kindness is a mark of faith" (Al-hanan 'allamat al-iman). May we learn to understand and be good to each other.

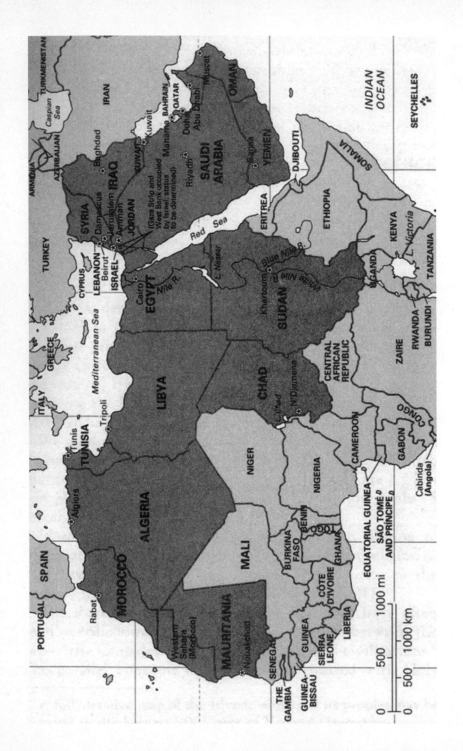

# PREFACE

*Understanding Arabs: A Contemporary Guide to Arab Society* is a handbook, intended to be read, easily and quickly, by people who are not specialists in the Middle East. The purpose of this book is to assist ordinary people, especially Westerners in America and Europe, to *understand* modern-day Arabs. This includes looking at the thought patterns, social relationships, and ways of life of urban Arabs in the twenty-first century. The majority of today's Arabs, the people we are likely to encounter in the media or in person, are mostly middle class (or slightly above or below), not exotic Bedouins from the desert. It is time to get away from "the Bedouin ethos."‡ When you picture an Arab in your mind, think of a computer programmer who lives in a high-rise building.

It is essential that we look at Arabs realistically as they are *today*, and not attempt to describe and explain them in terms of Middle East history that goes back centuries. Ancient and medieval history cannot be used to provide *reasons* for the present-day nature of Arab society—there have been too many changes, especially in the last one hundred years, approximately since the end of World War I. I think we have heard quite enough about pre-Islamic Arabia, the Muslim conquests, the eleventh-century Assassins, the twelfth- and thirteenth-century Golden Age, the harems, the House of War, the dragomans in Ottoman times, and the like. This information comes from outdated and sometimes discredited sources.

Most of us are aware of the degree to which different national and cultural groups stereotype each other, at a distance or in person-to-person

---

‡The Bedouin ethos is the basis for the code of chivalry brought to Europe in Crusader and post-Crusader times. It is no more relevant to the lives of modern Arabs than the Christian code of chivalry is to the lives of modern Westerners. Modern Arab society is not tied to the Bedouin ethos.

relations. When Westerners and Arabs interact, especially if neither understands the other, they often come away with impressions that are mutually negative.

Similarly, the Israeli-Palestinian conflict is about Israelis and Palestinians of today, who are not the same people referred to in the Bible as Hebrews and Ishmaelites (Arabians). Many Israelis are of European and other non-Semitic origins. The Palestinians are *Arabs* but not *Arabians* from the Arabian Peninsula.§ They are descended from indigenous populations such as Canaanites, Moabites, and Phoenicians. The current conflict is political, a clash over land, and has its origins entirely in the twentieth century.

It is important to understand that the conflict is *not* religious; Islam is far closer to Judaism than is Christianity. Muslims accept all of the Jewish prophets and many of their religious practices. Muslims have no historical grievance against Jews and did not engage in periodic persecutions as happened repeatedly in Europe, causing many Jews to flee south. However, after seventy years of bitter conflict, the religion of Judaism and the political ideology of Zionism have become mixed, by both sides. Still, I have never heard an Arab or a Muslim say anything negative about the Jewish faith, or Jews as people, *except in the context of Israel and its policies.*

The shared origins of Islam and Christianity have often been overshadowed by the historical conflicts between the two religions—the Crusader mentality, the clash of civilizations. Both religions have a concept of Holy War—Crusade and Jihad. Conflicts have accentuated the differences and polarized the West and the Middle East, obscuring the shared beliefs of the three great interrelated monotheistic faiths: Judaism, Christianity, and Islam.

A word about the title: *Arab* is a very general term, something like the word *European*. People in these groups have much in common, but

---

§The distinction between Arabs and Arabians is crucial and often blurred for political purposes. Confusing these groups leads to statements like "Jews . . . were settled in the country a thousand years before the coming of the Arabs [Arabians]" in A.D. 634. (1) Columnist Charles Krauthammer misspoke when he wrote: "Israel was the ancestral homesite of the first two Jewish commonwealths for a thousand years—long before Arabs [before the Arabian armies of the seventh century, but not the indigenous people], long before Islam, long before the Holocaust." (2) The reader can appreciate how explosive this simple factor is.

there are distinct regional differences. The term *Arab* is useful, though, in contexts such as the Arab League, the Arab world, and pan-Arabism. *Arab* refers not to ethnicity, but to *all Arabic-speaking people* regardless of origin or appearance.

*We must not confuse Arabs with Muslims.* There are eighteen Arab countries referred to here (it is a matter of definition; there are twenty-two members of the Arab League). There are 1.8 billion Muslims in the world and they are a majority in fifty-six countries. (3) There are currently about 360 million Arabs, 5 percent of whom are Christians or practice other religions. Owing primarily to immigration, Islam has become the second-largest religion in both the United States and Europe.¶ (4)

*Understanding Arabs* deals with the Arab countries in the Middle East and North Africa. It does *not* include the primarily Muslim but non-Arab populations in Turkey (where people speak a language of Mongolian origin) or the Middle Eastern countries in which people speak Aryan languages, which are part of the Indo-European language family: Iran (Persia), Afghanistan, Pakistan, and the Kurds. In contrast, Arabs outside of Africa, those in the center (Lebanon, Syria, Palestine, Jordan, Iraq) and the Arabian Peninsula, are Semitic in their ethnic origin. Semitic groups orginated in the Arabian Peninsula and include the Hebrews** and many Ethiopians.

Foreigners find very little material available to help them understand modern Arab society. Not much has been written on the subject of current cultural and social practices, either in Arabic or in Western languages. A great deal of the material that exists is thirty to forty years old and appears dated to anyone who is familiar with Arab society today.†† Some observations made two or three decades ago are no longer applicable. Many foreign writers and reporters have very limited contact with Arabs, often only government and military officials, intellectuals, the media, and

---

¶*Islam* is the name of the religion; the adjective is *Islamic* (like *Christianity, Christian*). A person who practices Islam is a *Muslim*.

**This is the origin of the term anti-Semitic.

††The well-known book *The Arab Mind* by Raphael Patai (5) was based on his residence in Jerusalem in the 1930s and 1940s, and his acquaintances during that era. He lived in the U.S. after 1947 and was a "frequent visitor" to the Jerusalem area. The book was outdated when it was published in 1973. It has continued to be published, most recently in 2002, *unchanged*. It is heavily based on the Bedouin ethos, and much other information is inaccurate, even outlandish. It should be read, if at all, with skepticism.

people who speak English. In recent years, changes in education, housing, health, technology, and the media (especially the Internet) have had a marked effect on attitudes and customs; this is well illustrated by the sudden appearance of uprisings and political opposition in many Arab countries in 2011, the so-called "Arab Spring."

The most serious deficiency in research about Arab society is the lack of attention given to the large majority of urban, educated (often Western-educated) Arabs. Researchers, especially anthropologists, have mostly focused on village life and nomadic groups and on the study of traditional, sometimes quaint, social patterns. Interesting as these studies are, they offer little directly applicable information for Westerners who will, for the most part, encounter Arabs who are well educated, well traveled, and sophisticated. Keep in mind that the large majority of the people (more than 95 percent) are never mentioned in the news, because they are getting on with their lives and do not engage in newsworthy activities.

This book is an attempt to fill that gap. It focuses on the middle and upper classes—businessmen and -women, bureaucrats, managers, scientists, professors, military officers, lawyers, banking officials, and intellectuals—and the way they interact with foreigners and with each other. At the same time, many traditions and customs still affect the Arabs' way of life, including their goals, values, and codes of accepted behavior. The many similarities among social groups and among the various Arab countries still outweigh the differences, so valid generalizations are possible. Any significant differences among groups will be pointed out.‡‡

Scholars have varying opinions about the sociological effort to characterize groups of people as the same, different, ahead, or behind. Multiculturalists say that all cultural practices are equally valid, so attempts at comparisons can be a form of racism. Other scholars are quick to criticize certain cultures and quick to draw their own conclusions, especially when compared to, in this case, the West. We hear of "cultural stagnation" and "cultural failure" and the justifications for creating such labels—it's amazing how observers, from historians to reporters to government officials,

---

‡‡The term *Arab* is so broadly used that many people wrongly assume that they are all one block of people. It is confusing, for example, to read about the "Janjaweed Arab militias" in south Sudan. They are called Arabs because they share the language and religion, but they have no other similarities, ethnically or culturally, with Arabs of the Middle East.

are never lacking in confidence when it comes to explaining what the Arabs think.

These opinions are often based on erudite references to events back through several centuries, and they come to sweeping conclusions such as "The fury of the Arab world is that it isn't really about us. It's about their own internal demons. . . . They prefer to blame others, to sleepwalk through history. . . . The truth is that Arabs have a deep inferiority complex. They're afraid they really might not be able to build a successful modern state, to say nothing of a postmodern, information-based society." (6) My goal, in contrast, is to present what most Arabs believe and leave it at that.

I hope that this book will help alleviate stereotyping in two ways:

1. By explaining some of the behavioral characteristics of Arabs in terms of cultural background, thereby deepening the reader's understanding and helping to avoid negative interpretations, and
2. By serving as a guide to cross-cultural interaction with Arabs, which will help Westerners avoid inadvertent insults and errors of etiquette, and help them make a favorable impression.

Westerners who interact with Arabs should be aware of the particular characteristics of Arab etiquette and patterns of behavior and thought, since the differences may be quite subtle and, initially, hard to identify. It is easy to be lulled into the security of assuming that the superficial similarities of appearance, dress, and lifestyle among educated Arabs mean that they are "just like us." One is more likely to remain alert for different social proprieties when seated in a tent or a village house; it is not so easy to remember the differences when seated in the living room of a modern Arab home, surrounded by Western-style furnishings and English-speaking Arabs.

Any attempt to describe the motives and values of an entire people is challenging. On the one hand, it leads to generalizations that are not true in all cases, and, on the other, it necessarily involves the observer's perspectives and interpretations and leads to emphasizing some traits over others. I hope to present a balanced view, one that is generally descriptive of Arabs throughout the entire cultural area of the Arab world. Most of the material in this book, including anecdotes (I have hundreds), comes from my own personal experiences and from interviews with others. These interviews have taken place in virtually all of the Arab countries—in North Africa, the Levant, the Fertile Crescent, and the Arabian Peninsula.

American college students return from a stay in the Arab world enthusiastic, even effusive, in their praise of the Arab people they have come to know, and they are anxious to find a way to go back. "They are so friendly . . . they were so nice to me . . . everyone was helpful . . . people in public would say 'Welcome' in English . . . I loved sitting in a cafe playing backgammon with Syrians and Iraqis"—not what we would expect based on media images.

There are many delightful surprises that await foreigners as they come to know more: the hospitality, the wonderful food, the kindness to children and elderly people, the large, loving families. But this is not a book for tourist agencies. We also need to look at the problem areas, as many of them as possible, in order for this book to be helpful. Many factors can lead to mistaken interpretations, on both sides, and perhaps *lead to serious errors in judgment.*

The Arabs have been subjected to so much direct or indirect criticism by the West that they are very sensitive to a Westerner's statements about them. I have made an effort here to be fair, honest, and at the same time, sympathetic to the Arab way of life, especially when contrasting Arab and Western cultural behavior. Value judgments do not belong here; there is no assumption that one cultural approach is better than another.

**Note:** Arabic words may be written in English in their conventional spelling, or spelled in a way that is closer to the actual Arabic pronunciation. Both ways are fine; it depends on your purpose. We see variant spellings: *Moslem/Muslim, Mohammed/Muhammad, Koran/Qur'an*, and names with *Abdul/Abdel*. You will also see the prefix *al-* (or *el-*, *il-*, *ul-*), which means *the* and is often included in names.

Finally, the word *Shiite* in English was coined so we could add *-s* and make it look like an English plural. In Arabic, the singular is *Shii* and the plural is *Shia*. *Shia* is the term used in this book.

# INTRODUCTION: PATTERNS OF CHANGE

Arab society has been subjected to enormous pressures from the outside world, particularly since World War II. Social change is evident everywhere because the effects of economic modernization and political experimentation have been felt in all areas of life. Even for nomads and residents of remote villages, the traditional way of life is disappearing.

## ❀ MODERNIZATION

Most social change has come through the adoption of Western technology, consumer products, healthcare systems, financial structures, educational concepts, and political ideas. These changes, necessarily, are controversial but inevitable and are present to varying degrees in all of the Arab countries.

The Arab nations have experienced an influx of foreign advisers, managers, businesspeople, teachers, engineers, healthcare and military personnel, diplomats, politicians, and tourists. Through personal contact and increased media exposure, Arabs have learned how outsiders live. Thousands of Arab students have been educated in the West and have returned with changed habits and attitudes. The spread of the Internet has had a major impact as well.

Tens of thousands of Westerners live, or have lived, in the Arab world, and most of them love the experience. Many stay on for years and have a wide circle of Arab friends. They comment that human relations seem deeper, and friendships, even business transactions, feel more personal and meaningful than in Western societies.

Arab governments are building schools, hospitals, housing units, airports, and industrial complexes so fast that entire cities and towns change their appearance in a few years—it is easy to feel lost in some Arab cities even if you have been away only a year or two. Modern hotels are found in any large city; the streets and roads are jammed with cars; and the telephone, fax, and Internet services are often overtaxed. Imported consumer products, ranging from white wedding dresses to goods in supermarkets, are abundant in most Arab countries. While these are surface changes, they also symbolize deeper shifts in values.

Overall rates of literacy have skyrocketed since the 1960s. In 1980, an Arab fund was created for eliminating illiteracy. (1) In the last fifty years, the number of educated people more than doubled in some countries and increased ten times or more in others. Literacy in the Arab countries has reached an average of 65 percent, (2) and literacy in the states of the Arabian Peninsula rose from about 10 percent in the 1970s to above 90 percent today. Literacy rates are much higher among youth than among older citizens, and they are higher in urban areas: 90 percent average for males and 81 percent for females. (This gender disparity is most prominent in Morocco, Egypt, and Yemen.) (3) The lowest literacy is in Yemen, and the highest is in the Palestinian Territories. The only country where literacy has declined is Iraq, which once had one of the highest rates.

Education at the university level is rising even faster, sometimes doubling or tripling in one or two decades. The following table shows what has happened since 1980.

❂ ❂ ❂ ❂ ❂ ❂ ❂ ❂ ❂ ❂ ❂ ❂ ❂ ❂ ❂ ❂ ❂ ❂ ❂ ❂ ❂ ❂ ❂

## PERCENTAGE ENROLLED IN UNIVERSITY EDUCATION (4)

|              | 1980      | 2001 | 2008 |
|--------------|-----------|------|------|
| Jordan       | 13        | 31   | 41   |
| Saudi Arabia | 7         | 22   | 30   |
| Tunisia      | 5         | 23   | 33   |
| Oman         | 0         | 7    | 27   |
| Lebanon      | 28 (1985) | 45   | 51   |

Arab women are becoming more educated and active professionally. In 1973 only 7 percent of women were employed in the workforce, (5) whereas currently the average is 25 to 30 percent. Arab women are aware that this percentage is still well below the worldwide rate. The industrial world, by comparison, averages from 40 to 50 percent female employment.

As more women enter the workforce, they will constitute a large, well educated, and largely untapped resource, which will greatly strengthen the societies of the region. More and more women are working as professionals.

❋ ❋ ❋ ❋ ❋ ❋ ❋ ❋ ❋ ❋ ❋ ❋ ❋ ❋ ❋ ❋ ❋ ❋ ❋ ❋ ❋ ❋ ❋ ❋

## PERCENTAGE OF WOMEN IN THE WORKFORCE (ECONOMICALLY ACTIVE) 2010 (6)

| | |
|---|---|
| Qatar | 52 |
| UAE | 44 |
| Kuwait | 43 |
| Bahrain | 39 |
| Sudan | 31 |
| Libya | 30 |
| Oman | 28 |
| Morocco | 26 |
| Tunisia | 25 |
| Yemen | 25 |
| Egypt | 24 |
| Lebanon | 23 |
| Saudi Arabia | 17 |
| Algeria | 15 |
| Jordan | 15 |
| Iraq | 14 |
| Palestine | no statistics available |

Improved health care—including the vast number of new hospitals, clinics, and medical graduates—is changing the quality of life. Life expectancy has increased dramatically, as well.

❄ ❄ ❄ ❄ ❄ ❄ ❄ ❄ ❄ ❄ ❄ ❄ ❄ ❄ ❄ ❄ ❄ ❄ ❄ ❄ ❄ ❄ ❄ ❄ ❄

## LIFE EXPECTANCY (7)

|  | 1955 | 2011 |
|---|---|---|
| Morocco | 43 | 76 |
| Egypt | 42 | 73 |
| Kuwait | 55 | 77 |
| Saudi Arabia | 34 | 74 |

This increased longevity is reflected in population statistics. Since the 1950s, the average rate of population growth has ranged between 2.5 to 3 percent, as high as anywhere in the world. In the four years between 1986 and 1990, the overall Arab population grew 5 to 7 percent (8 percent in the UAE and 10 percent in Oman); it has leveled out to 2.3 percent. An increase in education and the availability of contraception accounts for the lowering of the birthrate. U.N. data show a dramatic fall in rates in the last five to ten years, especially among women under age 20. (8) Birthrates in the UAE, Bahrain, Kuwait, Lebanon, and Tunisia have almost reached the low European levels.

By 2009, over 30 percent of the entire Arab population was age fifteen or under; over 50 percent was under age twenty-four. The World Bank estimates that the population of the Middle East, including non-Arab nations, will increase from 450 million to 650 million by 2050. (9) With youth unemployment at about 30 percent, the region will need 51 million more jobs by 2020 to avoid a further increase in unemployment. (10) Currently, 100 million people are between ages fifteen and twenty-nine. (11)

All over the Arab world, the population has been shifting from farms and villages to large urban areas, most dramatically during the period from the end of World War II to 1980. The magnitude of urbanization is illustrated by comparing the rates in recent years (numbers rounded off). Some countries are among the most urbanized in the world.

❄ ❄ ❄ ❄ ❄ ❄ ❄ ❄ ❄ ❄ ❄ ❄ ❄ ❄ ❄ ❄ ❄ ❄ ❄ ❄ ❄ ❄ ❄ ❄

## PERCENTAGE URBANIZED (12) (13)

|  | 1970 | 1995 | 2010 |
|---|---|---|---|
| Saudi Arabia | 49 | 79 | 82 |
| Libya | 50 | 76 | 78 |

*(continues)*

|         | 1970 | 1995 | 2010 |
|---------|------|------|------|
| Jordan  | 56   | 78   | 79   |
| Tunisia | 43   | 61   | 67   |
| UAE     | 78   | 78   | 84   |

Throughout the Arab world, 85 to 90 percent of the land is uninhabitable desert.

Urbanization brings its own problems. Except in the Gulf countries, governments face housing shortages, overuse of municipal services, and overburdened social services, such as schools and healthcare centers. For example, Amman, Jordan, has water only a few hours per day; public transportation is almost impossible in Cairo; everywhere traffic is far more than the roads were designed for. In the poorer countries, notably cities such as Casablanca, Algiers, and Cairo, unauthorized housing proliferates; in fact, 20 percent of Cairo's population live in illegal housing, not registered with the municipality. And occasional political crises contribute to problems. At the end of 1990, after the invasion of Kuwait, four to five million people left the Gulf region, exacerbating the problems of housing, schools, and unemployment in their home countries. (14) In 2011, refugees were created from Libya, Syria, and Yemen, who fled to neighboring countries and put more strain on their resources.

Internet access and usage illustrate the current situation well. In the poorer countries, 5 to 10 percent of the people have access; in the rich countries, 20 to 30 percent access the web, with a high of 55 percent in the UAE and 50 percent in Kuwait. (15) This is compared to 55 percent in the U.S. and 40 to 50-plus percent in the developed world. (16)

Some of the other major social changes and trends in the Arab world include the following:

> People have far more exposure to newspapers, television, radio, computers, and the Internet.
> Entertainment outside the home and family is increasingly popular.
> More Arabs travel, work, and study abroad.
> Political awareness and aspirations have greatly increased.
> International trade is booming.
> More people are working for large, impersonal organizations and industries.

Educational and professional opportunities for women have
changed family life.

Parents are finding that they have less control over their children's
choice of career and lifestyle.

Family planning is promoted and increasingly practiced in most
Arab countries, and it is accepted as permissible by most
Islamic jurists.

## ❊ THE ARAB HUMAN DEVELOPMENT REPORTS

The publication of the *Arab Human Development Report* in 2002 was the
first of its kind, a major event in Arab self-appraisal. It was written by a
group of Arab intellectuals from the twenty-two countries in the Arab
League and funded by the Arab Fund for Economic and Social Development, which is part of the United Nations. The report was notable for its
frankness in pointing out the region's lack of freedom, economic development, and achievements in science and technology,§§ as well as gender
inequality, and the high rate of illiteracy. In the report it was stated, "There
is a serious failing in the Arab world, and this is located specifically in the
political sphere." (17) It called for greater political freedom, a sharing of
absolute ruling power, and a curtailment of corruption. It also expressed
complete acceptance of "liberal democratic ideals."

The 2002 report¶¶ also mentioned that the Arab world had lost
25 percent of its university graduates to emigration because of poor
economic conditions. Between 1998 and 2000, 15,000 medical doctors
emigrated. Today, economic conditions remain poor in many countries,
and the "brain drain" to Europe, America, Australia, and the Arabian
Gulf is still very real.

## ❊ THE EFFECTS OF CHANGE

The disruptive effects of the sudden introduction of foreign practices
and concepts on traditional societies are well known. The social strains

---

§§It is refreshing to see a frank analysis of the current situation without reference to the
glories of the Golden Age of Islamic civilization in medieval times. It is important to
acknowledge these contributions, but it is also time to move on.
¶¶Reports since then have dealt with various other topics.

among groups of people who represent different levels of education and exposure to Western ideas can be intense. In fact, mutual frustrations exist to a degree that can hardly be imagined by Westerners.

Both modernist and traditionalist ways of thinking are present at the same time in modern Arab society, forming a dualism. Modern science and technology are taught side by side with traditional law and religious subjects.

Arabs, particularly the younger generation, are *very attracted to* and *appreciative of* American culture and its products, including entertainment, music, clothing, and liberal ideals such as freedom and equal opportunity. The generation gap is very painful for some communities and families. Some of the younger people are liberal and influenced by the West, while others have become more conservative and religious. All this affects family decisions. A Westernized Arab once equated the feelings of an Arab father whose son refuses to accept the family's choice of a bride with the feelings of a Western father who discovers that his son is on drugs.

A common theme of Arab writers and journalists is the necessity for scrutinizing Western innovations. They emphasize the need to adopt those aspects that are beneficial to their societies (for example, scientific and technical knowledge) and reject those that are harmful (such as lessening concern for family cohesion or social morality).

Arabs have long been concerned that Westernization is often a part of modernization. They want to modernize, but not at the expense of certain traditions. It is a mistake to assume that Arabs aspire to create societies identical to Western models. Many Americans, in particular, find it surprising that most foreigners are not interested in the ways Americans do things, in personal life or in society. At the same time, it's important to note that although Arabs often disapprove of what they hear about American or European social problems and moral standards (understood correctly or not), they have no interest in changing the Western way of life. They just don't want it imposed on them.

The issue for Arabs is how they will be able to adopt Western technology without adopting the Western values and social practices that go with it, and thereby retain their cherished traditional values. Their ideal society would retain its Islamic character, relying on Islamic values while undertaking reform. Most Arabs do not want an Iranian-style theocracy or a completely Western-style democracy. The large majority both reject the militants and have serious reservations about the West—they want a "soft revolution" within their own cultural and religious context.

## ❈ THE MUSLIM VIEW

*Interpretations of Islamic practices vary widely.* Many of the customs that distinguish Middle East countries stem from *local cultural practices* (family relationships, women's role in society, people's manner of dress, child-rearing practices, female circumcision), *not religion.* Because Sunni Islam has no organized hierarchy and no central authority, decisions by religious scholars often vary as well.

Most educated people want to "renew" Islam, in order to face the new conditions of modern life. But this is more easily said than done, particularly in light of the recent emphasis on traditional Islam.

All over the Arab world and the entire Middle East, religious studies have increased in universities, as has the publication of religious tracts, and more religious orations are heard in public. This has been going on for a long time—the number of religious broadcasts and Islamic newspapers and books tripled in the 1980s alone. (18) There has also been a steady increase in Islamic-oriented organizations, laws, social welfare services, educational institutes, youth centers, publishers, and even Islamic banks. Many tradition-oriented Muslims have entered politics. A more visible Islamic dimension has become a part of everyday life.

The resurgence of conservative religion further supports the views of the traditionalists, who oppose any reinterpretations of Islam, and this group contains many government authorities, military officers, teachers, journalists, and intellectuals. *But traditionalists are not fundamentalists* if we use the term *fundamentalist* to mean "militant Islamist." Traditionalists want to maintain cultural and religious authenticity; they are exactly like traditionalists in other religions. The Muslim traditionalist view is that while Islam must accommodate modernity, modernity must also accommodate Islam. (19)

Muslims are determined to deal with change their own way. They believe they can contribute to the changing world, to a possible new global order. While the West excels at progress through the development of technology, Islam can provide a humanizing factor—morality. The goal is a universally *moral and materially advanced* global world order. Many non-Westerners believe that the Western exercise of world power lacks a strong underpinning of morality that leads to preferences for their own interests, without consideration of whether the policies are right or wrong for all people.

Benazir Bhutto, the eleventh prime minister of Pakistan, once characterized two groups of Muslims—reactionary and progressive:

> I would describe Islam in two main categories: reactionary Islam and progressive Islam. We can have a reactionary interpretation of Islam, which upholds the status quo, or we can have a progressive interpretation of Islam, which tries to move with a changing world. (20)

Islamic societies will change, but they will always reflect diverse influences, lifestyles, and ideologies.

## ❁ ISLAMIC EDUCATION

There has long been discussion about how Islamic education could or should differ from Western education, and this subject is often mentioned in the media. Of particular concern is how science and technology relate to traditional Islamic values and ways of looking at the world, and how these values can be retained. Many Muslim commentators believe that Western education relies too exclusively on process, without the spiritual dimension. They contend that the search for knowledge about the world constantly changes, but values do not change.

Many Muslims believe that textbooks should be prepared so that they reflect the Islamic outlook even as they present pertinent modern theories and discoveries. One educator, for example, suggested that, in the natural sciences, the word *nature* could be replaced with *God* so that it is clear that God is the source of natural growth and development, of the properties of chemicals, of the laws of physics and astronomy, and the like. Historical events are to be evaluated not for military or political significance but by their success in furthering the spiritual aims of humanity; for example, an agnostic society that amassed a great empire would not be judged as successful. (21) It seems to me that evangelical Christians would find very little to differ with in these kinds of statements.

The relationship between Islam and science is uncertain and attracts many opinions. Some assert that "Islamic science" does not exist, saying that Islam does not encourage free, creative inquiry, while others are confident that the two can be reconciled. (22) Some Muslims find Western science lacking in that it asks "what" and "how" but not "why," the latter bringing in a religious and philosophical dimension.

Muslim intellectuals everywhere are actively seeking Islamic alternatives for their societies. In many countries young people belong to informal groups in which the role and contributions of Islam to modern society are avidly discussed.

## ❊ Facing the Future

Outside pressure toward change is glaringly visible in the Arab countries' architecture and city planning. Skyscrapers and air conditioning have replaced thick-walled traditional houses that were designed to condition the air themselves by means of a wind tower. Many crowded "old city" districts, with twisted lanes and jumbled markets and houses, have been destroyed; those that are left are in stark contrast with the newer parts of cities, built with wide streets on a city-block plan. Unfortunately, modern housing often does not address the needs of families and communities: there is no daily gathering place for women or separate living and entertainment areas for men and women. In most Arab cities, it is difficult nowadays for members of an extended family to find housing in one place or even in one area.

Many young people in particular agonize about their identity (family? nation? Arab region? religious group or secular?) and what constitutes appropriate lifestyle choices, a dilemma that is simply unknown among Westerners. Balancing between the modern and the authentic traditional way of life in their own personal lives is a concern among Arabs at all levels in society.

Westerners may perceive a dual personality present in many educated Arabs, who have the ability to synthesize two diverse ways of thinking and appreciate both. Few of us in the West have to contend with a dualism of this kind.

It is clear that a great deal of confusion and upheaval is still to be experienced. Consider the questions that modernity raises in the mind of an Arab: How do you compare the relative value of a communications satellite with the wisdom of a village elder? What good is a son who is a computer expert but lacks filial respect? How do you cope with a highly educated daughter who announces that she never intends to marry?

This is the context in which Westerners encounter Arabs today. This is the background for Arabs' choices and aspirations.

## CHAPTER 1

# BELIEFS AND VALUES

When we set ourselves the task of coming to a better understanding of groups of people and their culture, it is useful to begin by identifying their most basic beliefs and values; these determine their outlook on life and govern their social behavior. We have to make broad generalizations in order to compare groups of people—here, Arabs and Westerners. Bear in mind that this generalizing can never apply to all individuals in a group; the differences among Arabs of the eighteen nations described here are numerous, although all have an Arab identity.

Westerners tend to believe, for instance, that the individual is the focal point of social existence, laws apply equally to everyone, people have a right to certain kinds of privacy, and the environment can be controlled by humans through technological means. These beliefs have a strong influence on what Westerners think about the world around them and how they behave toward each other.

Arabs characteristically believe that many, if not most, things in life are controlled, ultimately, by fate rather than by humans; that everyone loves children, wisdom increases with age, and the inherent personalities of men and women are vastly different. These beliefs play a powerful role in determining the nature of Arab culture.

One might wonder whether there is, in fact, such a thing as Arab culture, given the diversity and spread of the Arab region. Looking at a map, one realizes how much is encompassed in the phrase "the Arab world." The Arab countries cover a vast territory, almost all of it desert or wilderness; if the uninhabitable land were removed, the Arab world would be *very small* for its 360 million people. Much of the inhabited land is along coasts and rivers. Sudan is larger than Western Europe, yet its population was 44 million in 2011 (as compared with 400 million in Western Europe); Saudi Arabia is bigger than Texas and Alaska combined, yet had only 26 million people in 2010. Egypt, with 83 million people in 2011, is 95 percent desert.* One writer has stated, "A true map of the Arab world would show it as an archipelago: a scattering of fertile islands through a void of sand and sea. The Arabic word for desert is *sahara* and it both divides and joins." (3)

The differences among Arabs in various regions are immediately obvious—they have different foods, manners of dress, housing, decorative arts, and architectural styles. The political diversity is also notable; governmental systems include monarchies, military governments, "socialist republics," and now, the possibility of participatory democracies.

But despite the differences, the Arabs are more homogeneous than Westerners in their outlook on life. All Arabs share basic beliefs and values that cross national and class boundaries. Social attitudes have remained relatively constant because Arab society is conservative and demands conformity from its members. Arabs' beliefs are influenced by Islam, even if they are not Muslims. Many family and social practices are cultural, some are pre-Islamic; child-rearing practices are nearly identical; and the family structure is essentially the same. Arabs have not been as mobile as people in the West, and they have a high regard for tradition. Here are some features shared by all Arab groups: the role of the family, class structure, religious and political behavior, standards of social morality, the presence of change, and the impact of economic development on people's lives. (4)

Initially, foreigners may feel that Arabs are difficult to understand, or that sometimes their behavior patterns are not what was expected (Arabs feel the same about Westerners). In fact, though, their behavior is very comprehensible, even predictable. For the most part it conforms to certain patterns that make Arabs consistent in their reactions to other people. *It is important for a foreigner to be aware of these cultural patterns and distinguish them from individual traits.*

By becoming aware of patterns, one can achieve a better understanding of what to expect and thereby cope more easily. The following lists

---

*Like many Arab countries, Egypt is large; statistics on population density reflect that. In terms of total area, Egypt's population density is 200 persons per square mile. (1) If considering only the habitable area, it is 3,820 persons per square mile. (2)

of Arab values, religious attitudes, and self-perceptions are central to the Arab culture and will be examined in detail in subsequent chapters.

## Basic Arab Values

- ❈ One should behave at all times in a way that will create a good impression on others.
- ❈ A person's dignity, honor, and reputation are of paramount importance, and no effort should be spared to protect them. Honor (or shame) is often viewed as collective, pertaining to the entire family or group.
- ❈ Loyalty to one's family takes precedence over personal preferences.
- ❈ Social class and family background are the major determining factors of personal status, followed by individual character and achievement.
- ❈ Conservative social morality standards should be maintained, through laws if necessary.

## Basic Arab Religious Attitudes

- ❈ Everyone believes in God, acknowledges His power, and has a religious affiliation.
- ❈ Humans cannot control events; some things depend on God's will, that is, fate.
- ❈ Piety is one of the most admirable characteristics in a person.
- ❈ There should be no separation between church and state; religion should be taught in schools and promoted by governments (this is the Islamic view, not necessarily shared by Arab Christians).
- ❈ Established beliefs and practices are sacrosanct. Liberal interpretations or indiscriminate imitations of Western culture can lead to social disorder, lower moral standards, and a weakening of traditional family ties, so they must be rejected.†

---

†Often cited are the West's tolerance of youthful rebellion, alcohol, drugs, pornography, homosexuality, unchaperoned dating, and the rate of illegitimate births (currently 41 percent in the U.S.). (5) In America, half a million children are in foster care. Surveys indicate that the dominant perception in Arab and Muslim countries is that religion and family are not very important in Western societies. Arabs value social morality far more than individual choice.

*Basic Arab Self-Perceptions*

- ❊ Arabs are generous, humanitarian, polite, and loyal. Arabs see these traits as characteristic of themselves and as distinguishing them from some other groups.

- ❊ Arabs have a rich cultural heritage, as illustrated by their contributions in medieval times to philosophy, literature, medicine, architecture, art, mathematics, and the natural sciences (some of which were made by non-Arabs living within the Islamic empire). Most of these outstanding accomplishments are largely unknown and unappreciated in the West.

- ❊ Although there are many differences among Arab countries, the Arabs are a clearly defined cultural group and perceive themselves to be members of the Arab Nation (*al-umma al-'arabiyya*).

- ❊ The Arab peoples see themselves as having been victimized and exploited by the West. For them, the experience of the Palestinians represents the most painful and obvious example, although recent suffering by Iraqi civilians is now a close second. They believe that Arabs are misunderstood and wrongly characterized by most Westerners, and that many people in the West are anti-Arab and anti-Muslim. Most Westerners do not distinguish between Arabs and Muslims.

# CHAPTER 2

# FRIENDS AND STRANGERS

Relationships are very personalized in the Arab culture. Friendships start and develop quickly. But the Arab concept of friendship, with its rights and duties, is quite different from that in the West.

## THE CONCEPT OF FRIENDSHIP

Westerners, especially Americans, usually think of a friend as someone whose company they enjoy. A friend can be asked for a favor or for help if necessary, but it is considered poor form to cultivate a friendship primarily for what can be gained from that person or his or her position. Among Arabs, also, a friend is someone whose company one enjoys. *However, equally important to the relationship is the duty of a friend to give help and do favors to the best of one's ability.*

Differences in expectations can lead to misunderstandings and, for both parties, a feeling of being let down. The Westerner feels set up to do favors, and the Arab concludes that no Westerner can be a true friend. In order to avoid such feelings, we must bear in mind what is meant by both sides when one person calls another *friend.*

## RECIPROCAL FAVORS

For an Arab, good manners require that one never openly refuse a request from a friend. This does not mean that the favor must actually be done, but rather that the response must not be stated as a direct "no." If a friend asks you for a favor, do it if you can—this keeps the friendship flourishing. If it is unreasonable, illegal, or too difficult, the correct form is to listen carefully and suggest that while you are doubtful about the outcome, you will at least try to help. Later, you should express your regrets and offer instead to do something else in the future. In this way you have not openly refused a favor (as if you didn't care), and your face-to-face encounters have remained pleasant.

I once talked to an Egyptian university student who told me that he was very disappointed in his American professor. The professor had gratefully accepted many favors while he was getting settled in Egypt, including assistance in finding a maid and buying furniture. When the Egyptian asked him to use his influence in helping him obtain a graduate fellowship in the United States, the professor told him that there was no point in trying because his grades were not high enough to be competitive. The Egyptian took this as a personal affront and felt bitter that the professor did not care about him enough to help him work toward a better future. The more appropriate response by the professor would have been to make helpful gestures. For example, he might have helped the student obtain information about fellowships, assisted him with applications, and offered encouragement—even if he was not optimistic about the outcome.

In Western culture, actions are far more important and more valued than words. In the Arab culture, *an oral promise has its own value* as a response. If an action does not follow, the other person cannot be held entirely responsible for a failure because it is assumed that he or she at least tried.

If you fail to carry out a request, you will notice that no matter how hopeful your Arab friend was that you would succeed, he or she will probably accept your regrets graciously without asking precisely why the favor could not be done (which could embarrass you and possibly force you to admit a failure). You should be willing to show the same forbearance and understanding in inquiring about one of your requests. Noncommittal answers probably mean there is no hope. This is one of the most frustrating cultural patterns Westerners confront in the Arab world. You must learn to work with this idea rather than fighting against it.

When Arabs say "yes" to your request, they are not necessarily certain that the action will or can be carried out. Etiquette demands that your request have a positive response. The result is a separate matter. A positive response to a request is a declaration of intention and an expression of goodwill—no more than that. *Yes* should not always be taken literally. You will hear phrases such as *Inshallah* (If God wills) used in connection with promised actions. This is called for culturally, and it sometimes results in lending a further degree of uncertainty to the situation.

It is more polite on both sides to express goodwill rather than to criticize a person's ideas or refuse a request bluntly. Arabs are responding to a different culturally defined concept of politeness; it does not mean that they are "lying" or that they are not dependable. This is a subtle point, and it depends on the situation.*

Sometimes an Arab asks another person for something and then adds the phrase, "Do this for my sake." This phrasing sounds odd to a foreigner, especially if the persons involved do not know each other well, because it appears to imply a very close friendship. In fact the expression means that the person requesting the action is acknowledging that he will consider himself indebted to return the favor in the future. "For my sake" is very effective in Arab culture when added to a request.

An Arab expects loyalty from anyone who is considered a friend. The friend is therefore not justified in becoming indignant when asked for favors, once it is understood from the beginning that giving and receiving favors is an inherent part of the relationship. Arabs will not form or perpetuate a friendship unless they also like and respect you; their friendship is not as calculated or self-serving as it may appear. The practice of cultivating a person only in order to use him or her is no more acceptable among Arabs than it is among Westerners.

❀ INTRODUCTIONS

Arabs quickly determine another person's social status and connections when they meet. They will, in addition, normally give more information about themselves than Westerners will. They may indulge in a little (or

---

*This is from a recording I made of a Qatari woman's speech: "There is no polite flattery or indirectness—I liked this in Europe. They tell the truth when they talk. If someone likes something, he tells you, 'Yes.' If he doesn't like it, he says, 'No.' I might get irritated, but it's the truth." (1)

a lot of) self-praise and praise of their relatives and family, and they may present a detailed account of their social connections. When Westerners meet someone for the first time, they tend to confine personal information to generalities about their education, profession, spouse and children, and interests.

To Arabs, information about the extended family and social connections is important, possibly even more important than the information about themselves. Family information and social connections are also what they want from you. They may find your response so inadequate that they wonder if you are hiding something, while your impression is that much of what they say is too detailed and largely irrelevant. Both parties give the information they think the other wants to know.

Your Arab friends' discourse about their influence network is not bragging, and it is not irrelevant. This information may turn out to be highly useful if you are ever in need of high-level personal contacts, and you should appreciate the offer of potential assistance from insiders in the community. Listen to what they have to say.

## ❀ VISITING PATTERNS

Arabs feel that good friends should see each other often, at least every few days, and they offer many invitations to each other. Westerners who have Arab friends sometimes feel overwhelmed by the frequent contact and wonder if they will ever have any privacy. There is no concept of privacy among Arabs. In translation, the Arabic word that comes closest to *privacy* means "loneliness"!

A British resident in Beirut once complained that he and his wife had almost no time to be alone—Arab friends and neighbors kept dropping in unexpectedly and often stayed late. He said, "I have one friend who telephoned and said, 'I haven't seen you anywhere. Where have you been for the last three days?' "

By far the most popular form of entertainment in the Arab world is conversation (although television and the Internet are making inroads). Arabs enjoy long discussions over shared meals or many cups of coffee or tea. You will be expected to reciprocate with invitations, although you do not have to keep pace precisely with the number you receive. If you plead for privacy or become too slack in socializing, people will wonder if they have offended you, if you don't like them, or if you are sick. You can say that you have been very busy, but resorting to this too often without sufficient explanation may be taken as an affront. "Perhaps," your friends may think, "you are just too busy for us."

I once experienced a classic example of the Arab (and especially Egyptian) love of companionship in Cairo. After about three hours at a party where I was surrounded by loud music and louder voices, I stepped onto the balcony for a moment of quiet and fresh air. One of the women noticed and followed immediately, asking "Is anything wrong? Are you angry at someone?"

An Arab American was quoted as saying:

> In the United States . . . you can have more personal space. I guess this is about the best way to put it. You have privacy when you want privacy. And in Arab society they don't really understand the idea that you want to be alone. That means that you're mad, you're angry at something, or you're upset and you should have somebody with you. (2)

People want to be surrounded by others when they are sick in the hospital or in a state of mourning, times when a Westerner might prefer to be alone. All hospital rooms have facilities for relatives, and a patient cannot possibly keep them out, even if he or she wanted to. Arabs feel terribly lonely in a new place where they don't know anyone; a comfortable security has been lost. This is a description of an Arab woman who had just arrived in England, written by her daughter:

> She hated the cold weather and the rain and she complained she could scarcely keep the house warm. She was lonely and longed for company. In the Arab world, you were never alone for a moment. Your neighbors or friends were always there to call on every day and, in any case, there was the family around you at all times. (3)

If you are not willing to increase the frequency or intensity of your personal contacts, you may hurt your friends' feelings and damage the relationship. Ritual and essentially meaningless expressions used in Western greetings and leave-taking, such as "We've got to get together some time," may well be taken literally, and you have approximately a one-week grace period in which to follow up with an invitation before your sincerity is questioned.

Some Westerners, as they learn about the intricate and time-consuming relationships that develop among friends, decide they would rather keep acquaintances at a distance. If you accept no favors, you will eventually be asked for none, and you will have much more time to yourself, but you will soon find that you have no Arab friends. Arab friends are generous with their time and efforts to help you, are willing to inconvenience themselves for you, and are concerned about your welfare. They will go to great lengths to be loyal and dependable. If you spend much time in an Arab country, it will be a great personal loss if you develop no Arab friendships.

## ❁ Business Friendships

In business relationships, personal contacts are much valued and quickly established. Arabs do not fit easily into impersonal roles, such as the "business colleague" role (with no private socializing offered or expected) or the "supervisor/employee" roles (where there may be cordial relations during work hours but where personal concerns are not discussed). For Arabs, all acquaintances are personal friends.

*A good personal relationship is the most important single factor in doing business successfully with Arabs.* A little light conversation before beginning a business discussion can be extremely effective in setting the right tone. Usually Arabs set aside a few minutes at the beginning of a meeting to inquire about each other's health and recent activities. If you are paying a business call on an Arab, it is best to let your host guide the conversation in this regard—if he is in a hurry, he may bring up the matter of business almost immediately; if not, you can tell by a lull in the conversational amenities when it is time to bring up the purpose of your visit. If an Arab is paying a call on you, don't be in such a rush to discuss business that you appear brusque.

The manager of the sales office of a British industrial equipment firm based in Kuwait told me about his initial inability to select effective salesmen. He learned that the best salesmen were not necessarily the most knowledgeable, eager, or efficient but were instead those who were relaxed, personable, and patient enough to establish friendly personal relations with their clients.

You will find it useful to become widely acquainted in business circles, and if you learn to mix business with pleasure, you will soon see how the latter helps the former proceed. *In the end, personal contacts lead to more efficiency than following rules and regulations.* This is proven over and over again, when a quick telephone call to the right person cuts through lengthy procedures and seemingly insurmountable obstacles.

## ❈ OFFICE RELATIONS

When Westerners work with the same people every day in an office, they sometimes become too casual about greetings. Arabs are conscientious about greeting everyone they see with "Good morning" or "Good afternoon" if it is the first encounter of the day, and they will go out of their way to say "Welcome back" when you return after an absence. Some Westerners omit greetings altogether, especially if they are distracted or hurried, and Arab coworkers invariably take notice. They usually understand and are not personally offended, but they interpret it as a lack of good manners. They are simply more formal; it is a matter of *adab*, good manners.

An American nurse at a hospital in Taif, Saudi Arabia, had an enlightening experience on one occasion when she telephoned her Saudi supervisor to report arrangements for an emergency drill. She was enumerating the steps being taken when the Saudi said, "That's fine, but just a moment—first of all, how are you today?"

If you bring food or snacks into the office, it is a good idea to bring enough to share with everyone. Arabs place great value on hospitality and would be surprised if you ate or drank alone, without at least making an offer to share. The offer is ritual, and if it is obviously your lunch or just enough food for yourself, it is usually politely refused; it depends on the situation.

Remember to inquire about business colleagues and coworkers if they have been sick, and ask about their personal concerns from time to time. Arabs do mention what is happening in their lives, usually good things like impending trips, weddings, and graduations. You do not need to devote much time to this; it is the gesture that counts.

In Arab offices supervisors and managers are expected to give praise to their employees from time to time, to reassure them that their work is noticed and appreciated. Direct praise, such as "You are an excellent employee and a real asset to this office," may be a little embarrassing to a Westerner, but Arabs give it frequently. You may hear "I think you are a wonderful person, and I am so glad you are my friend" or "You are so intelligent and knowledgeable; I really admire you." Statements like these are meant sincerely and are very common.

I was once visiting an American engineering office in Riyadh and fell into conversation with a Jordanian translator. I asked him how he liked his work. He answered in Arabic so that the Americans would not understand, "I've been working here for four years. I like it fine, but I wish they would tell me when my work is good, not just when they find something wrong." Some Westerners assume that employees know they are appreciated simply because they are kept on the job, whereas Arab employees, and friends, for that matter, expect and want praise when they feel they have earned it. Even when a Westerner does offer praise, it may be insufficient in quantity or quality for the Arab counterpart.

## ✿ CRITICISM

Arab employees usually feel that criticism of their work, if it is phrased too bluntly, is a personal insult. A foreigner is well advised to take care when giving criticism. It should be indirect and include praise of any good points first, accompanied by assurances of high regard for the individual. To preserve the person's dignity, avoid criticism in front of others, and consider using an intermediary. (A discussion of intermediaries follows this section.) The concept of constructive criticism truly cannot be translated into Arabic—forthright criticism is almost always taken as personal and destructive.

The need for care in criticism is well illustrated by an incident that occurred in an office in Amman. An American supervisor was discussing a draft report at some length with his Jordanian employee. He asked him to rewrite more than half of it, adding, "You must have entirely misunderstood what I wanted." The Jordanian was deeply hurt and said to one of the other employees, "I wonder why he doesn't like me." A far better approach would have been, "You are doing excellent work here, and this is a good report. We need to revise some things, however; let's look at this again and work through it together, so we can make it even better."

I remember overhearing a dramatic confrontation in an office in Tunis, when an American supervisor reprimanded a Tunisian employee because he continually arrived late. This was done in front of other employees, some of whom were his subordinates. The Tunisian flared up in anger and responded, "I am from a good family! I know myself and my position in society!" Clearly he felt that his honor had been threatened and was not at all concerned with addressing the issue at hand.

## ❀ INTERMEDIARIES

The designation of one person to act as an intermediary between two other persons is very common in Arab society. Personal influence is helpful in getting decisions made and things done, so people often ask someone with influence to represent them. In Arabic this process is called *wasta*.

If you are a manager, you may find that some employees prefer to deal with you through another person, especially if that person knows you well. An intermediary may serve as a representative of someone with a request or as a negotiator between two parties in a dispute.

Mediation or representation through a third party also saves face in the event that a request is not granted, and it gives the petitioner confidence that maximum influence has been brought to bear. You may want to initiate this yourself if an unpleasant confrontation with someone appears necessary. But because you, as an outsider, could easily make a mistake in selecting an intermediary, it is best to consult with other Arab employees of a higher rank than the person with whom you have a conflict.

Foreign companies have local employees on their staff who serve as liaisons with government offices and help obtain permits and clearances. The better acquainted the employee is with government officials, the faster the work will be done and the better the service will be. Arab "government relations" employees are indispensable; no foreigner could hope to be as effective with highly placed officials.

You will observe the wide use of intermediaries in Arab political disputes. Mediators, such as those who try to intervene when a political problem arises (the recent clashes between revolutionaries and leaders come to mind) may be able to establish personal contact and influence that makes consensus possible. Their success depends on the quality of the personal relationship that is established. If mediators are recognized by both parties as being honorable and trustworthy, they have already come part of the way in solving the problem. That is why some negotiators and diplomats are more effective than others; personalities and perceptions, not issues, may determine their relative success.

## ❀ PRIVATE AND PUBLIC MANNERS

*In the Arab way of thinking, people are clearly divided into friends and strangers.* The manners required when dealing with these two groups are very different. With friends and personal acquaintances, it is essential to be polite, honest, generous, and helpful at all times. These are "private manners." However, when Arabs are dealing with strangers, "public manners" are applied; these do not call for the same kind of considerateness.

It is accepted practice for many Arabs to do such things as crowd into lines, push, drive aggressively, and overcharge tourists. If you are a stranger to the person or persons you are dealing with, many of them will respond to you as they do to any stranger. Resenting this public behavior will not help you function better in Arab societies, and judging individuals as ill-mannered because of it will inhibit the development of needed relationships.

All over the Arab world, people drive fast, cross lanes without looking, turn corners from the wrong lane, and honk their horns impatiently. Yet, if you catch a driver's eye or ask his or her permission, the driver will graciously motion for you to pull ahead or will give you the right-of-way.

While shopping in a tourist shop in Damascus, I watched a busload of tourists buy items at extremely high prices. When they were gone, I chatted with the shopkeeper for a few minutes and then bought some things. After I had left, a small boy came running after me—the shop owner had sent him to return a few more pennies in change.

Whenever I am in a crowded airport line, I try to make light conversation with the people around me. Never has anyone with whom I talked tried to push in front of me; in fact, they often motion for me to precede them.

*Personal contact makes all the difference.* If you feel jostled while you are waiting in line, the gentle announcement "I was here first" or "Please wait in line" (along with a smile, if you can possibly manage it) will usually produce an apology, and the person will at least stand behind you, if not others. Keep calm, avoid scenes, and remember that none of the behavior is directed at you personally.

## CHAPTER 3

# EMOTION AND LOGIC

How people deal with emotion and what value they place on objective versus subjective behavior is culturally conditioned. *While objectivity is given considerable emphasis in Western culture, the opposite is true in Arab culture.* Among Arabs, though, whatever you encounter, there are always reasons; no behavior is random.

## ❊ OBJECTIVITY AND SUBJECTIVITY

Westerners are taught that objectivity, the examination of facts in a logical way without the intrusion of emotional bias, is the mature and constructive approach to human affairs. One of the results of this belief is that in Western culture, subjectivity—a willingness to allow personal feelings and emotions to influence one's view of events—represents immaturity. Arabs believe differently. They place a high value on the display of emotion, sometimes to the embarrassment or discomfort of foreigners. It is not uncommon to hear Westerners label this behavior as immature, imposing their own values on what they have observed.

A British office manager in Saudi Arabia once described to me his problems with a Palestinian employee: "He is too sensitive, too emotional about everything," he said. "The first thing he should do is grow up." In stark contrast, Arabs may find Westerners cold and inscrutable.

*Arabs consciously reserve the right to look at the world in a subjective way,* particularly if a more objective assessment of a situation would bring to mind a too-painful truth. There is nothing to gain, for example, by pointing out Israel's achievements in land reclamation or comparing the quality of some Arab-made consumer items with imported ones. Such comments will generally not lead to a substantive discussion of how Arabs could benefit by imitating others; more likely, Arab listeners will become angry and defensive, insisting that the situation is not as you describe it and bringing up issues such as Israeli occupation of Arab lands or the moral deterioration of technological societies. They would have to do this, because you have offended their pride and failed to observe polite conventions (*adab*).

## ❀ FATALISM

Fatalism, a belief that people are powerless to control events, is part of traditional Arab culture. It has been much overemphasized by Westerners, however, and is far more prevalent among traditional, uneducated Arabs than it is among the educated elite today. Nevertheless, it still needs to be considered, since it is often encountered in one form or another.

For Arabs, fatalism is based on the belief that God has direct and ultimate control of all that happens. If something goes wrong, people can absolve themselves of blame or can justify doing nothing to make improvements or changes by assigning the cause to God's will. Indeed, too much self-confidence about controlling events is considered a sign of arrogance tinged with blasphemy. The legacy of fatalism in Arab thought is most apparent in the ritual phrase *Inshallah* ("If God wills"), noted in Chapter 2.

Western thought has essentially rejected fatalism. Although God is believed by many Westerners to intervene in human affairs, Greek logic, the humanism of the Enlightenment, and cause-and-effect empiricism have inclined the West to view humans as having the ability to control their environment and destiny.

## ❀ WHAT IS REALITY?

Reality is what you perceive—if you believe something exists, it is real to you. If you select or rearrange facts and if you repeat these to yourself often enough, they eventually become reality.

The difference between Westerners and Arabs arises not from the fact that this selection takes place, but from the manner in which each

makes the selection. Arabs are more likely to allow subjective perceptions to determine what is real and to direct their actions. This is a common source of frustration for Westerners, who often fail to understand
why people in the Middle East act as they do. This is not to say that
Arabs cannot be objective—they can. But there is often a difference in
outward behavior.

If Arabs find that something threatens their personal dignity, they
may be obliged to deny it, even in the face of facts to the contrary. A Westerner can point out flaws in their arguments, but that is not the point. If
they do not want to accept the facts, they will reject them and proceed
according to their own views of the situation. Arabs will rarely admit to
errors openly if doing so will cause them to lose face. *To Arabs, honor is
more important than facts.*

Any Arab would understand if someone felt obliged to deny an obvious fact due to pride, and would never suggest that the other person is
lying ("Lying" is a common Western accusation). Nor would he insist
on proving the facts and thus humiliate the other person. Here are
some examples.

An American woman in Tunis realized, when she was packing to
leave, that some of her clothes and a suitcase were missing. She confronted
the maid, who insisted that she had no idea where they could be. When
the American found some of her clothes under a mattress, she called her
employer's security officer. They went to the maid's house and found more
missing items. Despite the proof, the maid was adamant that she could
not account for the items being in her home. The security officer said
that he felt the matter should not be reported to the police (who would
have been brutal); the maid's humiliation in front of her neighbors was
sufficient punishment.

An American diplomat recounted an incident he had observed in
Jerusalem. An Israeli entered a small Arab-owned cafe and asked for
some watermelon, pointing at it and using the Hebrew word. The Arab
proprietor responded that it should be called by the Arabic name, but
the Israeli insisted on the Hebrew name. The Arab took offense at this
point. He paused, shrugged, and instead of serving his customer, said,
"There isn't any!"

At a conference held to discuss Arab and American cultures, Dr.
Laura Nader related this incident:

The mistake people in one culture often make in dealing with another culture is to transfer their functions to the other culture's functions. A political scientist, for example, went to the Middle East to do some research one summer and to analyze Egyptian newspapers. When he came back, he said to me, "But they are all just full of emotions. There is no data in these newspapers." I said, "What makes you think there should be?" (1)

Another way of influencing the perception of reality is the choice of descriptive words and names. The Arabs are very careful in naming or referring to places, people, or events; slogans and labels are popular and provide an insight into how things are viewed. The Arabs realize that *names have a powerful affect on perception.*

For example, there is a big psychological gap between opposing labels like "Palestine/Israel," "the West Bank/Judea and Samaria," and "freedom fighters ('hero martyrs' if they are killed)/terrorists." Even the establishment of Israel has its own name in Arabic: the Catastrophe (as in, "ten years after the Catastrophe . . .").

Be conscious of names and labels—they matter a great deal to the users.* If you attend carefully to what you hear in conversations with Arabs and what is written in their newspapers, you will note how precisely they select descriptive words and phrases. You may find yourself being corrected by Arab acquaintances ("It is the Arabian Gulf, not the Persian Gulf," for example), and you will soon learn which terms are acceptable and which are not.

## ❈ THE HUMAN DIMENSION

Arabs look at life in a personalized way. They are concerned about people and feelings, and they place emphasis on human factors when they make decisions and analyze events. They feel that Westerners are too prone to look at events in an abstract or theoretical way and that many Westerners lack sensitivity toward people.

---

*They matter in America too. "The Department of Homeland Security" sounds much better than "The Department of Defense Against Terrorism." America refers to its "Revolutionary War," whereas it is called "the War of the American Rebellion" in England.

In the Arab world, a manager or an official is always willing to reconsider a decision, regulation, or problem in view of someone's personal situation. Any regulation can be modified or avoided by someone who is sufficiently persuasive, particularly if the request is justified on the grounds of unusual personal need. This is unlike most Western societies, which emphasize the equal application of laws to all citizens. *In the Arab culture, people are more important than rules.*

T. E. Lawrence stated it succinctly: "Arabs believe in persons, not in institutions." (2) They have a long tradition of personal appeal to authorities for exceptions to rules. This is commonly seen when they attempt to obtain special permits, exemptions from fees, acceptance into a school when preconditions are not met, or employment when qualifications are inadequate. They do not accept predetermined standards if these standards are a personal inconvenience.

Arabs place great value on personal interviews and on giving people the opportunity to state their case. They are not comfortable filling out forms or dealing with an organization impersonally. They want to know the name of the top person who makes the final decision and are always confident that the rejection of a request may be reversed if top-level personal contact can be made. Frequently, that is exactly what happens.

## ❀ PERSUASION

Arabs and Westerners place a different value on certain types of statements, which may lead to decreased effectiveness on both sides when they negotiate with each other. Arabs respond much more readily to personalized arguments than to attempts to impose "logical" conclusions. When you are trying to make a persuasive case in your discussions with Arabs, you will find it helpful to supplement your arguments with personal comments. You can refer to your friendship with each other or emphasize the effect approval or disapproval of the action will have on you or other people.

In the Middle East, negotiation and persuasion have been developed into a fine art. Participants in negotiations enjoy long, spirited discussions and are usually not in any hurry to conclude them. Speakers feel free to add to their points of argument by demonstrating their verbal cleverness, using their personal charm, applying personal pressure, and engaging in personal appeals for consideration of their point of view.

The display of emotion also plays its part; indeed, one of the most commonly misunderstood aspects of Arab communication involves their "display" of anger. Arabs are not usually as angry as they appear to be. Raising the voice, repeating points, even pounding the table for emphasis may sound angry, but in the speaker's mind, they merely indicate sincerity. A Westerner overhearing such a conversation (especially if it is in Arabic) may wrongly conclude that an argument is taking place. *Emotion connotes deep and sincere concern for the substance of the discussion.*

Foreigners often miss the emotional dimension in their cross-cultural transactions with Arabs. A British businessman once found that he and his wife were denied reservations on a plane because the Arab ticketing official took offense at the manner in which he was addressed. The fact that seats were available was not an effective counterargument. But when the Arab official noticed that the businessman's wife had begun to cry, he gave way and provided them with seats.

Arabs usually include human elements in their arguments. In arguing the Palestine issue, for instance, they have often placed the greatest emphasis on the suffering of individuals rather than on points of law or a recital of historical events. This is beginning to change, however, with a growing awareness of how to relate effectively to the way Westerners think and argue.

## CHAPTER 4

# GETTING PERSONAL

The concept of what constitutes personal behavior or a personal question is culturally determined, and there are marked differences between Westerners and Arabs. This is a subject that is rarely discussed openly, since how one defines what is personal or private seems so natural to each group. On the whole, Westerners feel that Arabs become too personal, too soon.*

## ❊ PERSONAL QUESTIONS

Arabs like to discuss money and may ask what you paid for things or what your salary is; this is more common among Arabs with less experience around Westerners. If you don't wish to give out the information, consider responding without answering. You can speak on the subject of money in general—how hard it is to stay ahead, high prices, inflation. After a few minutes of this, the listener will realize that you do not intend to give a substantive answer. This is the way Arabs would respond if they were asked a question they did not really want to answer.

If you are unmarried, married and childless, or married but have no sons, Arabs may openly ask why. They consider it unusual for an adult to be unmarried, since marriage in Arab society is arranged for most people by their families and, in any event, is expected of everyone. Arab people want children, especially sons, to enhance their prestige and assure them of care in their old age.

---

*By the same token, take care that you are not so reticent that you appear unfriendly.

Unmarried Westerners may well find themselves subjected to well-intentioned matchmaking efforts on the part of Arab friends. If you wish to avoid being "matched," you may have to resort to making up a fictitious long-distance romance. You might say, "I am engaged and we're working out the plans. I hope it won't be long now." Statements such as "I'm not married because I haven't found the right person yet" or "I don't want to get married" make little sense to many Arabs.

When you explain why you don't have children, or more children, don't say, "We don't want any more children" (impossible to believe) or "We can't afford more" (also doubtful). A more acceptable answer is "We would like to have (more) children, and if God wills, we will have."

Just as Arabs may pose questions that Westerners find too personal, Westerners should avoid asking questions that Arabs consider too personal, particularly those pertaining to women in the family, if asked by a man. If you are a man, it is best to talk about "the family," referring to a man's wife, sister, or grown daughter. It is acceptable for women to discuss these issues, especially with other women.

## ❊ SENSITIVE SUBJECTS

There are two subjects that Arabs favor in social conversation with foreigners—religion and politics—and these can be sensitive, on both sides.

Muslims enjoy discussing religion with non-Muslim Westerners because they are curious about Western religious beliefs and because they feel motivated to share information about Islam with friends as a favor to them. They are secure in their belief about the completeness of Islam, since it is accepted as the third and final refinement of the two previously revealed religions, Judaism and Christianity. They like to teach about Islam, which eventually leads them to ask, "Why don't you consider conversion?" A Westerner may feel uncomfortable and wonder how to give a gracious refusal. The most acceptable response is to state that you appreciate the information and respect Islam as a religion but that you cannot consider conversion because it would offend your family. Or, if you are seriously committed to your religion, simply state that this is the case. There is a widespread perception that most Westerners are not religious; if you are, people will be very impressed.

Arabs like to talk politics with Westerners, and they will readily bring up controversial topics like the Palestine issue, the Iraq wars, and the legacies of colonialism and imperialism. Yet they are not prepared for frank statements of disagreement with their positions on these questions or even inadvertent comments that sound negative toward their point of view or supportive of the opposing side of the argument. The safest response, if you cannot agree fully, is to confine yourself to platitudes and wait for the subject to change, expressing your concerns for the victims of war and your hope for a lasting peace. *A frank, two-sided discussion is usually not constructive if the subject is an emotional one*, and you may find that Arabs remember only the statements you made in support of the other side.

You will be able to tell when you have brought up a sensitive subject by the way your Arab friend evades a direct answer to your questions or comments. If you receive evasive answers, don't press further; there is a reason why the person does not want to pursue the subject.

If a sensitive subject arises, it is useful to introduce other topics into the conversation if you can; the best approach is to change the subject. These are suggested topics that most Arabs love to discuss, and you can bring them up whether you are actually interested or not:

- The Golden Age of the Arabs and their contributions in the Middle Ages
- The culturally required traits of an "ideal person"
- The experience of making the Hajj (pilgrimage)
- The person's extended family
- The Arabic language, its literature, and poetry

## ❀ SOCIAL DISTANCE

Arab and Western cultures differ in the amount of touching they feel comfortable with in interpersonal relations and in the physical distance they maintain when conversing. These norms are largely unconscious, so both Arabs and Westerners may feel uncomfortable without knowing exactly why.

In general, Arabs tend to stand and sit closer and to touch other people (of the same sex) more than Westerners do. It is common to see two men or two women holding hands as they walk down a street, which is simply a sign of friendship. You must be prepared for the possibility that an Arab will take your hand, especially when crossing the street. Similarly, after shaking hands in greeting, Arabs may continue to hold your hand while talking if the conversation is expected to be brief. They will then shake it again when saying good-bye.

Kissing on both cheeks is a common form of greeting (again, only with members of the same sex)†, as is embracing. It is also common to touch someone repeatedly during a conversation, often to emphasize a point. Western children, especially if they are blond, should be prepared to have their heads rubbed by well-meaning adults.

Arab culture does not have the same concept of public and private space as do Western cultures. Westerners, in a sense, carry a little bubble of private space around with them. Arabs, on the other hand, are not uncomfortable when they are close to or touching strangers.

Westerners are accustomed to standing in an elevator in such a way that maximum space is maintained between people. In the Arab world, it is common for a person to board an elevator and stand close beside you rather than moving to the opposite corner, even if the elevator is not crowded. When Arabs board a bus or select a seat on a bench, they often sit beside someone rather than going to an empty seat or leaving a space between themselves and others.

Here is a typical example. An American was standing on a street corner in Beirut waiting for a friend. He had a good view of the intersecting streets—until a Lebanese man also came to wait on the corner and stood directly in front of him.

When Arabs and Westerners are talking, they may both continually shift position, in a kind of unconscious dance, as the Arab approaches and the Westerner backs away, each trying to maintain a comfortable social distance. For Arabs, the space that is comfortable for ordinary social conversation is approximately the same as the space that Westerners reserve for intimate conversation.

Anthropologist Edward T. Hall was the first to write about the concept of personal space in his classic book *The Hidden Dimension*, never since equaled:

---

†Unless the Arabs are very Westernized, but this is rare.

For the Arab, there is no such thing as an intrusion in public. Public means public. In the Western world, the person is synonymous with an individual inside a skin. And in northern Europe generally, the skin and even the clothes may be inviolate. You need permission to touch either if you are a stranger. . . . For the Arab, the location of the person in relation to the body is quite different. The person exists somewhere down inside the body. . . . Tucking the ego down inside the body shell not only would permit higher population densities but would explain why it is that Arab communications are stepped up as much as they are when compared to northern European communication patterns. Not only is the sheer noise level much higher, but the piercing look of the eyes, the touch of the hands, and the mutual bathing in the warm moist breath during conversation represent stepped-up sensory inputs to a level which many Europeans find unbearably intense. (1)

You do not have to adopt Arab touching patterns, of course; just be aware that they are different from your own and accept them as natural and normal.

*Note:* In Saudi Arabia and the Arabian Peninsula countries, touching other people is not nearly so common and can even be viewed as offensive.

## ❁ GESTURES

Arabs make liberal use of gestures when they talk, especially if they are enthusiastic about what they are saying. Hand and facial gestures are thus an important part of Arab communication. If you are able to recognize them, you will be able to get the full meaning of what is being said to you.

Listed here are some of the most common gestures used in Arab countries. There are variations among countries, but most are in wide use. Men use gestures more than women do, and less educated people use them more than the educated do. You should not try to use these gestures (foreigners often use gestures in the wrong place or situation), but you should learn to recognize them.

- ❁ Moving the head slightly back and raising the eyebrows means "no." Moving the head back and the chin upward also means "no." Moving the chin back slightly and making a clicking sound with the tongue means "no."

- ❋ After shaking hands, placing the right hand to the heart or chest means the greeting is given to someone with respect or sincerity.
- ❋ Holding the right hand out, palm downward, and moving it as if scooping something away from you, toward the listener, means "go away."
- ❋ Holding the right hand out, palm upward, and opening and closing it means "come here."
- ❋ Holding the right hand out, palm upward, then closing the hand halfway and holding it means "give it to me."
- ❋ Holding the right hand out, palm downward, and moving it up and down slowly means "quiet down."
- ❋ Holding the right hand out, palm upward, and touching the thumb and tips of fingers together and moving the hand up and down slowly means "calm down," "be patient," or "slowly."
- ❋ Holding the right forefinger up and moving it from left to right quickly several times (the "windshield wiper") means "no, never."
- ❋ Holding the right hand out, palm downward, then quickly twisting the hand to show the palm upward means "what? why?"

## ❋ NAMES

In many Western societies, one indication of the closeness of a personal relationship is the use of first names. In Arab society the first name is used immediately, even if it is preceded by "Miss," "Mrs.," or "Mr." Arabs do not refer to people by their third, or "last," name. Arab names, for both men and women, consist of a first name (the person's own), the father's name, and the paternal grandfather's name, followed by a family name (in countries where family names are used). In other words, an Arab's name is simply a string of names listing ancestors on the father's side. A Western example might be John (given name) Robert (his father) William (his grandfather) Jones.

Because names reflect genealogy on the father's side, women have masculine names after their first name. Some people include *ibn/bin* (son of) or *bint* (daughter of) between the ancestral names. This practice is common in the Arabian Peninsula. Examples include Abdel-Aziz ibn Saud (son of Saud), the founder of the Kingdom of Saudi Arabia, and Khalifa bin Zayed Al Nahyan, the ruler of the UAE If there is no hyphen, the word *Al* often means "family," as in Al Saud, translated as the House of Saud, and Al Nahyan, the Nahyan family. In North Africa, the words *Ben* or *Ould* are used to mean "son of"; *Bou* (father of) is also a common element of a family name. Examples are political figures such as Abdelaziz Bouteflika, the president of Algeria; Mohamed Ould Abdel Aziz, the president of Mauritania; and Zein Al-Abidin Ben Ali, the former president of Tunisia.

Because a person's first name is the only one that is really his or hers, Arabs use it from the moment they are introduced, including with a title. A Western man can expect to be called "Mr. Bill" or "Mr. John." If he is married, his wife would be called "Mrs. Mary," or possibly "Mrs. Bill." An unmarried woman would be "Miss Mary." First names are also used with titles such as "Doctor" and "Professor," as well as with military ranks.

A person may retain several names for legal purposes but may omit them in daily use. A man named Ahmad Abdullah Ali Muhammad, for example, would be commonly known as Ahmad Abdullah; if he has a family or tribal name, let's say Al-Harithi, he would be known as Ahmad Abdullah Al-Harithi or possibly Ahmad Al-Harithi. Similarly, a woman whose full name is Zeinab Abdullah Ali Muhammad Al-Harithi may be known as Zeinab Abdullah or Zeinab Al-Harithi. People are not always consistent when reciting their names on different occasions.‡

When a genealogical name becomes too long, after four or five generations, some of the older names will be dropped. The only pattern that is really consistent is that the father's name will be retained along with the family name, if there is one. It is entirely possible that full brothers and sisters may be registered with different combinations of names.

In Arabian Peninsula countries the telephone books list people under their family names. In some Arab countries, however, the telephone book lists people under their first names, because the first name is the only one

---

‡An article in the *Washington Post* on May 5, 2011, referring to Saddam Hussein, was titled "Hussein trial court to be disbanded." Arabs unused to the Western naming system would not understand who this referred to. (2) This is why you usually hear Arabs say his name as simply Saddam. In Egypt, the name of former president Mubarak was used by the West to the point that the Egyptians adopted it; in a face-to-face situation, he was called "President Hosni."

that can be depended on to be consistently present (and telephone books don't work well; they are rarely consulted). Some business organizations find it easier to keep payroll records by first name.

A family or tribal name identifies a large extended family or group whose members still consider themselves tied by bonds of kinship and honor. A family name may be geographical (Hejazi, "from Hejaz"; Halaby, "from Aleppo"); denote an occupation (Haddad, "smith"; Najjar, "carpenter"); be descriptive (Al-Ahmar, "red'"; Al-Taweel, "tall"); denote tribe (Al-Harithi, Quraishi); or sound like a personal name because it is the name of an ancestor (Abdel-Rahman, Ibrahim).

An Arab Muslim woman does not change her name after marriage, since she does not take her husband's genealogy. Arabs are very proud of their mother's family and want her to retain the name and refer to it. Only informally is a wife called "Mrs." with her husband's first or last name.

When people have children, an informal but very pleasing and polite way to address the parents is by the name of the oldest son or oldest child: *Abu* (father of) or *Umm* (mother of) the child; for example, Umm Ahmad (mother of Ahmad). These terms of address are considered respectful, and *Umm* is especially useful when talking to a woman because it provides a less personal way of addressing her.

Arabs do not name their sons after their father, but naming a child after his paternal grandfather is common. You will meet some men whose first and third names are the same.

Titles are used more widely in Arabic than in English. Anyone with an M.D. or a Ph.D. degree is addressed as "Dr." ("Duktor" for a man, "Duktora" for woman). It is important to find out any titles a person may have; omitting the title will be noticed. "Sheikh" is a respectful title for a wealthy, influential, or elderly man. Government ministers are called *Ma'ali*, and senior officials are given the honorary title *Sa'ada* before their other titles and name. There are a large number of titles and formulas when addressing royalty.

Most Arab names have a meaning and can be clues to certain facts about a person. Many names indicate religion or country of origin. Because the exchange of personal information is so important, some people introduce themselves with various long combinations of names, especially if their first and last names are ambiguous or used by more than one group.

It is useful for foreigners to be able to place people, at least partially, upon hearing their names. Here are a few guidelines:

- ❁ If a name sounds Western (George, Antoine, Mary), it marks a Christian.
- ❁ If a name is that of a well-known figure in Islamic history (Muhammad, Bilal, Salah-Eddeen, Fatima, Ayesha), it marks a Muslim.
- ❁ Most hyphenated names using "Abdel-" are Muslim. The name means "Servant (Slave) of God," and the second part is one of the attributes of God (Abdullah, "Servant of God/Allah"; Abdel-Rahman, "Servant of the Merciful"; Abdel-Aziz, "Servant of the Powerful"). There are a few Christian names of this pattern (Abdel-Malak, "Servant of the Angel"; Abdel-Massih, "Servant of the Messiah"; Abdel-Qaddous, "Servant of the Most Holy"), but over 90 percent of the time you can assume that a person with this type of name is Muslim. Of the ninety-nine attributes for God (the Knowing, the Compassionate, the Wise, the Generous, etc.), most are currently in use as names.
- ❁ Names containing the word *deen* (religion) are Muslim (Sharaf-Eddeen, "The Honor of Religion"; Badr-Eddeen, "The Moon of Religion"; Salah-Eddeen, "the Rightness of Religion").
- ❁ Many names are simply descriptive adjectives (Saeed, "happy"; Amin, "faithful"; Jameela, "beautiful"). Such descriptive names do not mark religion.
- ❁ Names that derive from both the Qur'an and the Bible (Ibrahim, "Abraham"; Suleiman, "Solomon"; Daoud, "David"; Yousef, "Joseph") do not distinguish whether the person is Muslim, Christian, or Jewish. Issa (Eisa), "Jesus," is a common name among Muslims.

## CHAPTER 5

# MEN AND WOMEN

In Arab society the nature of interaction between men and women depends on the situation. Continual interaction is expected at work or in professional situations, although it remains reserved by Western standards, and in Saudi Arabia it is actually restricted. However, in social situations, interaction between men and women is very carefully controlled. The degree of control differs among Arab countries, depending on their relative conservatism, but nowhere is it as free and casual as it is in Western societies.

## ❊ SOCIAL INTERACTION

The maintenance of family honor is one of the highest values in Arab society. Many Westerners fail to understand an important concept: Because misbehavior by women is believed to do more damage to family honor than misbehavior by men, clearly defined patterns of behavior have been developed to protect women (in the traditional view) and help them avoid situations that may give rise to false impressions or unfounded gossip. Women interact freely only with other women and close male relatives.

Arab men and women are careful about appearances when they meet. They avoid situations where they would be alone together, even for a short time. It is improper to be in a room together with the door closed, to go out on a date as a couple, or to travel together, even on a short daytime trip. Guarding a woman's image is neither a personal nor a family choice;

it is imposed by the culture, just as chaperones were once required in Western society. The point is not the woman's character, or what does or does not happen—the point is how it looks.

Shared activities take place with other people present. At mixed social events, women are accompanied by their husbands or male relatives. In Saudi Arabia (only), "religious police" may question couples who are at a restaurant or in a car together and ask for proof that they are married.

Foreigners must be aware of the restrictions that pertain to contact between Arab men and women and then consider their own appearance in front of others. *Arabs quickly gain a negative impression if you behave with too much (presumed) familiarity toward a person of the opposite sex.* They will interpret your behavior on their own terms and may conclude that you are a person of low moral standards. If an embarrassing incident involves a Western man and an Arab woman, they may feel that the Westerner insulted the woman's honor, thereby threatening the honor of her family.

A Western man can feel free to greet an Arab woman at a social gathering (though it is not a common practice in Saudi Arabia), but their subsequent discussion should include other people rather than just the two of them. A married Western woman may greet and visit with Arab men, provided she is not alone. If a woman is unmarried or if her husband is not present, she should be more reserved.

In many Arab countries, men and women separate into their own conversation groups shortly after arrival at a social gathering; this depends on the customs of a given area. In Saudi Arabia, women are often excluded from social gatherings altogether, or they may be more restricted in their behavior when they are included; they usually sit separately. It is important to point out that social separation is not practiced merely because it is required by custom; it is often preferred by both men and women because they feel more comfortable. Westerners can expect to spend much of their social time in all-male or all-female groups.

Western men and women should also give thought to their appearance in front of others when they interact among themselves. Behavior such as overly enthusiastic greetings, animated and joking conversations, and casual invitations to lunch are easily misinterpreted by Arabs and reinforce their stereotype of the morally lax Westerner.

## ✤ DISPLAYING INTIMACY

*The public display of intimacy between men and women is strictly forbidden by the Arab social code*, including holding hands or linking arms or any gesture of affection such as kissing or prolonged touching. Such actions, even between husband and wife, are highly embarrassing to Arab observers.

A public display of intimacy is a particularly serious offense in Saudi Arabia, and incidents of problems and misunderstandings are frequent. One such incident occurred when an American woman was observed getting into a car with an American man, sliding over to his side, and kissing him on the cheek. A captain of the Saudi National Guard, who happened to see this, demanded proof that they were married. They were, but not to each other. The woman was deported, and the man, who compounded his problem by being argumentative, was sent to jail. Even behavior such as holding hands (especially among young people) is still viewed by most people everywhere with disapproval.

## ✤ THE STATUS OF WOMEN

The degree to which women have been integrated into the workforce and circulate freely in public varies among the Arab countries. In Morocco, Algeria, Tunisia, Egypt, Lebanon, Syria, Jordan, and Iraq, educated women have been active at all levels of society. Women have been heads of state in four non-Arab Islamic countries: Pakistan, Bangladesh, Indonesia, and Turkey.

In the Arabian Gulf states, about half of the educated women work outside the home, and the government is encouraging women's education and participation in the workplace. Those who do work are mainly in professions such as law, medicine, or academia. They work in all-female environments; an exception is made for the medical professions. All Arab governments now support efforts to increase women's educational opportunities.

In the area of domestic law, Arab women have traditionally not fared so well. Weighing Islamic law (*Sharia*) against current Western criteria of what constitutes women's equality has become very controversial, and an impassioned discussion of this issue is ongoing virtually everywhere. Traditional Islamic law restricts the rights of women, and this seems to many people to be seriously outdated. The various points of view rest on interpretations of the Qur'an, which, like any holy book, can be obscure and unclear. Like the Bible, the Qur'an is a product of its times, and it does not reflect modern concepts on issues such as slavery and women's rights.

Morocco and Tunisia have been outstanding in efforts to blend Sharia law with women's rights. There is a Muslim organization in Europe, the LibForAll Foundation, that promotes moderate interpretations of Sharia throughout the Islamic world. Dr. Abu Zayd at the foundation has asserted that the Qur'an need not be interpreted literally; when interpreted "sensibly in context," it carries a strong message of social justice and women's rights. (1) There is a project to retranslate the Qur'an in light of modern academic scholarship, which is yielding interpretations in keeping with "the ethics of the modern age" and fighting against cultural practices that are justified as religious. (2) Much more discussion and many adjustments are coming, because Muslim societies are so culturally, socially, ethnically, and, to an extent, religiously diverse.

Feminism in the Middle East is not the same as in the West. Muslim women do not expect an all-at-once liberation from traditional restrictions, and certainly not from gender roles. They are working *within* religious values, picking their battles, and taking it step by step.

Westerners have an exaggerated image of the status of Arab and Mulsim women, having seen so many lurid stories in the news. A kind of folk knowledge has grown up—the image of Muslim women as oppressed, servile, and without rights. Much information about Arab women, in print and online, is very dated; anything over five years old should be viewed with skepticism and checked. Some stories have dealt with unusual, newsworthy events, and many are based on the worst possible examples—the Taliban in Afghanistan, the Wahhabis in Saudi Arabia, the strict rules in post-revolutionary Iran. It is natural to generalize from certain incidents and arrive at a distorted view of this issue. In fact, most Muslim women are happy in their lives, all the while working to make them better.

In 2006, a Gallup poll asked whether the men and women interviewed in the Middle East agree that women should have leadership roles. Of the Moroccans who participated in the survey, 74 percent were in favor. In Jordan, it was 55 percent. Lebanon came in at 92 percent; 54 percent of the Egyptians also agreed. Only Saudi Arabia was below the halfway mark, at 40 percent.* (3)

Arab first ladies have been active in promoting women's rights for years. Arab Women's Conferences were held in 2005 and 2008, where many prominent women (activists, journalists, writers, and parliamentarians) called for greater awareness and efforts to protect women's rights. (4) Although few in the West have heard of the Arab Women's Organization set up in Egypt in 2002, fifteen out of twenty-two first ladies in the region are members. A conference titled "National Plans on Gender Equality: The Role of Women Parliamentarians" was held in Bahrain in December 2009. (5)

Arab Women's Day is commemorated annually on February 1. On Arab Women's Day in 2011, the first lady of Lebanon, Wafaa Suleiman, stated, "There can be no advancement whatsoever, at whatever level, if women are not among its key components." (6) These alliances are breaking taboos and getting feminist issues on the political agenda. The director of the U.N. Development Program's Arab Bureau said in 2006, "Women are making gains, but they are not realizing their full potential yet in contributing to the prosperity and strength of their societies." (7)

Despite strong efforts over the years, things could certainly be better, and women constantly confront obstacles. After the 2011 revolution in Tunisia, only two women were included in the transitional government. In Egypt, no women at all participated in revamping the constitution. This makes women worry that conservatives may try to repeal or reinterpret progressive family laws. (8)

In March 2011 there was an annual Women of the World conference in New York City, in which women from all over the world discussed the effects of the Arab revolutions on women's status. Factors considered were women's long-standing participation in protests (it's not really a new role for Arab women), the nature of the religiously conservative societies in the Arab region, and the need to renegotiate between emergent conservatives and progressives when the situation is more stable. (9)

Impediments to change are political and traditional, *not religious*. Because the laws are subject to change (forward or backward), the role of women in Arab society and in Islam is by no means static or fixed, even

---

*The non-Arab countries included were Turkey, 96 percent, and Pakistan, 58 percent.

in Saudi Arabia. And the Internet and expanded media communications are facilitating region-wide contacts and making both men and women open to new ideas. (10)

## ❈ WOMEN'S RIGHT TO VOTE

In most Arab countries women have the right to vote. Progress in this sphere is evident, and any differences among Arab countries are social, certainly not related to Islam. In Kuwait, there was a large protest demonstration in March 2005, which resulted in women gaining the right to vote (it was the parliament, not the ruler, that opposed it). In Saudi Arabia, women were given the vote in September 2011, but have not yet participated in elections. In the UAE, women still do not have the right to vote, but pressure is growing. The table that follows is a summary of the current situation.

❈ ❈ ❈ ❈ ❈ ❈ ❈ ❈ ❈ ❈ ❈ ❈ ❈ ❈ ❈ ❈ ❈ ❈ ❈ ❈

### DATE WOMEN'S SUFFRAGE GRANTED (11)

| | |
|---|---|
| Iraq | 1948 |
| Syria | 1949/1953 |
| Lebanon | 1952 |
| Egypt | 1956 |
| Tunisia | 1957/1959 |
| Algeria | 1962 |
| Morocco | 1963 |
| Libya | 1964 |
| Sudan | 1964 |
| Jordan | 1974 |
| Yemen | 1993 |
| Oman | 1994 |
| Qatar | 1998/2003 |
| Bahrain | 2001/2002 |
| Kuwait | 2005 |
| Saudi Arabia | 2011 |

## ❄ WOMEN IN GOVERNMENT POSITIONS

Arab women are increasingly represented at various levels of government. Women serve in the cabinets of most countries, except the most conservative. Women are generally well represented in parliaments, where most countries have a quota for a minimum number of seats for women.

❄ ❄ ❄ ❄ ❄ ❄ ❄ ❄ ❄ ❄ ❄ ❄ ❄ ❄ ❄ ❄ ❄ ❄ ❄ ❄ ❄ ❄

### ARAB WOMEN IN PARLIAMENT AS OF MARCH 2011 (12)

| Iraq | 82 |
| --- | --- |
| Egypt | 64 |
| Tunisia* | |
| Morocco | 40 |
| Algeria | 37 |
| Libya | 36 |
| Syria | 31 |
| Jordan | 22 |
| Oman | 14 |
| UAE | 9 |
| Bahrain | 12 |
| Kuwait | 5 |
| Lebanon | 4 |
| Yemen | 3 |
| Qatar | 0 |
| Saudi Arabia | 0 |
| Sudan* | |

*Information not available.

## ❄ WOMEN'S POWER IN THE FAMILY

In traditional Arab society, men and women have well-defined spheres of activity and decision making. Do not assume that because Arab women are not highly visible in public, their influence is similarly restricted in private life.

Inside the family, women have a good deal of power. They usually have the decisive voice in matters relating to household expenditures, the upbringing and education of children, and sometimes the arrangement of their children's marriages. Men are responsible for providing the family's material welfare, so even if a woman has her own money, she need not contribute to family expenses. In fact, many women do have their own money, and many own property, such as homes and businesses. Islamic law states clearly that they retain sole control of their money and inheritance after marriage.

The older a woman becomes, the more status and power she accrues. Men owe great respect to their mothers all their lives, and they must make every effort to obey their mother's wishes, even her whims. All older women in the family are treated with deference, but the mother of sons gains even more status.

## ❃ THE HEADSCARF AND THE VEIL

The wearing of the Hejab (the headscarf) is, of course, controversial, both inside and outside the Middle East.† Yet the number of women wearing the Hejab has increased enormously in the last twenty-five years. It began with the Islamic revival in the 1980s and 1990s, and it has gradually and steadily spread throughout society.

Most Westerners see the Hejab as a symbol of women's oppression, but not all Muslims agree. It may only be a sign that the wearer is conservative. Whether or not there is a political significance attached may depend on the wearer. A woman is (theoretically) making a free choice, since the Hejab *is not required by the Islamic religion.* However, there is growing *social* pressure from family or friends to wear the head covering. On the other hand, some families are actually distressed that their daughters are doing so. While some Arab Muslim women see the Hejab as a religious, cultural, or political statement, other women strongly disagree and disapprove.

Some observers believe that the voluntary wearing of headscarves is a manifestation, in a person or in the whole society, of a growing sense of

---

†Covering the hair should not be referred to as "veiling," since that requires that the face be covered.

Muslim identity. Women often say that by masking their sexuality, they are far freer in their movements in society. They believe that the headscarf deters unwelcome attentions from men because they see it and respect it. Many women wear headscarves that are chic, expensive, and highly decorated.

The situation differs widely among countries and regions. The only two Muslim nations that forbid the Hejab are Tunisia and Turkey. However, it *is* being worn in Turkey, often as a "cultural" headscarf in order to bypass the law. In Tunisia, the authorities ban women in headscarves from schools, government buildings, and some public places. Police have been known to stop women and ask them to remove a Hejab.

The full face veil (the Niqab) is banned in Syria, but not the Hejab, which is in fairly wide use. Syria's current government is secular, so this could change. In Jordan, about half of the women wear a Hejab, but a face veil is rare. The Hejab is also seen in Lebanon, though at a much lower rate than in other Arab countries.

In Egypt the Hejab is widespread, worn by about 80 percent of the women. It is not encouraged by the current government, but it is not forbidden. In some cases the Hejab has been seen as a political symbol, but many Egyptian women use the Hejab for social acceptance among peers and as a fashion statement. A small number of women wear the face veil as well. In 2009 scholars at the Azhar University‡ stated that full veiling of the face is not required under Islam. They said, "It is a custom and not a form of worship." (13) (14) There was a ban against the veil on college campuses during examinations. After protests, the ban was lifted, and male professors have to bring in female aides to verify women's identification. A similar ruling was made by the Azhar regarding the Hejab, reiterated in May 2012. This, too, is causing pushback. (15)

In Morocco, the Hejab is not encouraged, and it is generally frowned upon by the urban middle and higher classes. It is not traditional, and its use is often viewed as a religious or political decision. It is more common in the north and in the workers' class; in one French-owned factory, more than 95 percent of the women covered their hair in 2005, compared with only 20 percent ten years earlier. (16)

---

‡ The Azhar is as close as Sunni Islam comes to having a central authority; it is recognized as the premier religious center.

Women in the conservative countries of the Arabian Peninsula all cover their hair, and most wear a face veil in public, although not necessarily indoors. The veil is more strictly required in Saudi Arabia than elsewhere.

In any case, Muslim women feel that Westerners are too concerned with the way Muslim women dress, considering the other issues they face. Many Muslim feminists defend their conservative dress in terms of nationalism, anti-imperialism, or as a matter of personal faith.

The Qur'an itself says nothing explicit about veiling. This was a later development that did not become widespread in the Islamic empire until three or four generations after the death of Muhammad. The custom of veiling and secluding women came into the Muslim world from Persia and Byzantium.§ (17)

The Qur'an is far more protective of women's rights and status than is the case with more recent social practices. It contains only three verses referring to women's modesty, none of which mentions hair. (18) Here are the two most cited. (The third refers to the Prophet's wives, who generally conversed with people from behind a curtain.)

> O Prophet, tell the wives and daughters that they should cast their outer garments over their persons when abroad, that is the most convenient, that they should be known and not molested. (33:59)
>
>     Say to the believing men that they should lower their gaze and guard their modesty... And say to the believing women that they should lower their gaze and guard their modesty; that they should not display their beauty and ornaments except what must appear thereof; that they should draw their veils over their bosoms and not display their beauty except to their husbands, their fathers... [it goes on to list male relatives, small children, etc.] (24:30-31)

Arab women generally wear clothing that is at least knee-length, with sleeves that cover at least half of their arms. However, the practice of wearing more conservative, floor-length, long-sleeved clothing is increasing, even in modern cities like Cairo and Amman.

---

§Certainly there were restrictions on women in Europe in past times. "In the Middle Ages the position was reversed: then the Muslims were horrified to see the way Western Christians treated their women in the Crusader states, and Christian scholars denounced Islam for giving too much power to menials like slaves and women." (19)

# ❀ POLYGAMY

The issue of polygamy in the Arab world is overemphasized in the West, where many people think it is a common practice and is widely condoned. In fact, though, polygamy is allowed only under certain conditions in most Arab countries and is outlawed altogether in others. About 1 or 2 percent of married men have more than one wife. Because laws are more traditional in the Arabian Peninsula and men have more money, polygamy is more common there. In other places, polygamy must meet conditions such as the following: the man must prove he can support all wives separately and equally; a judge's permission must be obtained in response to an unusual condition, such as a wife who cannot bear children; or the first wife must be informed and can obtain a divorce if she disapproves.

Many secular elements in governments disapprove of polygamy, as do the middle and upper classes in non-Peninsular countries. There is considerable variation among countries because it is a controversial issue. Nowadays almost nobody can afford the cost of maintaining more than one family, so polygamy is practiced only by the very rich or by villagers and peasants, who need help with labor and do not incur large expenses.

Polygamy was sanctioned in the seventh century, after a series of battles in which many men were killed and many widows and orphans were left behind. The following verse from the Qur'an refers to the aftermath of these battles:

> If you fear that you will not act justly towards the orphans, marry
> such women as seem good to you, two, three, four; but if you fear that
> you will not be able to deal justly (with them), then only one, or what
> your right hands own. That will be more suitable to prevent you from
> doing injustice. (4:3)

Most modern commentators take this verse to mean that polygamy is restricted to certain circumstances and monogamy is encouraged. "What your right hands own" refers to slaves or captives, common in the seventh century. The Qur'an continues:

> You will not be able to be fair and just between your wives, even if it
> is your ardent desire (4:129)

This is, at best, ambiguous, and it is easy to see how the verses could have multiple interpretations.

It is unfortunate that we see so many references in Western magazines and newspapers to polygamy, making it look commonplace.¶ Most
mainstream Muslims realize that it has outlived its time and purpose.
Polygamy was decreasing markedly for years, although with the recent
rise of religious conservatism, we may see it increase once again. It is no
surprise that Osama Bin Laden is said to have married eleven to sixteen
women, although only four at a time.

Polygamy is permitted in Saudi Arabia, Kuwait, the UAE, Libya,
Jordan, Morocco, Lebanon, and Egypt. It is conditionally permitted in
Iraq, Syria, and Algeria, and outlawed in Tunisia. (21) For the record,
polygamy is far more practiced in sub-Saharan Africa than anywhere
else in the world.

## ❋ TRADITIONAL GENDER ROLES

Westerners hear and read about events involving certain Muslim women
(forced marriages, family punishments, and seclusion) and perceive them
as typical of the subjugation of women in Islamic society as a whole. Some
of this is a valid criticism, and many people in the West and the Middle
East believe that legal redress is urgently needed. Nevertheless, even if we
Westerners disagree with the status quo, we must at least try to *understand* the traditional view and not be too quick to judge and condemn
motives and cultural practices, many of which are *not* related to religion.

---

¶A case in point is Bernard Lewis' article "Targeted by a History of Hatred: The United
States Is Now the Unquestioned Leader of the Free World, Also Known as the Infidels,"
which appeared in *The Washington Post* on September 10, 2002, during the first Gulf
War. (20) The subject was his explanation of Muslims (referring to all of them) hating
the United States and hating the West for centuries. It goes on to state that hatred has
been growing, and "one reason for the contempt with which they regard us" is due to
"what they perceive as the rampant immorality and degeneracy of the American way"
(the reference to "they" is unclear). Then polygamy is mentioned as a factor to explain
contempt toward Christianity and, more generally, toward the West. There follows a
quote from "a recent Arabic newspaper article in defense of polygamy." The quote is
explicit, detailed, and to Western ears offensive, yet the source is left vague and the
author gives the impression that polygamy is part of the modern Arab way of life, when
98 percent of Arab men are monogamous and most would not even consider polygamy.
I mention this because I think that making these statements without any qualifications
reinforces stereotypes about Middle Eastern Arabs and Muslims and may strengthen
a negative image.

Unlike Western assumptions about Arab society, *tradition-oriented* Arab men and women do not view social customs and restrictions as repressive but as *an appropriate acknowledgement of the nature of women*. They do not see this as cruel, nor do they despise women. They sincerely see the restrictions as providing protection for women so that they need not be subjected to the stress, competition, temptations, and possible indignities found in outside society. Most Arab women, even now, feel satisfied that the present social system provides them with security, protection, and respect.

Middle East gender roles have traditionally been governed by a patriarchal kinship system that had already existed in the regions to which Islam spread. Many of the variations in the status of women are due to local traditions (such as covering the entire face). Men are expected to provide for their families; women, to bear and raise children; children, to honor and respect their parents and grow up to fulfill adult roles (which include marriage). (22) It is important for an outsider to keep these points of view in mind when analyzing and discussing the status of Arab women. A woman who was elected to Iraq's National Assembly stated, "To tell you the truth, I am not a feminist. I don't want to commit the same mistakes Western women have committed. I like that family should be the major principle for women here." (23)

## ❋ WESTERN WOMEN

Western women find that they do not quite fit into Arab society; they are not accorded the full rights of men but they are not considered bound by all the restrictions of Arab women either.

Western women are expected to behave with propriety, but they are not required to be as conservative as Arab women in dress or in public behavior. They need not use full face veils in Saudi Arabia, for example, and can simply cover their hair. But all women are expected to dress conservatively, preferably in loose clothing. Western women may go shopping, attend public activities, or travel alone. The respectability of a Western woman will be judged by *the way she is groomed and dressed*.

Arabs accept professional Western women and admire them for their accomplishments. Women have had great success as diplomats in the region. Well-educated women find that their opinions are taken seriously, and they are often invited to all-male professional gatherings. When a woman has a work-related reason to call on someone or to be present at any event, she is usually welcomed, and men are comfortable with her presence.

## ❈ LOOKING TOWARD THE FUTURE

There is every reason to be optimistic, on the whole, about women's over-all progress in the Middle East. Trends are good. Arab women do not hesitate to call for more rights and recognition, and they are steadily becoming better integrated into public society.

## CHAPTER 6

# SOCIAL FORMALITIES AND ETIQUETTE

Social formalities and rules of etiquette are extremely important in Arab society. *Good manners constitute the most salient factor in evaluating a person's character.*

## ❋ HOSPITALITY

Arabs (and all Middle Easterners) are generous in the hospitality they offer to friends and strangers alike, and they admire and value the same in others. *Generosity to guests is essential for a good reputation.* It is a serious insult to characterize someone as stingy or inhospitable.

Arabs assume the role of host or hostess whenever the situation calls for it—in their office, home, or shop. Sometimes people say, "Welcome to my country" (in English) when they see a foreigner on the street or in a shop, thus assuming the role of host to a guest. Arabs are always willing to help a foreigner, again, because they take on the role of host. If you ask directions, some people may insist on accompanying you to your destination. One American tourist reported that when she and her husband were visiting Egypt, people sometimes took their hands to help with crossing the street in the midst of harrowing traffic. (1)

A guest in someone's home or in the workplace never stays long without being offered something to drink, and it is assumed that the guest will accept and drink at least a small quantity as an expression of friendship or esteem. When you are served a beverage, accept and hold the cup or glass with your right hand. The left hand is considered unclean.

No matter how much coffee or tea you have had elsewhere, never decline this offer. Some shops and business offices have employees whose sole duty is to serve beverages to guests. You will notice that while a Westerner would likely ask guests, "Would you care for coffee or tea?" which suggests that the guest may or may not want any, a Middle Easterner would ask, "What would you like—coffee or tea?" which simply gives the guests a choice. If someone comes to a home or place of business while food is being served, the people eating always offer to share the food. Usually an unexpected guest declines, but the gesture must be made.

The phrase *Ahlan wa Sahlan* or *Marhaba* (Welcome) is used when a guest arrives, and it is repeated several times during a visit. A guest is often given a seat of honor (this is particularly common as a gesture to a foreigner), and solicitous inquiries are made about the guest's comfort during the visit. Sometimes you may feel uncomfortable because you are getting so much attention.

Regardless of pressing circumstances, an Arab would never consider refusing entrance to a guest, even if the guest is unexpected and the visit inconvenient. The only excusable circumstance would be if a woman (or women) were at home alone when a man dropped by. In that case, the visitor would refuse to enter, even if his prospective host were expected back very soon.

Arabs are proud of their tradition of hospitality and have many anecdotes illustrating it. A favorite is the story of the Bedouin who killed his last camel (or sheep) to feed his guest. The word for "generous, hospitable" in Arabic is *kareem*, and this concept is so highly valued that its meanings extend to "distinguished, noble-minded, noble-hearted, honorable, respectable" (there are twenty-five meanings in the dictionary).

In turn, Arabs expect to be received with hospitality when they are guests, and your personal image and status will be affected by people's perceptions of your hospitality. The most important components of hospitality are welcoming a guest (including using the word *Welcome*), offering the guest a seat (in many Arab homes, there is a special room set aside for receiving guests, called the "salon"), and offering something to drink. As a host, stay with your guests as much as possible, excusing yourself for brief absences from the room only as necessary. This is a description of Arab hospitality, written by an Arab woman:

> For Arabs, hospitality is at the heart of who we are. How well one treats his guests is a direct measurement of what kind of a person she or he is. Hospitality is among the most highly admired of virtues. Indeed, families judge themselves and each other according to the amount of generosity they bestow upon their guests when they enter- tain. Whether one's guests are relatives, friends, neighbors, or relative strangers, they are welcomed into the home and to the dinner table with much the same kindness and generosity. (2)

A guest often does not see the rest of the house and meets only the family members who are presented. Privacy *within* a family is not valued, but privacy from *the outside* is essential. Most houses are set behind high walls.

Hospitality extends to the public sphere, too. In Tunis, Cairo, Beirut, and Amman I have asked for directions and been escorted to my des- tination, though in each instance it was a long walk and a considerable inconvenience for my guide. When thanking someone for such a favor, you will hear the response, "No thanks are needed for a duty." No task is too burdensome for a hospitable host.

## ❊ TIME AND APPOINTMENTS

Among Arabs, time is not as fixed and rigidly segmented as it tends to be among Westerners. It flows from past to present to future, and Arabs flow with it. Social occasions and appointments need not have fixed begin- nings or endings. Arabs are thus much more relaxed about the timing of events than they are about other aspects of their lives. Nevertheless, these attitudes are beginning to change as people respond to the demands of economic and technological development and modernization.

Some Arabs are careful to arrive on time (and are impatient with those who do not), and some are habitually late, especially for social events. Given these attitudes, a person who arrives late and has kept you waiting may not realize that you have been inconvenienced and expect an apology.

Frequently, an Arab shopkeeper or someone in a service trade fails to have something finished by a promised time. This also pertains to public services (such as getting a landline telephone connected), personal services, bus and train departures, customer services (where standing in long lines can be expected), and bureaucratic procedures. Be flexible; everyone expects delays. You will appear unreasonably impatient and demanding if you insist on having things finished at a precise time.

If you invite people for dinner or a social event, do not expect all of your guests to arrive at the specified time. A dinner should be served rather late, and plans should always be flexible enough to accommodate latecomers.

The Arabic word (and sentence) *Ma'alish* represents an entire way of looking at life and its frustrations. It means "Never mind" or "It doesn't matter" or "Excuse me—it's not that serious." You will hear this said frequently when someone has had a delay, a disappointment, or an unfortunate experience. Rather than give in to pointless anger, Arabs often react to impersonally caused adversity with resignation and, to some extent, an acceptance of their fate.

## ❈ DISCUSSING BUSINESS

Arabs mistrust people who do not appear to be sincere or who fail to demonstrate an interest in them personally or in their country. They also don't like to be hurried or to feel they are being pressured into a business agreement. If they like you, they will agree to work out an arrangement or a compromise; if they do not like you, they will probably stop listening. *Arabs evaluate the source of a statement or proposal as much as the content.*

Initial reactions by your Arab counterparts to your suggestions, ideas, and proposals can be quite misleading if taken at face value. Arabs are not likely to criticize openly but are more likely to hint that changes are needed or to give more subtle indications that the proposal is unacceptable—by inaction, for instance. They may promise to be in touch but fail to do so (which is more polite than a refusal), or they might offer a radical counterproposal that may constitute a position from which compromise is expected.

Don't take flattery and praise too seriously. It will more likely be adherence to good manners than an indicator of potential success in the business transaction. A noncommittal reaction to a proposal does not mean it has been rejected; nor does it guarantee ultimate acceptance. Some decisions simply require consultation with superiors (if you are not dealing with the top person). Only time will tell the outcome. More often than not, success will depend on patience and the cultivation of good personal relations.

Despite the frustration you may feel as a result of delays, *if you press for a specific time by which you want a decision, you may actually harm your chances of success.* Your counterpart may perceive it as an insult, especially if the person is a high-ranking manager or executive.

The vice president of an American engineering company was meeting with a high-level Saudi official in the Ministry of Planning in Riyadh. The company's local representative had been trying for several weeks to obtain approval for one of the company's proposals. The vice president decided to set a deadline. He asked to receive a definite answer during the week while he was still in town. The Saudi looked surprised and appeared irritated. Then he answered that he could not guarantee action within that time period. The proposal was never approved.

If a decision is coming slowly, it may mean that you need to reassess the proposal. Do not expect to conclude all of your business at once, especially if several decisions are required. Patience and repeated visits are called for. Arabs have plenty of time, and they see little need to accommodate foreigners who are in a hurry and trying to pressure them.

## ❊ SHARING MEALS

Arabs enjoy inviting guests to their homes for meals; a foreigner will probably be a guest at meals many times. Sharing food together provides an Arab host and hostess with a perfect opportunity to display their generosity and demonstrate their personal regard for you.

It is not an Arab custom to send written invitations or to request confirmation of acceptance. Invitations are usually verbal and often spontaneous.

If it is your first invitation, check with others for the time meals are usually served and for the time you are actually expected to arrive.

Westerners often arrive too early and assume the meal will be served earlier than is customary. In most Arab countries (but not all), a large midday meal is served between 2:00 and 3:00 P.M., and a supper (with guests) is served about 10:00 or 11:00 P.M. Guests should arrive about two hours before the meal, since most of the conversation takes place before the meal, not after it. If the dinner is formal and official, you may be expected to arrive at the specified time, and you can expect the meal to end within an hour or two.

Arabs serve a great quantity of food when they entertain—indeed, they are famous for their munificence and very proud of it. They do not try to calculate the amount of food actually needed; on the contrary, the intention is to present abundant food, which displays generosity. (The leftover food does not go to waste; it is consumed by the family or by servants for several days afterward.)

Most foreigners who have experienced Arab meals have their favorite hospitality stories. For example, I was told about a banquet once given by a wealthy merchant in Qatar who was known for his largess. After several courses the guests were served an entire sheep—one per person!

You can expect to be offered second and third helpings of food, and you should make the gesture of accepting at least once. Encouraging guests to eat is part of an Arab host or hostess's duty and is required for good manners. This encouragement to eat more is called *'uzooma* in Arabic, and the more traditional the host, the more insistently it is done. Guests often begin with a ritual refusal and allow themselves to be won over by the host's insistence. You will hear, for example,

"No, thanks."
*"Oh, but you must!"*
"No, I really couldn't!"
*"You don't like the food!"*
"Oh, but I do!"
*"Well then, have some more!"*

Water is often not served until after a meal is finished; some people consider it unhealthy to eat and drink at the same time. In any case, Arab food is rarely flavored to be "hot," although it may be highly seasoned.

A guest is expected to express admiration and gratitude for the food. Because you are trying to be polite, you will probably overeat. Many people eat sparingly on the day they are invited out to dinner because they know how much food will be served that evening.

When you have eaten enough, you may refuse more by saying, *Alhamdu lillah* (Thanks be to God). When the meal is over and you are about to leave the table, it is customary to say, *Dayman* (Always) or *Sufra dayma* (May your table always be thus) to the host and hostess. The most common responses are *Ti'eesh* (May you live) and *Bil hana wa shifa* (To your happiness and health).

After a meal, tea or coffee will be served, usually presweetened. Conversation continues for a while longer, perhaps an hour, and then guests prepare to leave. In some countries, bringing a tray of ice water around is a sign that dinner is over and guests are free to leave. In the Arabian Peninsula countries, incense or cologne may be passed around just before the guests depart. When guests announce their intention to leave, the host and hostess usually exclaim, "Stay a while—it's still early!" This offer is ritual; you may stay a few more minutes, but the expression need not be taken literally, and it does not mean that you will give offense by leaving. Generally, you can follow the example of other guests. However, since many Arab people prefer to stay out very late, you may be the first to leave. In most Arab countries, you do not have to stay after midnight.

When you are invited to a meal, it is appropriate, although not required, to bring a small gift. Flowers, candy, or cakes are the most common. You will see elaborately wrapped gifts of sweets displayed in stores; they are intended for hospitality gifts.

*If you invite Arabs to your home, consider adopting some of their mealtime customs.* It will improve their impression of you.

In the countries of the Arabian Peninsula, women rarely go out socially in mixed company. When you invite a man and his wife to your home, the wife may not appear. It depends largely on whether the couple is accustomed to socializing with foreigners and on who else will be there. It is considerate, when a man is inviting a couple, to say, "My wife invites your wife" and to volunteer information about who else is invited. This helps the husband decide whether he wishes his wife to meet the other guests, and it assures him that other women will be present. Don't be surprised if some guests do not come, or if someone arrives with a friend or two.

Always serve plenty of food, with two or three main meat dishes; otherwise you may give the impression of being stingy. I once heard an Egyptian describe a dinner at an American's home where the guests were served one large steak apiece. "They counted the steaks, and they even counted the potatoes," he said. "We were served baked potatoes—one per person!"

If you serve buffet style rather than a sit-down dinner with courses, your eating schedule will be more flexible and the visual impression of the amount of food served will be enhanced. Give thought to your menu, considering which foods are eaten locally and which are not. Serve foods in fairly simple, recognizable form, so guests won't wonder what they are eating in a foreigner's home. Arabs usually do not care for sweetened meats or for sweet salads with the main meal.

Muslims are forbidden to eat pork. Some foreigners serve pork as one of the choices at a buffet and label it. However, it is best not to serve pork at all. Even in a buffet, it can be disconcerting to Muslim guests, who may wonder if the pork has touched any of the rest of the food.

The consumption of alcohol is forbidden for Muslims. Do not use it in your cooking unless you either label or mention it. If you cook with wine or other alcohol, you will limit the dishes available to your Muslim guests—it does not matter that the alcohol may have evaporated during cooking. If you wish to serve wine or alcoholic beverages, have non-alcoholic drinks available too.

Be sure to serve your guests second and third helpings of food. Although you don't have to insist vigorously, you should make the gesture. Serve coffee and tea at the end of a meal.

## ❀ SMOKING

A majority of Arab adults smoke, although women seldom smoke in public. Smoking is considered an integral part of adult behavior and constitutes, to some extent, the expression of an individual's "coming of age." Arab men, in particular, view smoking as a right, not a privilege. Do not be surprised if you see people disregarding "no smoking" signs in airplanes, waiting rooms, or elevators.

Arabs are rarely aware that smoking may be offensive to some Westerners. You can ask someone to refrain from smoking by explaining that it bothers you, but he may light up again after a few minutes. If you press the point too strongly, you will appear unreasonable. If possible, have a place available where people are welcome to smoke; it will help them relax.

## ❧ RULES OF ETIQUETTE

Listed below are some of the basic rules of etiquette in Arab culture:

- ❧ It is important to sit properly. Slouching, draping the legs over the arm of a chair, or otherwise sitting carelessly when talking with someone communicates a lack of respect for that person. Legs are never crossed on top of a desk or table when talking with someone.
- ❧ When standing and talking with someone, it is considered disrespectful to lean against the wall or keep one's hands in one's pockets.
- ❧ Sitting in a manner that allows the sole of one's shoe to face another person is an insult.
- ❧ In many countries and homes, a guest removes his or her shoes at the door. This is especially common in the Arabian Peninsula, which is one reason that slip-on sandals are usually worn. You can tell if this is required in two ways. First, watch others. Second, note if there is a pile of shoes at the door. You may keep your socks on. Removing your shoes is a sign of respect; it is always required in a mosque.
- ❧ Failure to shake hands when meeting or bidding someone good-bye is considered rude. However, when a Western man is introduced to an Arab woman, it is the woman's choice whether to shake hands or not; she should be allowed to make the first move. (Pious Muslims may decline to shake hands with a woman; this is not an insult.)
- ❧ Casual dress at social events, many of which call for rather formal dress (a suit and tie for men; a dress, high heels, and jewelry for women) may be taken as a lack of respect for the hosts or the occasion. There are, of course, some occasions for which casual dress is appropriate. Ask in advance how people are expected to be dressed.

❖ One who lights a cigarette in a group must be prepared to offer cigarettes to everyone.

❖ Men stand when a woman enters a room; everyone stands when new guests arrive at a social gathering and when an elderly or high-ranking person enters or leaves.

❖ Men allow women to precede them through doorways, and men offer their seats to women if no others are available.

❖ It is customary to usher elderly people to the front of any line or to offer to stand in their place. Elderly people should be greeted first.

❖ When saying good-bye to guests, a gracious host accompanies them to the outer gate, or to their car, or at least as far as the elevator in a high-rise building.

❖ If a guest admires something small and portable, an Arab may insist that it be taken as a gift. Guests need to be careful about expressing admiration for small, expensive items.

❖ In many countries, gifts are given and accepted with both hands and are not opened in the presence of the donor.

❖ In some social situations, especially in public places or when very traditional Arabs are present, it may be considered inappropriate for women to smoke or to drink alcoholic beverages.

❖ When eating with Arabs, especially when taking food from communal dishes, guests should not use the left hand. As noted earlier, it is considered unclean. This "rule" is overemphasized by Westerners, though; it does not pertain if you have your own plate and are eating with a knife and fork.

❖ At a restaurant, Arabs will almost always insist on paying, especially if there are not many people in the party or if it is a business-related occasion. Giving in graciously after a ritual offer and then returning the favor later is an appropriate response. Announce in advance when you invite everyone as your guests.

❖ Arabs have definite ideas about what constitutes proper masculine and feminine behavior and appearance. They do not approve of long hair on men or mannish dress and comportment by women.

❖ Family disagreements and disputes in front of others or within hearing of others should be avoided.

- ❀ People should not be photographed without their permission.
- ❀ Staring at other people is not usually considered rude or an invasion of privacy by Arabs (especially when the object is a fascinating foreigner). Moving away is the best defense.
- ❀ When eating out with a large group of people where everyone is paying his or her own share, it is best to let one person pay and be reimbursed later. Arabs find the public calculation of a restaurant bill embarrassing.
- ❀ Most Arabs do not like to touch or be in the presence of household animals, especially dogs. Pets should be kept out of sight when Arab guests are present.

It is impossible, of course, to learn all the rules of a foreign culture. The safest course of action is to imitate. In a social situation, *never be the first one to do anything!*

## CHAPTER 7

# THE SOCIAL STRUCTURE

Arab society is structured into social classes, and individuals inherit the social class of their family. The governments of Libya and the former South Yemen have tried experimenting with classless societies, but this has not affected basic attitudes. It made little difference in Libya. South Yemen became the first country in the Arabian Peninsula to grant women the right to vote, but social classes remain even there.

## ❖ SOCIAL CLASSES

In most Arab countries, there are three social classes. The upper class includes royalty (in some countries), large and influential families, and some wealthy people, depending on their family background. The middle class is composed of professionals, government employees, military officers, and moderately prosperous merchants and landowners. Peasant farmers and the urban and village poor make up the lower class. Bedouins, of whom about 10 percent are nomadic, do not really fit into any of these classes; they are mostly independent of society and are admired for their preservation of Arab traditions. Bedouins live in Libya, Egypt (Sinai), Lebanon, Jordan, Syria, Iraq, and the Arabian Peninsula.

The relative degree of privilege among the classes and the differences in their attitude and way of life vary from country to country. Some countries are wealthy and underpopulated, with a large privileged class;

others are poor and overpopulated, with a high percentage of peasants and manual laborers.

There is usually very little tension among social classes. Arabs accept the social class into which they were born, and there is relatively little effort on the part of individuals to rise from one class to another. In any case it would be difficult for a person to change social class, since it is determined almost entirely by family origin. One can improve one's status through professional position and power, educational attainment, or acquired wealth, but the person's origins will be remembered. A family of the lower class could not really expect social acceptance in the upper class for two or three generations. Similarly, an upper-class family that squandered its wealth or influence would not be relegated to lower-class status for some time.

Foreign residents of Arab countries automatically accrue most of the status and privileges of the upper class. This is due to their professional standing, their level of education, and their income.

## ❁ IMAGE AND UPPER-CLASS BEHAVIOR

Certain kinds of behavior are expected of people in the upper class who wish to maintain their status and good public image. If you know the basic norms of upper-class behavior, you will be free to decide the extent to which you are willing to conform. While you risk giving a negative impression by breaking a rule, doing so will not necessarily be offensive. You may simply be viewed as eccentric or as having poor judgment. Still, some activities are simply not acceptable in public and, if seen, cause shock and surprise.

*No upper-class person engages in manual labor in front of others.* Arabs are surprised when they see Westerners cleaning their house, washing their cars or sweeping the sidewalk. While upper-class Arabs may do some menial chores inside their homes, they do not do them in public or in front of others.

A white-collar or desk job in an office is much desired by Arabs because of the status it confers. There is an enormous difference between working with one's hands and working as a clerk. Arabs who have white-collar jobs will resent being asked to do something they consider beneath their status. If, in an office situation, you find that your requests are not being carried out, you should consider if you have been asking a person to do something that is demeaning or threatening to his or her dignity. If that is the case, employees won't wish to offend you, so they will be hesitant to tell you. Instead, they may simply disregard the request.

An Egyptian interpreter in an American-managed hospital once told me that she was insulted when a Western doctor asked her to bring him a glass of water. She felt that her dignity had been threatened and that she had been treated like the "tea boy" who took orders for drinks.

Manual work is acceptable if it can be classified as a hobby—for example, sewing, painting, or craftwork. Refinishing furniture might get by as a hobby (though it would probably raise eyebrows), but repairing cars is out. If you decide to paint the exterior of your house or to refinish the floors yourself, expect to be the object of conversation.

*Upper-class Arabs are careful about their dress and appearance whenever they are in public, because the way a person dresses indicates his or her wealth and social standing.* Arab children are often dressed in expensive clothes, and women wear a lot of jewelry, especially gold. The men are partial to expensive watches, cuff links, pens, and cigarette lighters. Looking their best and dressing well are essential to Arabs' self-respect, and they are surprised when they see well-to-do foreigners wearing casual or old clothes (faded jeans, a tattered T-shirt). Why would a person dress poorly when he or she can afford better?

Usually, upper-class Arabs do not socialize with people from other classes, at least not in each other's homes. They may enjoy cordial relations with the corner grocer and newsstand vendor, but, like most Westerners, they would not suggest a dinner or an evening's entertainment together. (A possible exception is a big occasion like the celebration of a wedding.)

*When you plan social events, do not mix people from different social classes.* You can invite anyone from any class to your home, and the gesture will be much appreciated, but to invite a company director and your local baker at the same time would embarrass both parties.

## ❀ DEALING WITH SERVICE PEOPLE

Westerners living in an Arab country usually have one or more household servants. You may feel free to establish a personal relationship with your household help; they appreciate the kindness and consideration they have come to expect from Westerners—"Please" and "Thank you" are never out of place. You may, in fact, work right alongside the servant, but you will notice that the relationship changes if Arab guests are present. The servant will then want to do all the work alone so as not to tarnish your social image. If a glass of water is spilled, for example, you should call the servant to clean up, rather than be seen doing it yourself. Inviting your servant to join you and your guests at tea or at a meal would be inappropriate and embarrassing to everyone.

Servants expect you to assume some responsibility for them; you may, for example, be asked to pay medical expenses and to help out financially in family emergencies. Give at least something as a token of concern, then ask around to find out how much is reasonable for the situation. If you feel that the expense is too high for you to cover completely, you can offer to lend the money and deduct it from the person's salary over a period of time. Be generous with surplus food and with household items or clothing you no longer need, and remember that extra money is expected on holidays. All this is in keeping with the cultural and religious requirement to be generous with charity.

Make the acquaintance of shopkeepers, doormen, and errand boys. Such acquaintances are best made by exchanging a few words of Arabic and showing them that you like and respect them.

If you become friendly with people who have relatively little money, limit the frequency of your social visits. They may be obliged to spend more than they can afford to receive you properly, and the problem is far too embarrassing to discuss or even admit. It is enjoyable to visit villages or the home of a taxi driver or shopkeeper, but if you plan to make it a habit, bring gifts with you or find other ways to compensate your hosts.

## CHAPTER 8

# THE ROLE OF
# THE FAMILY

A rab society is built around the extended family system. Individuals feel a strong affiliation with all of their relatives—aunts, uncles, and cousins—not just with their immediate family. The degree to which all blood relationships are encompassed by a family unit varies among families, but most Arabs have over a hundred "fairly close" relatives.

## ❋ FAMILY LOYALTY AND OBLIGATIONS

*Family loyalty and obligations take precedence over loyalty to friends or the demands of a job.* Relatives are expected to help each other, including giving financial assistance if necessary. Family affiliation provides security and assures a person that he or she will never be entirely without resources, emotional or material. Only the most rash or foolhardy person would risk being censured or disowned by his or her family. Family support is indispensable in an unpredictable world; the family is a person's ultimate refuge.

Members of a family are expected to support each other in disputes with outsiders. Regardless of personal antipathy among relatives, they must defend each other's honor, counter criticism, and display group cohesion, if only for the sake of appearances. Internal family disputes rarely get to the point of open, public conflict.

Membership in a well-known or influential family ensures social acceptance and is often crucial in obtaining a good education, finding a good job, or succeeding in business. Arabs are very proud of their family connections and lineage.

The reputation of any member of a family group reflects on all of the other members. One person's indiscreet behavior or poor judgment can damage his or her relatives' pride, social influence, and marriage opportunities. For this reason family honor is the greatest source of pressure on an individual to conform to accepted behavior patterns, and one is constantly reminded of his or her responsibility for upholding that honor.

The family is the foundation of Middle Eastern society. The security offered by a stable family unit is greatly valued and considered essential for the spiritual growth of its members. A harmonious social order is created by the existence of close extended families. Strong families create strong communities and underpin social order.

An employer must be understanding if an employee is late or absent because of family obligations. *It is unreasonable to expect an Arab employee to give priority to the demands of a job if those demands conflict with family duties.*

The description of Syrian society found in the book *Syria: A Country Study*, is applicable to Arab societies in general:

> Syrians highly value family solidarity and, consequently, obedience of children to the wishes of their parents. Being a good family member includes automatic loyalty to kinsmen as well. Syrians employed in modern bureaucratic positions, such as government officials, therefore find impersonal impartiality difficult to attain because of a conflict with the deeply held value of family solidarity.
>
> There is no similarly ingrained feeling of duty toward a job, an employer, a coworker, or even a friend. A widespread conviction exists that the only reliable people are one's kinsmen. An office-holder tends to select his kinsmen as fellow workers or subordinates because of a sense of responsibility for them and because of the feeling of trust between them. Commercial establishments are largely family operations staffed by the offspring and relatives of the owner. Cooperation among business firms may be determined by the presence or absence of kinship ties between the heads of firms. . . . There is no real basis for a close relationship except ties of kinship. (1)

## ❀ RELATIONS AMONG FAMILY MEMBERS

An Arab man is recognized as the head of his immediate family, and his role and influence are overt. His wife also has a clearly defined sphere of influence, but it exists largely behind the scenes. Although an Arab woman is careful to show deference to her husband in public, she may not always accord him the same deference in private.

In matters where opinions among family members differ, much consultation and negotiation take place before decisions are made. If a compromise cannot be reached, however, the husband, father, or older men in the family prevail.

Status in a family increases as a person grows older, and most families have patriarchs or matriarchs whose opinions are given considerable weight in family matters. Children are taught profound respect for adults, a pattern that is pervasive in Arab society at all ages. It is common, for example, for adults to refrain from smoking in front of their parents or older relatives. This is a sign of respect.

Responsibility for other members of the family rests heavily on older men in the extended family and on older sons in the immediate family. Children are their parents' "social security," and grown sons, in particular, are responsible for the support of their parents. In the absence of the father, brothers are responsible for their unmarried sisters.

Members of a family are very dependent on each other emotionally, and these ties continue throughout a person's life. Some people feel closer to their brothers and sisters and confide in them more than they do their spouses. A directive written for foreign social workers in the Muslim Arab world stated:

> A family's involvement in individual helping may be considerable, and could make the social worker's task more complex. In Muslim Arab communities, many are raised to consider the family unit as a continual source of support. Extended family members may be highly valued as well. They may be expected to be involved and may be consulted in times of crisis. When a family member experiences a problem, the person's restoration may be of concern to many other members . . . although Muslim Arab peoples may value privacy and guard it vehemently, their personal privacy within the family is

virtually non-existent. Decisions regarding health care are made by
the family group and are not the responsibility of the individual. (2)

In the UAE, a conference was held on the subject "Role of the Family
and Welfare of the Elderly," in which the ruler's wife stated:

> We believe our sons and daughters are responsible toward God and
> our nation, for their parents when they grow old. We believe that
> undertaking this responsibility is one of the essential anchors of our
> society. . . . We have noticed, regretfully, some family members who
> do not care for the elderly. These contravene our values and tradi-
> tions. We hope this seminar will help in fighting these trends and
> suggest necessary legislation to punish those who are responsible for
> contravening our values and traditions. (3)

In the traditional Arab family, the roles of the mother and the father
are quite different as they relate to their children. The mother is seen
as a source of emotional support and steadfast loving-kindness. She is
patient, forgiving, and prone to indulge and spoil her children, especially
her sons. The father, while seen as a source of love, may display affection
less overtly; he is also the source of authority and punishment. Some
Arab fathers feel that their status in the family is best maintained by
cultivating awe and even a degree of fear in other members of the family,
but this is quite rare.

In most Arab families, the parents maintain very close contact with
their own parents and with their brothers and sisters. For this reason,
Arab children grow up experiencing constant interaction with older
relatives, including their grandparents, who often live in the same home.
This contributes to the passing on of social values from one generation
to another, as the influence of the older relatives is continually present.
Relatively few Arab teenagers and young adults rebel against family
values and desires, certainly not to the extent common in Western societies. Even people who affect modern tastes in dress, reading material,
and entertainment subscribe to the prevailing social values and expect
their own family lives to be very similar to that of their parents. Many
Arab extended families living in the West gather together every weekend
if possible.

## ❧ MARRIAGE

Most Arabs still prefer family-arranged marriages. Though marriage customs are changing in some modern circles, couples still seek family approval of the person they have chosen. This is essential as an act of respect toward their parents, and people rarely marry in defiance of their families.

Many Arabs feel that because marriage is such a major decision, it is considered prudent to leave it to the family's discretion rather than to choose someone solely on the basis of emotion or ideas of romance. In almost all Arab countries and social groups, however, the prospective bride and bridegroom have the opportunity to meet and become acquainted—and to accept or reject a proposal of marriage. The degree to which the individuals are consulted will vary according to how traditional or modern the family is.

Among Muslim Arabs, especially in rural and traditional communities and in the Arabian Peninsula, the preferred pattern of marriage is to a first or second cousin. In fact, marriage to relatives is on the rise. On average, about a third of all marriages are between cousins or someone in the same kin group (the global average is about 20 percent). (4) Estimates vary, though, between 20 percent and 50 percent, higher in the Arabian Peninsula. Genetic problems occur in about 10 percent of these marriages. (5) Globally, Middle East countries rank high in percentage of birth defects.*

There are good reasons for this marriage pattern. Since an important part of a marriage arrangement is the investigation into the social and financial standing of the proposed candidates, it is reassuring to marry someone whose background, character, and financial position are well known. Marrying within the family is the principal means of reinforcing kinship solidarity. This is one reason many Arabs do not give their first loyalty to their nation and remain kin- and clan-oriented; even heads of state often place other loyalties ahead of national interests. Marrying a cousin acts as a protection for the wife, who is likely to have better

---

*Defects per 1000 births are 82 in Sudan and 81 in Saudi Arabia, and are in the 70s in Palestine, the UAE, Iraq, and Kuwait. The world average is around 50; Western nations have percentages in the 30s and 40s. (6)

relations with her in-laws than she would with outsiders and can win their support in time of need. Daughters who marry relatives will also be better able to care for elderly parents who are kin to the husband. If the bride is from outside the family, potentially her husband may develop more solidarity with her family and lessen his loyalty to his own. Marriage to a cousin also ensures that money, in the form of a dowry or an inheritance, stays within the family.

In contrast with Western couples, Arab couples do not usually enter marriage with idealistic or exaggerated romantic expectations. True, they are seeking companionship and love, but equally important, they want financial security, the social status of being married, and children. These goals are realistic and are usually attained. Arab marriages are, on the whole, very stable and characterized by mutual respect. Having a happy family life is considered a paramount goal in the Arab world.

## ❊ DIVORCE

Most Arab Christians belong to denominations that do not permit divorce. Among Muslims, divorce is permitted and regulated by religious law. In some countries, civil law also plays a part. Divorce is common enough that it does not carry a social stigma for the individuals involved, and people who have been divorced are eligible for remarriage.

Although a Muslim may divorce his wife if he wishes, he risks severe damage to his social image if he is arbitrary or hasty about his decision. The process in traditional Islam is quite simple: he merely recites the formula for divorce ("I divorce you") in front of witnesses. If he says the formula once or twice, the couple can still be reconciled; if he repeats it a third time, even on a separate occasion, it is binding. Almost every Middle Eastern country has modified this and now requires court proceedings, stipulating the wife's rights to alimony and child support.

A woman must go through court proceedings in order to divorce her husband. She is usually successful on grounds of childlessness, desertion, or nonsupport. In Jordan, Syria, and Morocco, she may write into her marriage contract the right to initiate divorce. Such protections are increasing.

When a Muslim woman is divorced, her husband must pay a divorce settlement, which is included in every marriage contract and is usually a very large sum of money. In addition she is entitled to financial support for herself for at least three months (a waiting period to determine that she is not pregnant) and more if she needs it, as well as support for her minor children when they are in her custody. Additional conditions can be written into a marriage contract.

A few Arab countries follow Islamic law entirely in matters of divorce; most have supplemented it. Laws pertaining to divorce have been widely discussed, and changes are constantly being proposed. For example, the custody of children is theoretically determined by Islamic law. They are to stay with their mothers to a certain age (approximately seven years for boys and nine years for girls, although it differs slightly among countries), and then they may go to their fathers, with the mothers having visitation rights. This shift is not always automatic, however, and may be ruled upon by a court or religious judge, according to the circumstances of the case.

## ❀ CHILD-REARING PRACTICES

Arabs dearly love children, and both men and women express that love openly. Arab children grow up surrounded by adoring relatives who share in child rearing by feeding, caring for, and even disciplining each other's children. Because so many people have cared for them and served as authority figures, and because the practice is so universal, Arabs are remarkably homogeneous in their experience of childhood. Arab children learn the same values in much the same way; their upbringing is not as arbitrarily dependent on the approach of their particular parents as it is in Western societies.

In traditional Arab culture there has always been a marked preference for boys over girls because men contribute more to the family's influence in the community. Arab children are provided different role models for personality development. Boys are expected to be aggressive and decisive; girls are expected to be more passive. This attitude toward boys and girls is starting to change now that women are being educated and becoming wage earners. Many Arab couples practice birth control and limit the size of their families to two or three children, even if they are all girls.

Most Arabs feel that while their childhood was, in many ways, a time of stringent training, it was also a time of indulgence and openly expressed love, especially from their mothers. Failure to conform is punished, but methods of discipline are usually not harsh.

*In Arab culture the most important requirement for a "good" child is respectful behavior in front of adults.* Unlike Westerners, all adults may share in correcting a child, because parents know that all adults have the same values. Children grow up without confusion about social requirements. Children must greet adults with a handshake, stay to converse for a few minutes if asked, and refrain from interrupting or talking back. Children often help to serve guests, and they learn the requirements of hospitality early. Westerners who want their children to make a good impression on Arab guests might wish to keep these customs in mind.

Among Arabs it is an extremely important responsibility to bring children up so that they will reflect well on the family. It is an insult to accuse someone of not being well raised. Children's character and success in life reflect directly on their parents—Arabs tend to give parents much of the credit for their children's successes and much of the blame for their failures. Parents readily make sacrifices for their children's welfare. They expect these efforts to be acknowledged and their parental influence to continue throughout the child's lifetime.

Many Western parents begin training their children at an early age to become independent and self-reliant. They give the children token jobs and regular allowance money, and they frequently encourage the children to make their own decisions. This training helps children avoid being dependent on their parents after they have reached adulthood.

Arab parents, on the other hand, welcome their children's dependence. Mothers, especially, try to keep their children tied to them emotionally. Young people continue to live at home until they are married. It is customary for the parents of a newly married couple to furnish the couple's home entirely and to continue to help them financially. In many cases, extended families live together.

## ❊ TALKING ABOUT YOUR FAMILY

Given this emphasis on family background and honor, you may want to carefully consider the impression you will make when giving information to Arabs about your family relationships. Saying the wrong thing can affect your image.

Arabs are very surprised if someone talks about poverty and disadvantages experienced in early life. Rather than admiring one's success in overcoming such circumstances, they wonder why anyone would admit to humble origins when it need not be known.

If your father held a low-status job; if you have relatives, especially female relatives, who have disgraced the family; or if you have elderly relatives in a nursing home (which Arabs find shocking), there is nothing to be gained by talking about it. If you dislike your parents or any close relatives, keep your thoughts to yourself. On the other hand, if you are from a prominent family or are related to a well-known person, letting people know this information can work to your advantage.

In sum, if you do not have positive things to say about your family, things that will incline Arabs toward admiration, it is best to speak in general terms or avoid the subject.

## CHAPTER 9

# RELIGION
# AND SOCIETY

Arabs identify strongly with their religious groups, whether they are Muslim or Christian and whether they participate in religious observances or not. A foreigner must be aware of the pervasive role of religion in Arab life in order to avoid causing offense by injudicious statements or actions.

## ❈ RELIGIOUS AFFILIATION

Religious affiliation is essential for every person in Arab society. There is no place for an atheist or an agnostic. If you have no religious affiliation or are an atheist, this should not be mentioned. Shock and amazement would be the reaction of most Arabs, along with a loss of respect for you. Arabs place great value on piety, and they respect anyone who sincerely practices his or her religion, no matter what that religion is.

## ❈ RELIGIOUS PRACTICES

An Arab's religion affects his or her whole way of life on a daily basis. Religion is taught in schools, the language is full of religious expressions, and people practice their religion openly, expressing it in numerous ways: religious names, decorations on cars and in homes, and jewelry in the form of gold crosses, miniature Qur'ans, or pendants inscribed with Qur'anic verses.

The Qur'an provides an all-encompassing code of interpersonal relations, beyond ethical teachings and exhortations to faith. Much of the Qur'an was revealed when the Prophet Muhammad was administering a community, so much of it deals with forming a just society, government, economic principles, laws, and conducting business. It is a religious text and a legal code, all in one.

Muslims say the Qur'anic formula "In the name of God, the Merciful, the Compassionate" (*Bismillah Ar-Rahman Ar-Raheem*) whenever they are setting out on a trip, preparing to undertake a dangerous task, or beginning a speech. This formula, sometimes called the Invocation, is printed at the top of business letterheads and included in the beginning of reports and personal letters—it even appears on receipts.

Islam does not permit pictures or statues in a place of worship (the same as in Judaism). For this reason, artistic decoration has taken the form of elaborate calligraphy and geometric "arabesque" patterns. Depictions of the Prophet Muhammad are rare, but some occur in miniature paintings, especially Persian and Mogul art from several centuries ago. Not all Muslims are upset by these pictures; it depends on their interpretations of customary practices.

For both Muslims and Christians, marriage and divorce are controlled by religious law. In some countries there is no such thing as a civil marriage; it must be performed by a religious official. For Muslims, inheritance is also controlled by religious law, and in conservative countries religious law partially determines methods of criminal punishment.

The practice of "Islamic banking" is gaining in popularity. The Islamic religion forbids lending money at a fixed rate of interest, viewing it as unfair and exploitative. Islamic banks, therefore, place investors' money in "shared risk" partnership accounts, with rates of return varying according to profits (or losses) on investments.

Marriage across religious lines is rare, although the Islamic religion permits a Muslim man to marry a Jewish or Christian woman without requiring that his wife convert. A Muslim woman, however, must marry a Muslim man; in this way, the children are assured of being Muslim because children are considered to have the religion of their father.

Never make critical remarks about any religious practice. *In Arab culture all religions and their practices are treated with respect.* If you are a Christian foreigner and ask Christian Arabs about accompanying them to church services, they will be very pleased. Non-Muslims do not normally attend Islamic religious services, however, and you should not enter a mosque until you have checked whether it is permitted, which varies from country to country and even from mosque to mosque.

## ❈ THE RELIGION OF ISLAM

To understand Arab culture, it is essential that you become familiar with Islamic history and doctrine. If you do, you will gain insights that few Westerners have, and your efforts will be greatly appreciated.

The Islamic religion had its origin in northern Arabia in the seventh century A.D. The doctrines of Islam are based on revelations from God to His last prophet, Muhammad, over a period of twenty-two years. The revelations were preserved and incorporated into the holy book of the Muslims, the Qur'an, which means "The Recitation."

The God Muslims worship is the same God Jews and Christians worship (*Allah* is simply the Arabic word for *God*; Arab Christians pray to *Allah).* Islam is defined as a return to the faith of Abraham, the prophet and monotheist who made a covenant with God.

The word *Islam* means "submission" (to the will of God), and the term *Muslim* (also spelled "Moslem," which is more familiar to Westerners but not as close to the Arabic pronunciation) refers to a *person* who practices Islam, "one who submits." The doctrines of the Islamic religion are viewed as a summation and completion of previous revelations to Jewish and Christian prophets. Islam shares many doctrines with Judaism and Christianity, and Jews and Christians are known as "People of the Book" (the Scriptures), which gives them a special status.

Shortly after the advent of Islam, the Arabians began an energetic conquest of surrounding territory and eventually expanded their empire from Spain to India in about one hundred years. The widespread conversion to Islam by the people in the Middle East and North Africa accounts for the fact that today 85 percent of the Arabs (Arabic speakers) are Muslims.

The basic tenets of the Islamic faith are known as "the Five Pillars," the primary obligations for Muslims:

1. *Reciting the Declaration of Faith: "There is no God but God and Muhammad is the Messenger (Prophet) of God."* The recitation of this declaration with sincere intent in front of two male Muslim witnesses is sufficient for a person to become a Muslim. There are no sacraments.

   Arabs, Muslims, and Christians alike intersperse their ordinary conversations with references to the will of God (see "Social Greetings" in the Appendix). To make a good impression, you are advised to do the same. The constant use of Arabic religious expressions acts as a formal acknowledgement of the importance of religious faith in Arab society.

2. *Praying five times daily.* The five prayers are said at dawn, noon, afternoon, sunset, and night, and their times differ slightly every day. Muslims are reminded to pray through a prayer call that is broadcast from the minaret of a mosque. A Muslim prays facing in the direction of the Kaaba* in Mecca. The weekly communal prayer service is the noon prayer in the mosque on Fridays, generally attended by men. (Women may go but it is not as common, nor is it expected.) The Friday prayer also includes a sermon.

   Prayer is regulated by ritual washing beforehand and a predetermined number of prostrations and recitations, depending on the time of day. The prayer ritual includes standing, bowing, touching the forehead to the floor (which is covered with a prayer mat, rug, or other clean surface), sitting back, and holding the hands in a cupped position, all while reciting sacred verses. Muslims may pray in a mosque, in their home or office, or in public places. Avoid staring at, walking in front of, or interrupting a person during prayer.

   The Call to Prayer, broadcast five times a day, contains the following phrases, the repetition of which varies slightly depending on the time of day:

   *God is Great.*
   *I testify that there is no God but God.*
   *I testify that Muhammad is God's messenger.*

---

*The Kaaba is the structure in the center of the Grand Mosque in Mecca which is covered with a black cloth. Muslims believe that the original structure was built by Abraham and his son Ishmael, to house a sacred black stone.

*Come to prayer.*
*Come to success.*
*God is great.*
*There is no God but God.*

If you learn the Call in Arabic, it will add to your pleasure in hearing it. Many Westerners become so accustomed to the Call that they miss it when they leave. The first statement, *Allahu Akbar*, "God is Great," is much used in Islam in other contexts as well. It is said when someone is very happy, to express approval, to praise a speaker, as a battle cry, and during times of extreme stress. (1)

3. *Giving alms (charity) to the needy.* Muslims are required to give as *Zakat* (a religious offering) 2.5 percent of their net annual income, after basic family expenses, for the welfare of the community in general and for the poor in particular. Some people assess themselves annually and give the money to a government or community entity; others distribute charity throughout the year.

   If you are asked for alms by a beggar, it is best to give a token amount. Even if you give nothing, avoid saying "no," which is rude. Instead, say *Allah ya'teek*, "God give you"; at least you have given the person a blessing. There is a very strong emphasis on charity in Islam; it is hugely important. Muslims see Islam as the religion of social justice.

4. *Fasting during the month of Ramadan.* Ramadan is the ninth month of the Islamic lunar calendar year (which is eleven days short of 365, so religious holidays move forward every year). During Ramadan, Muslims do not eat, drink, or smoke between sunrise and sunset. The purpose of fasting is to experience hunger and deprivation and to perform an act of self-discipline, humility, and faith. The Ramadan fast is not required of persons whose health may be endangered, and Muslim travelers are also excused; however, anyone who is excused must make up the missed fast days later when health and circumstances permit.

   Ramadan brings with it a holiday atmosphere. Work hours are shortened, shops change their opening and closing times, and most activities take place in the early morning or late at night. People gather with family and friends to break the fast at elaborate meals every evening. This meal is called the *Iftar*—by all means go if you are invited.

Be considerate of people who are fasting during Ramadan by refraining from eating, drinking, or smoking in public places during the fasting hours. To express good wishes to someone before or during Ramadan, you say *Ramadan Kareem* or *Ramadan Mubarak*, "Blessed Ramadan," to which the response is usually *Allahu Akram*, "God is most gracious."

5. *Performing a pilgrimage to Mecca at least once during one's lifetime if finances permit.* The Hajj pilgrimage is the peak religious experience for many Muslims. In the twelfth month of the Islamic year, Muslims from all over the world gather in Saudi Arabia to perform several activities, which are carried out at different sites in the Mecca and Medina area over a period of six days. The Hajj commemorates events in the life of the patriarch Abraham.

Pilgrims, men and women, wear white garments to symbolize their state of purity and their equality in the sight of God. A woman may *not* cover her face at this time. At the end of the Hajj period a holiday occurs, during which all families who can afford it sacrifice a sheep (or other animal) and, after taking enough for one meal, share the rest of it with the poor. The sacrifice relates to Abraham's test of faith—he was willing to sacrifice his son but was instructed to sacrifice a ram instead. Sharing on this holiday is such an important gesture that each year many governments send surplus sacrificial meat to refugees and to the poor in low-income Muslim countries around the world.

When someone is departing for the pilgrimage, the appropriate blessing is *Hajj Mabroor*, "Reverent Pilgrimage." When someone returns, offer congratulations and add the title *Hajj* (*Hajja* for a woman) to the person's name. Thus, a man may be known as Hajj Ahmad, for example. This title is not used in Saudi Arabia.

The Qur'an contains doctrines that guide Muslims to correct behavior so that they will find salvation on the Day of Judgment, narrative stories illustrating God's benevolence and power, and social regulations for the Muslim community. It is the single most important guiding force for Muslims, and it touches on virtually every aspect of their lives.

The Qur'an is supplemented by the *Hadith*, "Traditions of the Prophet," which are collections of sayings and decisions that the prophet was reported to have made, many gathered together in the ninth century. Because the Hadith are so variable and some are of arguable authenticity, many differences of opinion exist among scholars. The Hadith Project has been undertaken in Turkey to reevaluate Hadith, some of which are controversial, unsubstantiated, or invented to manipulate society. (2) It is one of several investigations into Islam's role in the twenty-first century. The Sunni and Shia have different sets of Hadith.

Another source of law is the Sunnah, more accounts of the prophet's practices, especially how to deal with friends, family, and government. The name Sunni is derived from this word. Some of the practices in the Sunnah predate Islam, and some are based on local customs. The Sunni and Shia both acknowledge the Sunnah, although they accept different parts of it and differ in ritual practices.

## ❁ SUNNI AND SHIA

Most of the Muslim Arabs are *Sunni* (also called "orthodox"), and they constitute 90 percent of Muslims. Ten percent are *Shia*, and they are found in large numbers in Lebanon, Iraq, and the Arabian Gulf (Iran, the most important Shia country, is not Arab). The separation of the Muslims into two groups stems from a dispute over the proper succession of authority (the "caliphate") after the death of the Prophet Muhammad. Sunnis and Shia differ today in terms of their religious practices and emphases on certain doctrines, but both groups recognize each other as Muslims.

The Shia have five principles: religion, unity (of God), prophecy, resurrection, and divine justice. (3) They also accept *Imams* as successors to the Prophet (the Sunnis do not), who have a redemptive quality between man and God.

## ❁ THE SHARIA, ISLAMIC LAW

About 90 percent of Islam's *Sharia* law comes from the Hadith. (4) The most infamous rules in the Sharia (the lower status of non-Muslims, seclusion of women, the ban on fine arts, and many violent punishments for sinful behavior)† come from *the Hadith, not* the Qur'an. (5) This means that rules are open to discussion and amendment. (6) Sunni jurists also use analogy and consensus when interpreting and applying Islamic law.

The application of Islamic law differs by country and local interpretations of the Sharia. Some countries (Saudi Arabia, Yemen, Kuwait, Bahrain, the UAE, Sudan) follow it almost exclusively in domestic and criminal law, but most countries have modified or supplemented it. In many countries, the legal system is secular, and Muslims can choose to bring familial and financial disputes to Sharia courts.

Islamic jurists are faced with new issues on which there has not been final agreement or consistency. Birth control, for instance, which is permitted in most Islamic countries, is openly promoted by some and discouraged by others. In Pakistan and Bangladesh (Muslim, non-Arab countries), for example, birth control is a social taboo based on the local interpretation of religious principles. There have been Islamic conferences where issues such as population control, abortion, women's dress, capital punishment, nuclear and biological warfare, terrorism, human rights, and societal pluralism are discussed. Among the Sunnis, however, there is no binding central authority to enforce agreed-upon decisions.

The Sharia can be narrowly interpreted by fundamentalists as requiring Muslims to live the way they lived 1,300 years ago, or, by most, as simply the law that Muslims follow, but that does not have a specific format and shifts over time. There are instances in the West of Muslims requesting that female police officers cover their hair when entering a mosque, requesting women-only hours at swimming pools, and creating the option of Islamic banking (without predetermined interest).

But some Westerners see any instance of Sharia compliance as threatening; a pamphlet at a Tea Party gathering in Florida in August 2010 stated, "Why do Muslims want to take over the world and place us under Sharia law?" (8) In several venues, there is "an eager promotion by anti-Islamic zealots of a growing conspiracy theory about 'creeping Sharia law,'" which includes conservatives of varying types. (9) In fact, Muslims do not want to apply Sharia law to outsiders; it is even optional for Muslims who live in some countries in Europe—they can choose to use it or not.

---

†Stoning for adultery is from the Hadith, but it was cited as Qur'anic by a conservative Anglican cleric. (7)

In the U.S., a coalition of Muslim groups has petitioned for a ban on Islamic law by the courts. They do not want cases in domestic law referred to the Sharia for resolution, even for Muslims.‡ They stated that they want to protect Muslims and non-Muslims alike from "extremist attempts" to use Sharia and institute "a highly politicized and dangerous understanding of Islam" in the West. One woman said, "Many of us fled the Muslim world to escape Sharia law. . . . We do not wish these laws to follow us here." (10)

A state representative in Tennessee, Rick Womick, has stated that the Sharia legal system seeks world domination. (11) Presidential candidates Michelle Bachman and Newt Gingrich signed a pledge to "reject Sharia law," apparently believing that this is necessary. (12)

## ❈ THE QUR'AN AND THE BIBLE

Much of the content of the Qur'an is similar (though not identical) to the teachings and stories found in the Old and New Testaments of the Bible. Islamic doctrine accepts the previous revelations to Biblical prophets as valid, but states, as the Bible does, that the people continually strayed from these teachings. Correct guidance had to be repeated through different prophets, one after the other. By the seventh century, doctrines and practices again had to be corrected through the divine revelations to Muhammad, who is known as the last, or "seal," of the prophets.

The Qur'an is divided into 114 chapters, arranged in order of length, longest to shortest (with a few exceptions). The chapters are not in chronological order, although the reader can identify whether a chapter was revealed in Mecca (earlier) or Medina (later). Each chapter is made up of verses. If you decide to read the Qur'an in translation, it is a good idea to obtain a list of the chapters in chronological order and read through them in that order so that the development of thought and teachings becomes clear.§

---

‡There are precedents. If religious law is deemed "unfair" by the courts, it will not be considered. In all cases, state law prevails over the laws of any religion. Orthodox Jews, for example, have asked judges to enforce their laws on divorce, but the courts have refused to do it; they won't be involved in interpreting religion.

§A list of the Qur'an's chapters in chronological order may be found in Richard Bell's *Introduction to the Qur'an* (1953). It is also available on the Internet.

Most of the chapters of the Qur'an are in cadenced, rhymed verse, while some (particularly the later legalistic ones) are in prose. The sustained rhythm of the recited Qur'an, combined with the beauty of the content, account for its great esthetic and poetic effect when heard in Arabic. The Qur'an is considered the epitome of Arabic writing style, and when it is recited aloud, it can move listeners to tears. The elegance and beauty of the Qur'an are taken as proof of its divine origin—no human being could expect to produce anything so magnificent.

The three most often cited characteristics of the Qur'an are these: it is inimitable, it is eternal (it always existed but was not manifested until the seventh century), and it is Arabic (the Arabic version is the Word of God, so translations of the Qur'an into other languages are not used for prayer). Verses from the Qur'an are much used for decoration, usually the same ones over and over, so learning to identify part of the verse can lead to deciphering the whole thing.

It is common for Muslims to memorize the Qur'an, or large portions of it; a person who can recite the Qur'an is called a Hafiz. Reading and reciting the Qur'an was once the traditional form of education, and it was often the only education many people received. In most Arab schools today, memorization of Qur'anic passages is included in the curriculum (for Muslim students).

The Qur'an and the Bible have much in common:

- The necessity of faith
- Reward for good actions and punishment for evil actions on the Day of Judgment
- The concepts of Heaven (Paradise) and Hell
- The existence of angels who communicate between God and man
- The existence of Satan (*Shaytan* in Arabic)
- The recognition of numerous prophets❡

---

❡The Qur'an recognizes eighteen Old Testament figures as prophets (among them Adam, Noah, Abraham, Ishmael, Isaac, Jacob, Moses, Joseph, Job) and three New Testament figures (Zachariah, John the Baptist, and Jesus), and it mentions four Arabian prophets who do not appear in the Bible. Of all these prophets, five are considered the most important. In order of chronology, these are Noah, Abraham, Moses, Jesus, and Muhammad.

- ❧ The prohibition of the consumption of pork and the flesh of animals not slaughtered in a ritual manner—this is very similar to kosher dietary laws in the Old Testament
- ❧ The teaching that Jesus was born of a virgin; Mary is called "Miriam" in Arabic—the theme is the same, although details differ
- ❧ The teaching that Jesus worked miracles, including curing the sick and raising the dead

There are some notable differences between the Qur'an and the Bible as well:

- ❧ Islam does not recognize the concept of intercession between God and man; all prayers must be made to God directly. Jesus is recognized as one of the most important prophets, but the Christian concept of his intercession for man's sins is not accepted.
- ❧ Islam teaches that Jesus was not crucified; instead, a person made to look like him was miraculously substituted in his place on the cross; God would not allow such an event to happen to one of His prophets.
- ❧ Islam does not accept the doctrine of Jesus' resurrection and divinity.
- ❧ Islam is uncompromisingly monotheistic and rejects the Christian concept of the Trinity.

Some of the biblical stories that are retold in the Qur'an (in a shortened version) include the following:

- ❧ The story of the Creation
- ❧ The story of Adam and Eve
- ❧ The story of Cain and Abel
- ❧ The story of Noah and the Flood
- ❧ The story of the covenant of Abraham and his willingness to sacrifice his son as an act of faith**

---

**Islam holds that Abraham was ordered to sacrifice Ishmael, whereas the Bible states that it was Isaac. Abraham is recognized as the ancestor of the Arabs through Ishmael.

❖ The story of Lot and the destruction of the evil cities
❖ The story of Joseph, son of Jacob, told in much detail,
❖ The story of David and Goliath
❖ The story of Solomon and the Queen of Sheba
❖ The story of the afflictions of Job
❖ The story of the birth of Jesus††

Muslims feel an affinity with the Jewish and Christian religions and find it unfortunate that so few Westerners understand how similar the Islamic religion is to their own. Islam is a continuation of the other two religions, and Muslims view it as the completed true faith.

## ❖ Passages from the Qur'an

Selected passages from the Qur'an are presented here to give the reader an idea of the tone and content of the book (from *The Koran Interpreted*, by A. J. Arberry, 1955). Titles of chapters refer to key words in that chapter, not to content. Chapter 93 begins with an oath, which is common in the Qur'an.

### Chapter 1: The Opening

In the name of God, the Merciful, the Compassionate.
Praise belongs to God, the Lord of all Being
the all-Merciful, the All-compassionate
the Master of the Day of Judgment.
Thee only we serve; to Thee alone we pray for help.
Guide us in the straight path,
the path of those whom Thou has blessed,
not of those against whom Thou art wrathful,
nor of those who are astray.

---

††In the Qur'anic version, Jesus was born at the foot of a palm tree in the desert and saved his unmarried mother from scorn when, as an infant, he spoke up in her defense and declared himself a prophet, saying "... Peace be upon me, the day I was born, and the day I die, and the day I am raised up alive" (referring to his resurrection on the Day of Judgment). This is a miracle of Jesus not recorded in the Bible.

### Chapter 5: The Table

(Verse 3)
Today the unbelievers have despaired of
your religion; therefore fear them not,
but fear you Me.
Today I have perfected your religion
for you, and I have completed My blessing
upon you, and I have approved Islam
for your religion.

(Verse 120)
To God belongs the kingdom of the heavens
And of the earth, and all that is in them,
and He is powerful over everything.

### Chapter 93: The Forenoon

In the name of God, the Merciful, the Compassionate.
By the white forenoon and the brooding night!
Thy Lord has neither forsaken thee nor hates thee
and the Last [life] shall better for three than the First.
Thy Lord shall give thee, and thou shalt be satisfied.
Did he not find thee an orphan, and shelter thee?
Did he not find thee erring, and guide thee?
Did he not find thee needy, and suffice thee?
As for the orphan, do not oppress him,
and as for the beggar, scold him not;
and as for thy Lord's blessing, declare it.

## CHAPTER 10

# COMMUNICATING
# WITH ARABS

This chapter is about how speech is used in the Arab culture, and it contains basic information about the Arabic language. Though you may never learn Arabic, you will need to know something about the language and how it is used. Arabic is the native language of 360 million people and the official language of some twenty countries. In 1973 it was named the fourth official language of the United Nations,* and it is the fifth most widely spoken language in the world.†

Arabic originated in the Arabian Peninsula as one of the northern Semitic languages. The only other Semitic languages still in wide use today are Hebrew (revived as a spoken language a century ago) and Amharic (Ethiopian), which is from the southern Semitic branch. There are still a few speakers of the other northern Semitic languages (Aramaic, Syriac, and Chaldean) in Lebanon, Syria, and Iraq.

Many English words have come from Arabic. The most easily recognizable are those that begin with *al* (the Arabic word for "the"), such as *algebra, alchemy, alcove, alcohol,* and *alkali.* Many pertain to mathematics and the sciences; medieval European scholars drew heavily on Arabic source materials in these fields. Other Arabic words include *cipher, algorithm,* and *almanac.* Some foods that originated in the East brought

---

*There are six official languages at the United Nations: Arabic, Chinese, English, French, Russian, Spanish.
†The ranking of the top ten languages is: Mandarin Chinese, Spanish, English, Hindi-Urdu, Arabic, Bengali, Portuguese, Russian, Japanese, Punjabi.

their Arabic names west with them: *coffee, sherbet, sesame, apricot, ginger, saffron*, and *carob*.‡

## ❀ VARIETIES OF ARABIC

Spoken Arabic in all its forms is very different from written Arabic. The written version is Classical Arabic, the language that was in use in the seventh century A.D. in the Hejaz area of Arabia. It is this rich, poetic language of the Qur'an that has persisted as the written language of all Arabic-speaking peoples since that time. Classical Arabic, which has evolved into Modern Standard Arabic to accommodate new words and usages, is sacred to Muslims. It is esthetically pleasing, and far more grammatically complex than the spoken (or colloquial) dialects.

The spoken languages are "Formal Spoken Arabic" (a classicized style of speech comprehensible to all educated Arabs), and colloquial Arabic; the latter includes many dialects and subdialects. Although some of them differ from each other as much as Spanish does from Italian or the Scandinavian languages do from each other, they are all recognized as Arabic. When Arabic spread throughout the Middle East and North Africa with the Arabian conquests, it mixed with and assimilated local languages, spawning the dialects that are spoken today.

An overview of Arabic language usage reveals the following:

*Classical (Modern Standard) Arabic.* Modern Standard Arabic is used for all writing and for formal discussions, speeches, and news broadcasts but not for ordinary conversation. It is the same in all Arab countries, except for occasional variations in regional or specialized vocabulary.§

*Colloquial Arabic (dialects).* Colloquial Arabic is used for everyday spoken communication but not for writing, except sometimes in very informal correspondence, in film or play scripts, or as slang in cartoons and the like.

---

‡For more examples see the *Mawrid* dictionary (1) 101–112, or Al-bab.com, which lists some 200 words. Mounir Al-Ba'albaki. 2004. Al-Mawrid: A Modern English-Arabic Dictionary. Beirut: Dar El-Ilm lil-Malayen, 101–12.

§ Classical and Modern Standard Arabic differ, but differences are technical.

*Formal Spoken Arabic.* Formal Spoken Arabic (Educated Spoken Arabic) is improvised, consisting principally of Modern Standard Arabic terminology within the structure of the local dialect; it is used by educated people when they converse with Arabs whose dialect is very different from their own. It is an acquired skill, with no hard-and-fast rules.

## ❁ The Superiority of Arabic

It is not an exaggeration to say that *Arabs are passionately in love with their language.* Just speaking and hearing it can be a moving esthetic experience. Arabs are secure in the belief that their language is superior to all others. This attitude about one's own language is held by many people in the world, but in the case of the Arabs, they can point to several factors as proof of their assertion:

Most important, they note that when the Qur'an was revealed directly from God, Arabic was the medium chosen for His message; its use was not an accident.

Arabic is also extremely difficult to master, and it is complex grammatically; this is viewed as another sign of superiority.

Because its structure lends itself to rhythm and rhyme, Arabic is pleasing to listen to when recited aloud.

Finally, it has an usually large vocabulary, and its grammar allows for the easy coining of new words, so that borrowing from other languages is less common in Arabic than in many other languages. In other words, Arabic is richer than other languages, or so it is argued.

While most Westerners feel an affection for their native language, the pride and love Arabs feel for Arabic are much more intense. The Arabic language is their greatest cultural treasure and achievement, an art form that cannot be accessed or appreciated by outsiders.

Arabic, if spoken or written in an ornate and semi-poetic style, casts a spell. Hearing the words and phrases used skillfully is an esthetic, poetic experience, and people respond as much to the style as to the content. A talented orator can wield power in this subtle way. Beautiful

Arabic conjures up images of once-memorized Qur'an passages or bits of poetry, and it can be just as intricate orally as the most complex Arabic calligraphy designs are visually. Arabs love poetry, which in ancient times was the nomadic Arabs' chief means of artistic expression and still has a powerful place in their culture.

## ❊ THE PRESTIGE OF CLASSICAL ARABIC

The reverence for Arabic pertains only to Classical Arabic, which is what Arabs mean by the phrase "the Arabic language." This was illustrated by the comment of an Egyptian village headman who once explained to me why he considered the village school to be important. "For one thing," he said, "that's where the children go to learn Arabic."

To the contrary, Arabic dialects have no prestige. Some people go so far as to suggest that they have "no grammar" and are not worthy of serious study. The dialects differ from each other as much as the Romance languages do, but now they are on the way to becoming more mutually intelligible and less of a block to communication. Satellite television has exposed everyone to other dialects, through programs from other countries and through frequent news interviews, often among people of mixed nationalities. Even speech from distant areas is commonly heard now. Committees of scholars have coined new words and tried to impose conventional usages to partially replace the dialects, but they have had no more success than language regulatory groups in other countries.

A good command of Classical Arabic is highly admired in the Arab culture because it is difficult to attain. Few people other than scholars and specialists in Arabic have enough confidence to speak extemporaneously in Classical Arabic or to defend their written style. In Arabic, the classical language is called "The Most Eloquent Language."

To become truly literate in Arabic requires more years of study than are required for English literacy. The student must learn new words in Classical Arabic (more than 50 percent of the words are different from the local dialect in some countries) and a whole new grammar, including case endings and new verb forms. A significant part of the literacy problem in the Arab world stems from the difficulty of Classical Arabic. Even people who have had five or six years of schooling are still considered functionally illiterate, unable to use the language for anything more than rudimentary needs, such as signing one's name or reading simple prose.

On the other hand, the written language is not entirely a foreign language to illiterates or even to preschool children. They hear it passively on a constant basis, in news broadcasts, in speeches and formal discussions, on their version of *Sesame Street,* and in children's books and recordings.

From time to time Arab scholars have suggested that Classical Arabic be replaced by written dialects to facilitate education and literacy. This idea has been repeatedly and emphatically denounced by the large majority of Arabs and has almost no chance of acceptance in the foreseeable future. The most serious objection is that Classical Arabic is the language of the Qur'an. Another argument is that if it were supplanted by the dialects, the entire body of Arabic literature and poetry would become inaccessible, and the language would lose much of its beauty. There has also been some talk of simplifying the language, but this is not popular either.

There is a political argument for Classical Arabic—it is a cultural force that unites all Arabs. To discard it, many fear, would lead to a linguistic fragmentation that would exacerbate the tendencies toward political and psychological fragmentation already present. As one language expert said, "The Arabic language becomes instrumental in preserving our cultural hemisphere and protecting our heritage, religion, and values." (2)

## ❧ ELOQUENCE OF SPEECH

Eloquence is emphasized and admired in the Arab world far more than in the West, which accounts for the flowery prose in Arabic, both in written and spoken form. *Instead of viewing rhetoric in a disparaging way, as Westerners often do, Arabs admire it.* The ability to speak eloquently is a sign of education and refinement.

Foreign observers frequently comment on long-winded political speeches and the repetition of phrases and themes in Arabic, failing to understand that the speaker's style of delivery and command of the language often appeal to the listeners as much as does the message itself. Nationalistic slogans, threats, and promises are meant more for momentary effect than as statements of policy or belief, yet foreigners too often take them literally, especially when encountered in the cold light of a foreign language translation. *In the Arab world, how you say something is as important as what you have to say.*

Eloquence is a clue to the popular appeal of some nationalistic leaders whose words are far more compelling than their deeds. Much of the personal charisma attributed to them is due in large part to their ability to speak in well-phrased, rhetorical Arabic. Repetition of refrains is common, as is exaggeration, which sometimes expresses wish fulfillment and provides a satisfying substitution of words for action.

Arabs devote considerable effort to using their language creatively and effectively. This is from a Christmas card I received from an Iraqi refugee, who had interviewed for a teaching position:

> When fate bestows on a person, lost in a distant land, a drop of tenderness, a bouquet of love, that person's health and trust in others is restored.
>
> I found in you true brotherhood, when you planted in my heart, which beats and which is not able to be still in its anxieties and its yearnings, that tenderness.
>
> Perhaps I will meet you some day in my beautiful Baghdad in order to return to you some of the kindness which you have shown me.
>
> May this Christmas be the right occasion to realize our shared dream to build a world driven by friendship, love, and peace, so that the people of the earth will be blessed with justice, democracy, and the solidarity of mankind.

Leslie J. McLoughlin, a British specialist in Arabic, has written:

> Westerners are not in everyday speech given, as Arabs are, to quoting poetry, ancient proverbs and extracts from holy books. Nor are they wont to exchange fulsome greetings. . . . Perhaps the greatest difference between the Levantine approach to language and that of Westerners is that Levantines, like most Arabs, take pleasure in using language for its own sake. The sahra (or evening entertainment) may well take the form of talk alone, but talk of a kind forgotten in the West except in isolated communities such as Irish villages or Swiss mountain communities—talk not merely comical, tragic, historical, pastoral, etc., but talk ranging over poetry, storytelling, anecdotes, jokes, word games, singing, and acting. (3)

When the American television show "The Apprentice" was copied in the Arab world, it was felt too harsh to say to someone, "You're fired!" Instead, the candidates were refused with "God be good to you." (4) Viewers understood the message from the context.

## ❋ SPEECH MANNERISMS

Making yourself completely understood by another person is a difficult task under the best of circumstances. It is more difficult still if you each have dramatically different ways of expressing yourself. Such is the problem between Westerners and Arabs, which often results in misunderstanding, leaving both parties feeling bewildered or deceived.

Arabs talk a lot, repeat themselves, shout when excited, and make extensive use of gestures. They punctuate their conversations with oaths (such as "I swear by God") to emphasize what they say, and they exaggerate for effect. Foreigners sometimes wonder if they are involved in a discussion or an argument.

If you speak softly and make your statements only once, Arabs may wonder if you really mean what you are saying. People will ask, "Do you really mean that?" or "Is that true?" It's not that they do not believe you, but they need repetition. They need to hear "yes" emphatically and repeatedly to be reassured.

Arabs have a great tolerance for noise and interference during discussions; often several people speak at once (each trying to outshout the other), interspersing their statements with gestures, all the while being coached by bystanders. Businessmen interrupt meetings to greet callers, answer the telephone, and sign papers brought in by clerks. A foreigner may wish that he or she could insist on the precondition of being allowed to speak without interruption. *Loudness of speech is mainly for dramatic effect and in most cases should not be taken as an indication of aggression or insistence on the part of the speaker.*

In a taxi in Cairo once, my driver was shouting and complaining and gesticulating wildly to other drivers as he worked his way through the crowded streets. In the midst of all this action, he turned around, laughed, and winked. "You know," he said, "sometimes I really enjoy this!"

Some situations absolutely demand emotion and drama. In Baghdad I was once a passenger in a taxi that was hit from the rear. Both drivers leapt out of their cars and began shouting at each other. After waiting ten minutes, while a crowd gathered, I decided to pay the fare and leave. I pushed through the crowd and got the driver's attention. He broke off the argument, politely told me that there was nothing to pay, and then resumed arguing at full voice.

Loud and boisterous behavior does have limits, however. It is more frequent, of course, among people of approximately the same age and social status who know each other well. It occurs mostly in social situations, less often in business meetings, and is not acceptable when dealing with elders or social superiors, in which case polite deference is required. Bedouins and the Arabs of Saudi Arabia and the Gulf tend to be more reserved and soft-spoken. In fact, *in almost every respect, protocol is stricter in the Arabian Peninsula than elsewhere in the Arab world.*

## ❁ PLEASANT AND INDIRECT RESPONSES

In general, Arab speech is rich in color and emotion. It is vibrant and not tied down to sterile logic. Arab culture values hospitality and goodwill over precision and directness in conversation.

If you ask for directions, you will almost always get a response, even if the person is not sure. Arabs believe it is more important to make a token effort of helpfulness, even if the information is wrong, than to refuse the request (the person didn't misguide you, he helped). If bad news is imminent, it may be considered more ethical to engage in circumlocution rather than going directly to the brutal truth. Indirect speech is also called for when making a request of a prominent or elderly person; it is a sign of deference.

## ❁ THE POWER OF WORDS

To the Arab way of thinking (consciously or subconsciously), words have power; they can, to some extent, affect subsequent events. Arab conversation is peppered with blessings, which are like little prayers for good fortune, intended to keep things going well. *Swearing and use of curses and obscenities are very offensive to Arabs.* If words have power and can affect events, it is feared that curses may bring misfortune just by being uttered. There is no point in provoking fate.

The liberal use of blessings also demonstrates that the speaker holds no envy toward a person or object; in other words, that he or she does not cast an "evil eye" toward something. Belief in the evil eye (often just called "the eye") is common, and it is feared or acknowledged to some extent by most Arabs, although less so by the better educated. It is widely believed that a person or an object can be harmed if viewed, even unconsciously, with envy—with an evil eye. The harm may be prevented, however, by offering blessings or statements of goodwill. Students of Arabic learn a large number of what may be called "benedictions," and then must remember to use them.

Foreigners who do not know about the evil eye may be suspected of giving it. When a friend buys a new car, don't express envy. Instead, say, "May you always drive it safely." When someone moves to a new house, say "May you always live here happily." When meeting someone's children, say "May they always be healthy" or "May God keep them for you." All these are translations of much-used Arabic expressions. Omitting benedictions can be seen as rude.

## ❋ EUPHEMISMS

Arabs are uncomfortable discussing illness, disaster, or death. This trait illustrates how the power of words affects Arab speech and behavior. In their view, *a careless reference to bad events can lead to misfortune or make a bad situation worse.* Arabs avoid such references as much as possible; they use euphemisms instead.

Euphemisms serve as substitutes, and a foreigner needs to learn the code in order to understand what is really being said. For example, instead of saying that someone is sick, Arabs may describe a person as "a little tired." They avoid saying a word like *cancer*, saying instead, "He has 'it'" or "She has 'the disease.'" They will often wait until an illness is over before telling others about it, even relatives. Similarly, Arabs do not speak easily about death and sometimes avoid telling others about a death for some time; even then they will phrase it euphemistically.

Some years back I was visiting the owner of an Egyptian country estate when two men came in supporting a third man who had collapsed in the field. The landlord quickly telephoned the local health unit. He got through just as the man slipped from his chair and appeared to be having a heart attack. "Ambulance!" he screamed. "Send me an ambulance! I have a man here who's . . . a little tired!"

These are social manners. In technical situations, of course, where specificity is required (doctor to patient, commander to soldier), explicit language is used.

## ❋ THE WRITTEN WORD

Arabs have considerable respect for the written as well as the spoken word. Some very pious people feel that anything written in Arabic should be burned when no longer needed (such as newspapers) or at least not left on the street to be walked on or used to wrap things, because the name of God probably appears somewhere. Decorations using Arabic calligraphy, Qur'anic quotations, and the name *Allah* are never used on floors (unlike crosses in floors of churches, especially in Europe). They are often seen, however, in framed pictures or painted on walls. If you buy something decorated with Arabic calligraphy, ask what it means; you could offend Arabs by the careless handling of an item decorated with a religious quotation.

If you own an Arabic Qur'an, you must handle it with respect. It should be placed flat on a table or in its own area on a shelf, not wedged in with many other books. Best of all, keep it in a velvet box or display it on an X-shaped wooden stand; both are made for this purpose. Under no circumstances should anything (an ashtray, another book) be placed on top of the Qur'an.

Written blessings and Qur'anic verses are believed to be effective in assuring safety and preventing the evil eye, so they are seen all over the Arab world. Blessings are posted on cars and trucks and engraved on jewelry. You will see religious phrases in combination with the color blue, drawings of eyes, or pictures of open palms, all of which appear as amulets against the evil eye.

## ❈ PROVERBS

Arabs use proverbs far more than Westerners do, and they have hundreds. Many are in the forms of rhymes or couplets. A person's knowledge of proverbs and when to use them enhances his or her image by demonstrating wisdom and insight.

Here is a selection of proverbs that help illuminate the Arab outlook on life. Proverbs frequently refer to family and relatives, poverty and social inequality, fate and luck.

❈ Support your brother, whether he is the tyrant or the tyrannized.

❈ The knife of the family does not cut. (If you are harmed by a relative, don't take offense.)

❈ You are like a tree, giving your shade to the outside. (You should give more attention to your own family.)

❈ One hand alone does not clap. (Cooperation is essential.)

❈ The hand of God is with the group. (There is strength in unity.)

❈ The young goose is a good swimmer. (Like father, like son.)

❈ Older than you by a day, wiser than you by a year. (Respect older people and their advice.)

❈ The eye cannot rise above the eyebrow. (Be satisfied with your station in life.)

❈ The world is changeable, one day honey and the next day onions. (This rhymes in Arabic.)

❈ Every sun has to set. (Fame and fortune may be fleeting.)

❈ Seven trades but no luck. (This rhymes in Arabic. It means that even if a person is qualified, because of bad luck he or she may not find work.)

❈ It's all fate and chance.

❈ Your tongue is like a horse—if you take care of it, it takes care of you; if you treat it badly, it treats you badly.

❈ The dogs may bark but the caravan moves on. (A person should rise above petty criticism.)

❈ Patience is beautiful.

❈ The slave does the thinking and the lord carries it out. (Man proposes and God disposes.)

❈ Bounties are from God.

And finally, my very favorite:

❁ The monkey in the eyes of his mother is a gazelle.

## CHAPTER 11

# ISLAMIC
# FUNDAMENTALISM
# (ISLAMISM)

Islamic fundamentalism is a political and social issue, not part of the mainstream Islamic religion. For this reason, it is considered here rather than in the chapter describing Islam. This chapter is intended as a description of militant Islamism in the Middle East and in the West (the United States and Europe). Exploring the various ramifications of the Islamist phenomenon is the goal here.

## ❈ DEFINITIONS AND NUMBERS

The efforts to understand evolving Islamic thought have been completely overwhelmed by the (notorious) emergence of fundamentalism. (More accurate terms are *Islamism, militant Islam, political Islam*, and the latest term, *Jihadism*. However, *fundamentalism* has caught on as the most common word to designate extremist Islamic thought.)*

One problem with using *fundamentalism* in this way is that genuine Muslim fundamentalism refers to the same principles as in other religions: returning to original sacred writings and applying these to social issues in the present. The word *fundamentalist* in Arabic derives from the word that means *roots*. About 10 percent of Muslims describe themselves as

---

*There are also the Salafists, who are an even more ascetic fringe group, with a cult-like character.

true fundamentalists (religious conservatives, *not* extremist Islamists). I will use the term *Islamism* to refer to extreme militant Islam.

Extremists exist in every religion. There is no reasoning with people *who are convinced they know exactly what God wants.* All society can do is try to control them.

Militant Muslim groups who espouse violence cannot represent even 1 percent of Muslims in the United States (that would be 50,000) or in the world (that would be 18 million). If it was even 1 percent we would be overrun with wild-eyed fanatics. Islamists who resort to violence add up to *less than* one tenth of 1 percent; we have only to consider numbers.† But terrorists do act, they engage in violence, and they are certainly getting most of the publicity.

We need to step back for a moment from the television images— chanting mobs, bombings of innocent people, and violent killings. It is simply common sense to realize that *these groups cannot possibly represent Arab or Muslim societies and people as a whole.* There are 1.8 *billion* Muslims in the world, 600 *million* in North Africa and the greater Middle East (including non-Arabs), and over 340 *million* Arab Muslims. The vast majority of these people have no interest whatever in Jihad and militancy.

Some estimates claim that as many as 10 to 15 percent of the Muslims are fundamentalists, meaning Islamists who want a strictly Islamic government. But very few Islamists are violent. Daniel Pipes, a conservative analyst and writer, claims that the Islamist element includes some 100 to 150 million adherents worldwide, his estimate based on "election data, survey research, anecdotal evidence, and the opinions of informed observers," with no sources cited. It is not clear if he means sympathizers or activists, nor is it clear what they are adhering to. He also states (with no sources cited), "Reliable statistics on opinion in the Muslim world do not exist,‡ but my sense is that one half of the world's Muslims—or some 500 million persons—sympathize more with Osama bin Laden and the Taliban than with the United States. That such a vast multitude hates the United States is sobering indeed." (1)

---

† This is assuming that the identification of these terrorists is actually related to militant Islam. The definition of *terrorist* is in itself unclear; there are many national groups (such as Chechens and some Iraqis) who see themselves as nationalists.
‡ There are numerous excellent polls taken every year, all over the Middle East and the Muslim world.

I daresay that over half of the people in the entire *world*, Buddhists, Hindus, Chinese, and others, sympathize more with Osama bin Laden's anti-U.S. *grievances* than with U.S. *foreign policy* (which is not the same as "hating the United States").§ When making such grand claims, it is important to clarify the wording carefully unless the purpose is to scare people.

One U.S. congressman claimed that 85 percent of the mosques in the U.S. have extremist leadership. (2) The author of a 2002 book *American Jihad: The Terrorists Living Among Us* (3) claims that "fundamentalists" control 80 percent of the mosques, since many mosques are funded at least partially with Saudi money. The same author had stated in 1995 that Islam "sanctions genocide, planned genocide, as part of its religious doctrine." (4)

Unqualified statements like these are alarmist. They fan hysteria and they libel the entire Muslim community. When such comments are repeated in the media, most ordinary readers assume that such statements are true of *all* Muslims, or if they don't know the difference, "all those Arabs," unless the Islamist context is repeatedly made very clear and the difference explained. Islamists have created their own definition of *infidels* and *Jihad* that are totally unorthodox.

Ordinary Muslims do not go around referring to Christians and Jews as infidels or unbelievers. Nor do they think in these terms. They would no more do this than Westerners would use similar (embarrassing, degrading) Crusade-era terms about them. In forty-five years I have never heard the terms *infidels* or *unbelievers* used by ordinary Muslims to refer to Westerners or their society and institutions, not once. When some Western scholars insist on using terms like these (they are not quoting, they are just being emphatic),¶ it is insulting to ordinary Muslims. What politicians and the media rarely emphasize is the fact that such terms are used *only* by Islamists, who also refer to *mainstream Muslims*

---

§Bin Laden's statements bear this out. He repeatedly mentions policy issues (Palestine, Iraq, sanctions), not religious differences or a desire to destroy the American way of life. It is probable that these terrorists would take action even if there were *no* religious differences.

¶Examples: "The Western world, or as they would put it, the infidel countries"; "They had dealt with one of the infidel superpowers"; "We infidels are the only hope for Islam"; "... showing a lack of gratitude or total indifference when we infidels come to their rescue"; "... repeated commands for Muslims not to befriend infidels/unbelievers (all non-Muslims)."

as unbelievers. Westerners rightly take offense when characterized as infidels, so it is essential that they understand the source of such labels.

*Muslims all over the world—like most people everywhere—just want to get on with their lives, get an education, find a job, raise their children, and participate in family and community life.* They are not inscrutable. They are not mysterious or exotic. They are ordinary people with *no interest* in harming non-Muslims or interfering with their way of life. That Muslims have normal human priorities is so obvious that it should not need to be stated.

As for Islamists, however, criticism is justified and should not be euphemized if statements are the truth. Militant Islamists advocate violence, deny rights to women, and oppose individual freedom. They do not deserve to be protected by a regard for political correctness. *They are doing devastating harm to everyone*, including the Arabs and Muslims, whom they have killed by the thousands. When Osama Bin Laden was hunted down and killed, this news brought satisfaction and relief that he was gone to millions around the world, including Muslims.

Every society has deviant groups. We as Westerners understand the reasoning and motives of such groups in our own society, yet that does not mean we condone them. Some scholars have compared extremist Islamists to the Ku Klux Klan in the U.S., which is Christian but definitely not mainstream (it has about 6,000 members today). (5) I think a better analogy is the white Aryan groups and militias, because they are more active and they, too, are committed Christians with grievances. They had their own reasons to support Timothy McVeigh's bombing of the federal building in Oklahoma City. A more recent notable incident was the bombing of a government building and the killing of seventy-seven people, carried out by Anders Breivik in Norway in July 2011. Breivik insisted that he was "100 percent Christian" and that he committed his acts in defense of Europe's "Christian heritage." Breivik is an unapologetic "Christian terrorist." (6) One commentator stated, "We should distinguish between true, peace-loving Christians and people like Anders Breivik, who would more properly be called a "Christianist." (7)

The number of hate groups in the U.S. jumped 54 percent between 2000 and 2008. (8) There are neo-Nazis, racist skinhead groups, and varying groups of separatists. Some militant groups are entirely political. Hate and vigilante groups number about 1,000. (9) (10) Federal law enforcement agencies are "more focused than at any time in the last ten years on the threat posed by homegrown terrorism," according to a Department of Homeland Security (DHS) counterterrorism official speaking in mid-2011. (11) A DHS domestic terror official said that the militia movement has "exploded" over the past two years, and "a Norway [the Anders Breivik] incident could definitely happen here; the same things that played into the Norway suspect's mindset are here in this country." (12) The number of U.S. patriot and militia groups rose to 1,274 in 2011, up from 824 in 2010 and 149 in 2008 (13).

There are two important factors in the case of Islamism that explain why it is growing quickly as compared with extremist groups in the U.S. and most other societies:

1. Their numbers will continue to grow rapidly because they act on perceived grievances *that are constantly being reinforced.*
2. There are many Muslims, especially the young, who feel lost, hopeless, alienated, and uncertain of their future. They need support from a group and a sense of purpose. They are idealists. They have a sense of moral outrage that resonates with their experiences. (14) They accept martyrdom as a kind of self-sacrifice, and once they belong to an extremist group, they feel it is shameful to turn back, so leaders can send them into battle. (15) Those who become cut off from other groups develop the most intense bond. (16)

It is understandable that Islamists receive a disproportionate amount of attention in the media. To uninformed Westerners such extremists appear to be numerous, but to the thousands of Westerners who visit or live in Muslim countries, these groups are no more a factor in life than are the fringe groups in our country. It was an error by our leaders to impute from the total number of Muslims a large number of terrorists. Al-Qaeda was always a small minority, even among Muslim dissidents. In his recent book, Charles Kurzman states, "Global Islamist terrorists have managed to recruit fewer than 1 in 15,000 Muslims over the past quarter century and fewer than 1 in 100,000 since 9/11." (17)

Here is an analogy. All Westerners readily understand the grievances of anti-abortion groups. Some agree and some disagree, some even join rallies, but this does not mean that these supporters are galvanized to condone or participate in violent acts.

Keep in mind that Islamists are primarily political, and looking for ways to fill power gaps. We see this notably in Egypt, Syria, Libya, and Yemen.

## ❀ JIHAD

*Jihad* is used here to mean "Holy War," which is how the term is used by Islamic militants and the Western media. In this sense, *Jihad* is the same concept as *Crusade*, that is, fighting in the name of a religion. A more accurate interpretation of Jihad refers to the "effort" that a Muslim makes to live and structure his or her personal life, and the wider society, on Islamic principles, which is a much more benign meaning. Anyone who combats temptations in order to live a righteous life can identify with this. A good definition of Jihad is "inner striving to live the Islamic life and attain a higher level of spiritual consciousness, or external armed confrontation with those seen as enemies of Islam." (18)

The concept of Jihad has undergone changes over time. The Hadith, which were collected beginning 150 years after the Prophet Muhammad's death, were all about fighting, and the original idea of internal struggle almost disappeared. (19) Over the next 400 to 500 years, when Islamic law was being codified, the notion of Jihad as fighting came to dominate. And it changed again in the nineteenth and twentieth centuries, away from emphasis on fighting. Jihad has become a wide-ranging cluster of ideas. (20)

Islamic historian Reza Aslan has stated, "These groups, in many ways, represent a wholly new sect that has arisen out of Islam. One in which all the multiplicity [and] diversity of Islamic thought, and the pillars upon which this faith and practice have rested for 14 centuries, [have] been diluted into this one single notion—Jihad and nothing else." (21)

In January 2002, in the wake of the September 11 attack, at a conference of the Muslim World League, scholars defined *terrorism* and *Jihad*. *Terrorism* is defined as "an unlawful action, acts of aggression against individuals, groups or states [or] against human beings, including attacks on their religion, life, intellect, property or honor." (22) Terrorism, then, is any violence or threat designed to terrorize people or endanger their lives or security. *Jihad* is "self-defense, meant for upholding right, ending injustice, ensuring peace and security and establishing mercy."

Muslims cannot *initiate* an attack and call it a Jihad—a Jihad *must be called in self-defense only*. Extremists have decided that because the West continues to oppress them, they are justified in a "self-defensive" Jihad.

Jihad is not a central prop of Islam, despite the Western perspective. But it was and remains a duty for Muslims to commit themselves to a struggle on all fronts—moral, spiritual, and political—to create a just and decent society. (23) This doctrine is, however, open to distortion.

## ❈ ISLAMISTS AND MUSLIM SOCIETY

Islamists do not recognize any interpretations of the Qur'an made by Islamic jurists over the centuries**; they want to "sweep away the cobwebs." They want to go back to a seventh-century "pure" society as they understand it, with no regard for the realities of the modern world. Some people agree with these unfounded interpretations; most people are dismayed. Many people attend mosques where they hear Islamists preach, but they are not necessarily Islamists themselves, or terrorists. The next steps to extremist action are built on a *deviant* interpretation of religious doctrines. Those who commit to extremist groups belong to a *cult*.

Much has been written by Muslims about the Islamists and their ideology. The ideology is anti-intellectual and reactive, nihilistic, and lacking faith in all political systems, in history, and in past social developments. (25) Islamists demonize not just the West, but *mainstream Islamic*

---

**A good example is a verse often quoted in the Western press and by extremists, "Kill them [infidels] wherever you find them." (2:191) The context of this revelation was the twelve-year persecution of the nascent Muslim community by enemies intent on eradicating it, and it was directed toward the Arabian pagans. This verse in no way refers to noncombatant non-Muslims today. (24) The Prophet Muhammad himself sent a letter to the monks in St. Catherine's Monastery in Sinai, which is still preserved, assuring them that they would be protected by the Muslims. Muhammad also intentionally shielded Christian Ethiopia from conquest. When Caliph Omar entered Jerusalem, he issued an edict that all Christian lives and property would be safe, and he allowed the Jews to return (they had been expelled by the Byzantines). One wonders how Islamic zealots accommodate such precedents. They also have to account for this verse in the Qur'an: "Those who believe, and those who follow the Jewish scriptures, and the Christians and the Sabaens [Ethiopians], any who believe in God and the Last Day and work righteousness shall have their reward with their Lord." (2:62) *culture and philosophy* as well. As one scholar put it, "There is no vision [amongst Islamists] of economic, social, or foreign policy, or a legislature, just the caliph, territory, and Islamic law." (26) They don't know what a state would look like. (Muhammad did not create a state; he created a community of believers.) They believe a fantasy, based on a false reading of human nature and how the world works.

The Islamists' message is first and foremost directed at other Muslims, whom they believe have fallen away from God, and who, in their view, can be sacrificed if they do not accept Islamist tenets. Islamist leaders *presume to judge who is or is not a good Muslim.*

It has become quite clear that people do not join the Islamists because of poverty or oppression, or for religious reasons; it is not that simple. They join because they are in search of purpose, excitement, or status. Ideology is less important than group dynamics, and filling psychological and emotional needs; (27) the ideology tends to be acquired later. About one fourth who join have criminal backgrounds. (28)

The Internet has had a huge impact in recruiting. It is a community in itself: a place to exchange information, have one's ideas reinforced, and discuss how to promote the cause. It provides a do-it-yourself Islam cobbled together from websites and from self-taught leaders. (29)

Because these groups resemble cults, there has been considerable effort to "de-program" members. It is a battle of ideas, using theological ammunition. (30) Programs for this type of education were begun in Yemen, and they have been tried in Indonesia, Saudi Arabia, Egypt, Singapore, Iraq, the United States, and Britain. (31) They seem to achieve success in more than half of the cases, when individuals renounce violence.

Many Muslims have found themselves torn between two quite different worldviews. Most seek a synthesis. But others, usually poorly educated, commit totally to groups who tell them what to believe. The leaders of these groups are better educated and have a political-power agenda. Theirs is a war for *limited* purposes. (32)

Islamist groups can also gain followers through extensive charity work, rather than ideology. They provide social services that local governments cannot or will not undertake, notably in Egypt, Lebanon, Morocco, Tunisia, Algeria, and Yemen. (Helping the poor is considered an Islamic obligation on the part of the ruling power.) Many organizations, such as the Muslim Brotherhood, (33) have schools, training centers, clinics, dental services, pharmacies, job centers, food banks, welfare agencies, and scholarships. They are well organized and well financed, and have created an institutional structure that is parallel to the state. (34) It is significant that Hizbollah has a hospital, schools, discount pharmacies, groceries, and an orphanage. (35) It benefits an estimated 250,000 Lebanese and is the country's second-largest employer.

Some of these groups' interpretations of specific Islamic doctrines are bizarre indeed. Because suicide has *never* been condoned in Islam (the incidence of suicide in Muslim societies is lower than that of any other regional or religious group), (36) suicide has to be classified as "Jihad martyrdom" to gain any acceptance at all. A prominent writer said of Islamists, "The truth is that nothing is further from true Islam than this extremist and unilateral approach, because Islam is the only religion that requires its adherents to believe in other religions. Muslims have surprised the world. . . with their ability to accommodate other cultures and integrate them into Islam's great civilization." (37)

It is also time to put the "72 virgins" to rest; this is a quaint, lurid, provocative interpretation of an obscure passage in the Qur'an, avidly seized upon by Westerners who find it amusing and use it repeatedly to ridicule Islamic belief. Typical is an article in the *Washington Post* that opened, "He was promised a straight shot to Heaven and 72 maidens to wait on him once he got there, but Hoshir Sabir Hasan was not ready to die." (38) A brochure from the Institute of Islamic Education states, "The promise of '70 or 72 virgins' is fiction written by some anti-Islam bigots." (39) This belief is to mainstream Muslims as the belief that we will one day be issued wings and a harp, and walk on clouds, is to mainstream Christians.†† Yet I have never seen the "72 virgins" refuted in the Western media.

---

†† "[The] first proponents [of this imagery] had nothing to do with the anti-Islamic myth that martyrs are motivated by the hope of being greeted by dozens of virgins waiting in heaven. It began with Hindu Tamils in Sri Lanka...when it spread to Palestine over the past decade, it was an act of last-resort desperation by frustrated people. . . . Al-Qaeda has merely taken [up] an old technique." (40)

These are the relevant verses: "Facing each other on thrones, round which will be passed to them a cup from a clear-flowing fountain...and beside them will be chaste women, their glances, with big eyes." (37:44–48) This is very brief and vague, and it has given rise to many commentaries over the centuries. The Islamist interpretation is based on commentaries.

## ❊ MAINSTREAM MUSLIMS

Moderate Muslims are well aware that *mainstream Islam is also a target of the extremists.* The moderates issue press releases, hold conferences, and publicize their repudiation of Islamist violence, but usually they get little or no press coverage.

Muslim authors have written extensively (some will be quoted here), trying to disassociate mainstream Islam from the outrageous statements made by Islamists that invariably get into the Western press. The idea is to reclaim Islamic heritage and promote an "Islamic renewal," a diffuse but growing social, political, and intellectual movement whose goal is a profound reform of Muslim societies. (41) They recognize that throughout time, Muslims have had to revise or bypass Islamic law and some ancient practices to adapt their states and societies to changing realities. (This is the centuries-old concept of *Ijtihad*.) Outside the Islamic framework, there is no real chance of substantive reform in the Middle East. Independent, moderate Muslim thinkers and leaders are confronting violence, oppression, and intolerance *in the name of Islam*. (42)

A well-known spokesman for moderate Islam is Tariq Ramadan, a Swiss-born Islamic specialist who has written and spoken extensively. He believes in re-interpreting Islam, tailoring it to specific circumstances. He also advocates creating a "Western Islam" in the U.S. and Europe, taking into account cultural differences. He states that there is a difference between religion and citizenship; Muslims should participate and contribute to their community wherever they are. (43) Because of an isolationist tendency, Muslims have not been active in defending their image, even while many are quietly and successfully integrating with the West. (44)

There are several new "evangelical," wildly popular spokesmen for moderate Islam. Their televised sermons are watched by millions, and they reach an audience through writings, the Internet, CDs, tapes, and social media as well. Most prominent among them is Amr Khaled, an Egyptian who advocates a blend of conservative Islamic belief with what is compatible with Western culture, regardless of where one lives. He is among "the world's one hundred most famous televangelist," and came in at number thirteen in *Time*'s 2007 list of the world's one hundred most influential people. (45)

Amr Khaled emphasizes first putting one's own life in order, succeeding at studies and in adult life, and finding ways to contribute—teaching illiterates, distributing food and clothing, volunteering—these instill a sense of purpose and are part of everyday religion (46). (An example of this was seen when young people periodically picked up trash at Tahrir Square during the Egyptian demonstrations.) He appeals to the upper middle class, those truly capable of changing the Islamic world. He blends Islam with feel-good optimism; one can enjoy the world and still be religious, and have a "purpose-driven" life. According to Amr Khaled, Muslims in the West should not just take from the host country, but participate. Like evangelical Christian preachers, he blends self-help with management-training jargon and religion, a new phenomenon in the Muslim world. After the Danish-cartoon controversy,‡‡ Amr Khaled organized a conference to talk to young Europeans about Islam, press freedom, and tolerance. (47)

Other influential televangelists, with essentially the same message, include Ahmed Al-Shugairi of Saudi Arabia, who advocates equality for women and speaks against sectarianism. He has stated, "Islam is an excellent product that needs better packaging." (48) He sees the Qur'an as a modern ethical guidebook, not a harsh set of medieval rules. Moez Masoud, Khaled Gendy, and dozens of others are speaking out to change Islam's image. (49) (50) The Middle East has at least 370 satellite channels, nearly triple the number it had three years ago, twenty-seven of them dedicated to Islam. Women in their audiences wear everything from a veil to designer jeans.

The older generation are not as likely to become activists in adapting Islam. It is for the younger generation (ages fifteen to thiry-five) to work at changing Islam's image. They are opening up economic and political systems that had been tightly closed. The non-profit organization Free Muslims Coalition Against Terrorism was created "to eliminate broad-based support for Islamic extremism and terrorism and to strengthen democratic institutions in the Middle East." (51) In U.S. Muslim communities, members have been invited to send to U.S. authorities anonymous reports of any Muslim individuals or groups that "advocate Muslim

---

‡‡The Prophet Muhammad was depicted in cartoons in a Danish newspaper, which led to demonstrations and attacks in some Islamic countries.

extremist ideology, engage in apologetic support for terrorist organizations, or advocate Jihad." (52)

In Jordan, King Abdullah convened a conference in 2005 titled "True Islam and Its Role in Modern Society." (53) In Saudi Arabia, a fatwa (religious ruling) was issued condemning terrorism *and those who finance it.* (Much private Saudi money has gone to terrorist groups.) (54) General David Petraeus stated in 2010, "The Saudi role in taking on Al Qaeda, both by force but also using political, social, religious and educational tools, is one of the most important, least reported positive developments in the war on terror." (55)

To date, Muslims have been alarmed, embarrassed, and often incredulous at what is happening. They know that Islamism is causing a crisis in the image of their religion that needs to be addressed, and soon. Sunni Muslims do not have a central authority to make and enforce decisions to combat extremism—they must do it themselves as groups and communities. The moderates are fighting back and the tide is turning.

## CHAPTER 12

# ANTI-AMERICANISM

A guidebook about Arabs cannot ignore the growing sentiment of anti-Americanism* among Middle Eastern Arabs and Muslims today. It is an important trend, it is increasing, and we urgently need to try to understand it. Here are some statistics that lend a sense of reality to the worsening anti-American sentiment among Middle Eastern nations.

A Pew poll conducted between March 21 and April 26, 2011 surveyed four Arab nations (along with Turkey and Pakistan) on whether people are favorable toward the United States and whether they have confidence in it. These findings were compared to similar polls in 2009 and 2010.

## FAVORABILITY AND CONFIDENCE IN THE UNITED STATES (1)

| | Favorable Toward the U.S. | | |
| --- | --- | --- | --- |
| | 2009 | 2010 | 2011 |
| Lebanon | 55% | 52% | 49% |
| Palestine | 15% | — | 18% |
| Jordan | 25% | 21% | 13% |
| Egypt | 27% | 17% | 20% |
| | Confidence in the U.S. | | |
| | 2009 | 2010 | 2011 |
| Lebanon | 46% | 43% | 43% |
| Palestine | 23% | — | 14% |
| Jordan | 31% | 26% | 28% |
| Egypt | 42% | 33% | 35% |

---

*America refers to the United States in this book because America is used in the U.S. media and also in the Middle East.

Reasons given for these feelings included a perception that the U.S. acts unilaterally, an opposition to the war on terror, and fears of America as a military threat—in other words, political policy. The "Arab Spring" uprisings did not really change America's image.

In other questions, democracy was widely seen as the best form of government, by more than 70 percent of the Arabs. The people clearly value freedom of religion, free speech, and competitive elections. Some prioritize a good economy over democracy.

In July 2011 a poll was taken by Al-Jazeera television in Morocco, Egypt, Lebanon, Jordan, Saudi Arabia, and the UAE. It showed that the U.S.'s reputation in the Arab world had fallen to a record low. The main reason cited was "U.S. interference in the Arab world," which ranked as high in the respondents' concerns as the continuing occupation of Palestinian lands. (2)

Before we go further, it must be made clear that *Middle Eastern Muslims and Arabs do not "hate" America.* Nor do they hate the American people. But they are very *angry at* and *afraid of* America's government. It is only the extremist fringe that hates America. I have never heard any ordinary Arabs state that they hate America, nor have I heard such reports from others.

If the Arabs are *angry*, then there is hope. If we understand the reasons for their anger, we can address those reasons, and not misdirect our efforts to bring about change. If they truly *hated* America and America's values, we would have a permanent breach, a real clash of civilizations, and that would be a hopeless situation, one side trying to eradicate the other. *It's not that bad.*

On both sides, anti-American and anti-Arab/Muslim sentiments are as much about *perceptions* as they are about *reality*—who and what people listen to and the conclusions they reach. Both sides generalize, and by now, each has a mostly negative, stereotypical image of the other. If people don't know a region or its inhabitants, they have to depend on the media to form their beliefs.†

---

†Unlike the rest of the world, Americans do not see daily images of suffering Palestinians and Iraqis. It's not that other countries have news different from America—it's America that is different. "[A] young Arab sees appalling scenes of horror and destruction [mostly on television] . . . He sees them, but the young European or young American does not see them." (3)

Certainly in the past many Americans truly, sincerely did not understand how this all came about, although it is becoming clearer to many people. I think the most objective approach is to let Americans and Arabs speak for themselves. We can look at statements on both sides. One thing we can all agree on is that there are many misunderstandings. Some statements that are quoted in this chapter use *they* without explaining who "they" are. At times *they* may refer to terrorists; other references are broader, and, given the large amount of commentary and rhetoric, it is often hard to tell how many are intended to refer to Arabs and Muslims in general.

Much of what we read or hear is confusing, especially to people who don't know much about the Middle East. If, for example, any of the opinions you read here are difficult to understand, you can do several things: (1) Ask an Arab or a Muslim in your community for clarification (virtually everyone has Arabs or Muslims in their communities); (2) talk with someone knowledgeable who has been in the region; and (3) look it up and read about it. Most important is that you consider statements from all sources and then *make up your own mind* as to the nature of anti-Americanism.

Because we have already mentioned that most Arabs don't actually hate America but are very angry, let's begin right here. Statements about Arabs here refer to the *people*, not the elite or national leaders.

## ❈ REASONS FOR ARAB ANGER

### Arab/Muslim and Some Western Views‡

"Although the [State Department ad hoc advisory] committee found deep and abiding anger toward U.S. policies and actions, the criticism was not leveled across the board. The U.S. system of higher education, science, and technology were praised, as were the values of freedom, democracy, and individual dignity." (4)
"In much of the world, the United States is viewed as less a beacon of hope than a dangerous force to be countered." (5)
"When Obama talks of his desire 'to pursue the world as it should be' he does not mean according to the yearnings of its people,

‡This can include non-Arab Middle Easterners, and non-Muslim Arabs.

but according to U.S. interests. . . . Washington hopes that these rising forces can be stripped of their ideological opposition to U.S. hegemony and turned into pragmatists, fully integrated into the existing U.S.-led international order." (6)

Osama Bin Laden: "The events that affected my soul in a difficult way started in 1982 when America permitted the Israelis to invade Lebanon and the American 6th Fleet helped them in that. And the whole world saw and heard but did not respond. . . . And as I looked at those demolished towers in Lebanon it entered my mind that we should punish the oppressors in kind and that we destroy towers in America in order that they taste some of what we tasted and so that they be deterred from killing our women and children." (7)

Osama Bin Laden: "America and its allies are massacring us in Palestine, Chechnya, Kashmir, and Iraq. The Muslims have the right to attack America in reprisal. . . . The September 11 attacks were not targeted at women and children. The real targets were America's icons of military and economic power." (8)

A poll released in April 2007 by WorldPublicOpinion.org suggests a widespread negative outlook on the politics and practices of the United States. "[It is alleged that] the U.S. seeks to weaken and divide the Islamic world, and to achieve political and military domination to control Middle East resources. Yet, the majority of those surveyed stated that they support globalization, democratization, and religious freedom." (9)

"Not a single respondent who condoned the 9/11 attacks used the Qur'an as justification. Instead, they relied on political rationalizations, calling the U.S. an imperialist power or accusing it of wanting to control the world." (10)

Rami Khouri, Lebanese commentator: "Americans do not like to hear it, but their government has behaved like an imperial power in the Middle East [for] more than fifty years." (11)

Rashid Khaldi, American academic: "[There is] a history that is behind perceptions in the Middle East of the American role there, perceptions that may not match what Americans think of themselves and their country's role in the world." (12)

"As usual, investment and aid are conditional on the adoption of
the U.S. model in the name of liberalization and reform, and on
binding the region's economies further to U.S. and European
markets under the banner of 'trade integration.' One wonders
what would be left of the Arab revolutions in such infiltrated
civil societies, domesticated political parties, and dependent
economies. . . . In vain does the U.S. try to reconcile the irrec-
oncilable—to preach democracy, while occupying and aiding
occupation." (13)

Between 1980 and 2001, the United States engaged in fifteen direct
military operations in the Middle East, all of them directed against Muslims.§ There were an equal number of non-military actions such as the
imposition of punitive embargoes, threats through military build-up, policies in support of some regional states against others, support of selected
opposition groups, and provision of weapons (sometimes secretly). What
matters here is not the political issue of who America supported and why;
the result has been that *these actions are seen by local people as American
interference in their region, and resentment has continued to build.* We are
talking about perceptions. We are talking about America's image. Here
are some more quotes.

"One of the greatest dangers for Americans in deciding how to confront the Islamist threat lies in continuing to believe—at the urg-
ing of senior U.S. leaders—that Muslims hate us and attack us for
what we are and what we think, rather than for what we do." (15)
"American policies often kill, directly and indirectly—and this
is why people are willing to sacrifice themselves to kill us in
return." (16)

---

§This be viewed at the *Information Clearing House* website, "U.S. Intervention in
the Middle East" *(www.informationclearinghouse.info)*. Military aid to Muslim Bosnia,
Kosovo, and Somalia does not counterbalance the "anti-Muslim" activities in the Middle
East. In September 2011, the U.S. announced the creation of a "ring" of secret drone
bases to target Somalia and Yemen. "The U.S. government is known to have used drones
to carry out lethal attacks in at least six countries: Afghanistan, Iraq, Libya, Pakistan,
Somalia, and Yemen" (14)

Most Americans have had little interest in foreign policy in the past (compared with Europeans, for example). But this has to change. The United States' foreign policies now can have a direct effect on the American people's lives.

> "But there is one thing that we have not done that is crucial to our future: we still have not engaged in a true national dialogue about what our foreign policy should be and what constitutes our national interests and values. That is an issue of national security no less vital than protecting our ports or airlines. Throughout our history there has always been a kind of unspoken presumption that foreign policy was outside the purview of the people, that it needed to be in the hands of specialists and policy mandarins and that ordinary Americans were just not equipped to make decisions about such highfalutin matters. That is a mistake we can no longer afford. American citizens pay taxes to support our policies overseas and send their sons and daughters to fight for the nation, which means they should be damn well able to pass judgment on what our foreign policy ought to be." (17)

## Some American Views

*They Hate Our Freedom, Values, Way of Life*

> George W. Bush: "America was targeted for attack because we're the brightest beacon for freedom and opportunity in the world." (18) "I am amazed that there's such misunderstanding of what our country is about that people would hate us. I am like most Americans, I just can't believe it because I know how good we are." (19) "They hate our freedoms, our freedom of religion, our freedom of speech, our freedom to vote and assemble and disagree with each other." (20) "They hate our values. They hate what America stands for." (21)
>
> William J. Bennett and Alan M. Dershowitz: "When we were attacked on Sept. 11, we knew the main reason for the attack was that Islamists hated our way of life, our virtues, our freedom." (22)

Glenn Beck: "We were attacked by the enemies of freedom. We are
a good and decent people and we are free." (23)

Rudolph Giuliani: "American foreign policy had nothing to do
with September 11. September 11 happened to us because these
people who hate us, hate us because of the freedoms that we
have." (24)

## They Hate Our Success

Charles Krauthammer: "The fact is that the world hates the U.S. for
its wealth, its success, its power." (25)

Ralph Peters: "Jealous of our success and power, terrified and
threatened by the free, unstructured nature of our societies,
and incapable of performing competitively in the twenty-first
century, they have convinced themselves that our way of life is
satanic. . . ." "We are dealing with a delusional civilization." (26)

## They Don't Know Enough About Us

The American government, after 9/11, undertook a new initiative—
strengthening programs that present information about the country and
its values (public diplomacy). This was predicated on the assumption
that anti-Americanism can be lessened by presenting more accurate or
detailed information. The Bush White House had a stated policy that
"spreading the universal principle of human liberty" was the key to changing the conditions that spawn terrorism.

The American government set up a radio station, Radio Sawa, which
attracts young viewers to the music, but which they turn off when it
comes to the news; a television station, Al-Hurra, which has a very low
watching public, about 1 percent; and a glossy magazine called 'Hi,'
which was expensive and did not sell. Public diplomacy efforts described
Muslims' lives in America, but Muslims in the Middle East all have
friends or relatives in America, so they don't need this information. In
addition, it described American families and communities, but the Arabs
already know that Americans are nice people. Other efforts focused on
explaining the workings of democracy and elections in the U.S.; equality of opportunity; rewards based on merit; and sports, entertainment,
and education.

"The State Department spent 15 million dollars for a warm and
fuzzy TV advertising campaign called 'Shared Values' intended
for broadcast in Muslim countries. The ads . . . were ultimately
dropped after test audiences said they didn't touch on any
of the main issues that divide America and the Muslim
world." (27)

"Ever since the initial response to the 9/11 attacks, American public diplomacy strategists have spent too much time on 'Aren't
we wonderful?' campaigns. In the Arab world, people simply
don't care about such self-serving pronouncements. Anything
that does not relate directly to their own lives is wasted effort.
The State Department has been emphasizing the importance of
educational and cultural exchanges, which are valuable tools."
(28)

"The [GAO] report added that despite the ten billion dollars spent
to advance U.S. strategic interests abroad since 9/11, foreign
public opinion polling data shows that negative views towards
the United States persist." (29)

"A series of studies in the United States have criticized U.S.-funded
Arabic-language media, such as Radio Sawa and the satellite TV
station Al-Hurra, for failing to attract a large audience. U.S. officials made a push to boost America's image among Arabs and
Muslims after the Sept. 11 2001 attacks. But the efforts have
been hampered because many Arabs strenuously object to U.S.
foreign policies, particularly over the Israeli-Palestinian conflict
and the Iraq war. . . . The State Department, which sponsors
the $4.5 million annual publication and distribution through-
out the Arab world of the Arabic-language magazine 'Hi,' said
on Thursday it stopped the presses because it was unclear how
widely it was read." (30)

"Hurting more than helping is Al-Hurra, the official Arab-language
broadcasting outlet sponsored by the U.S. government—or at
least such is the jaundiced view of the overwhelming majority
of the journalists, academics, officials and business executives
attending the annual Arab Media Forum in Dubai this week. . . .
There was broad agreement that the U.S.-branded Al-Hurra has

been a very costly mistake. According to Zogby, who quoted surveys of broadcast viewers in the region, the estimated penetration for Al-Hurra is less than 1 percent.... Even President Obama avoided appearing on Al-Hurra when he inaugurated his outreach campaign to the Arab and Muslim world, sidestepping the U.S. network for an interview on Saudi-based Al-Arabiyya." (31)

## Anti-Americanism Is an Excuse

Barry Rubin: "The basic reason for the prevalence of Arab anti-Americanism, then, is that it has been such a useful tool for radical rulers, revolutionary movements, and even moderate regimes to build domestic support and pursue regional goals with no significant costs." (32)

"Anti-Americanism is how Arab leaders play the Arab people and the United States against each other to preserve their own hides. There is no incentive to be anything but anti-American, and it is very dangerous not to follow the pack." (33)

## We Share a Long History of Hatred

Bernard Lewis: "This is no less than a clash of civilizations—the perhaps irrational but surely historic reactions of an ancient rival against our Judeo-Christian heritage.... The struggle between these rival systems has now lasted for some fourteen centuries. What is truly evil and unacceptable is the domination of infidels over true believers."¶ (34)

Bernard Lewis: "The motive, clearly, is hatred ... the hatred has been growing steadily for many years.... It is difficult if not impossible to be strong and successful and to be loved by those who are neither the one or the other.... This feeling, with far deeper roots and greater intensity, affects attitudes in the

---

¶Millions of Middle Eastern Muslims migrate to Europe and America precisely because they want to live under a Western government.

Muslim world toward the Western world or, as they would put it, the infidel countries."** (35)

Unfortunately, it is not clear who is being described. Perhaps only the Islamists, but it reads as if referring to everyone caught up in "the roots of Muslim rage."

Samuel Huntington: "Conflict along the fault line between Western and Islamic civilizations has been going on for 1,300 years. . . . On both sides, the interaction between Islam and the West is seen as a clash of civilizations." (36) "A complex of factors has increased the conflict between Islam and the West in the late twentieth century. . . . Muslim population growth . . . the Islamic Resurgence . . . the West's simultaneous efforts to universalize its values and institutions, to maintain its military and economic superiority . . . and to intervene in conflicts in the Muslim world . . . the collapse of communism . . . increasing contact between . . . Muslims and Westerners." (37)

---

**Many authors, as well as most reports in the media, wrongly depict the thinking of people in the Modern Middle East. I select the writings of Bernard Lewis as an example, because he is widely read and quoted. In all his writings, Dr. Lewis speaks in generalities, not distinguishing historical or extremist views from those of ordinary Arabs and Muslims of the twenty-first century. Repeating and emphasizing insulting remarks about Westerners will resonate with readers and become associated in their minds with Arabs and Muslims, even if they are outdated by a thousand years. Dr. Lewis continually uses phrases like "the enemies of God," "the infidels of the West," and "the House of Islam and the House of Unbelief," which have nothing to do with how modern, educated people think (perhaps it helps to sell books). He writes that "America has become the archenemy, the incarnation of evil, the diabolic opponent of all this good," which must be limited to extremists unless the ordinary people think that the Western way of life and government are evil too (they don't). I cannot imagine why he would assure us that "studying under infidel teachers was inconceivable," when this is not explained and thousands of Muslims study in the West. He cannot be describing ordinary people, but the damage is done. Arabs and Muslims do not think this way. Language like this does not reflect what I have been hearing, or overhearing, in the Arab world for over forty years.

Most Western readers simply want to understand 9/11, the Iraqi insurgency, the uprisings, and the current political climate in the Middle East. They don't know what is historical, current, or extremist. Such careless writing does not clarify current issues for Western readers; on the contrary, it does incalculable damage.

Assertions of a "clash of civilizations" ignore the fact that most Muslims are trying to integrate into a globalizing world. The September 11 attacks caused many outside of the Middle East to try to segregate Muslims as "others," and obscured the Muslim quest for modernization and its struggle to reclaim Islam's central values from a small but virulent minority. Muslims want to create an identity that fits in with political changes globally. (38)

The statements in this section, "Some American Views," cannot be based on interviews with Arabs all across the region. Arabs are amazed when they read statements such as these, and they wonder where the authors found the information to justify what they have written. No Arabs believe such assertions. Regrettably, Arabs are accustomed to being maligned (some Arabs see the title of this book and are afraid to open it). They also suspect malicious intent.

## ❧ ARAB/MUSLIM VIEWS ON AMERICAN CULTURE

"There remains residual respect for American culture, technology, education, and resources. Almost every Arab college student I talk with speaks about his or her desire to come to the United States for graduate school, and those who have already studied in America are almost always more friendly and sophisticated in their attitude about the United States." (39)

"Americans are used to images of resentment and anger from the Arab world. A less familiar sight is Arabs buying hamburgers at the McDonald's in Cairo, lattes at the Starbucks in Beirut, or ice cream at the Baskin-Robbins in Yemen. Although there is widespread animosity toward America across the Arab world—especially over U.S. policy toward Israel and the Palestinians—many Arabs embrace aspects of American life and American culture. 'It is a love-hate relationship,' said Mustafa Harmaneh, a political analyst in Jordan. 'Culturally, American music is popular. American food is popular. American clothes are popular. People still wear jeans with American flags on them. They wear baseball hats and they don't see any contradiction in that.'" (40)

## ❋ VIEWS ON WESTERN-STYLE DEMOCRACY

Lately, with freedom-and-democracy demonstrations in the news, most Westerners have come to realize that the Arabs love the concepts of democracy and freedom after all. *Democracy has an overwhelmingly positive image throughout the world.* This is constantly emphasized in the Arab world, in speech and in writing.

> The Pew Report of 2003: "In most Muslim populations, large majorities continue to believe that Western-style democracy can work in their countries. . . . Although many Muslims around the world would like more religion in politics, this view does not contradict widespread support for democratic ideals among these publics. In fact, in a number of countries, Muslims who support a greater role for Islam in politics place the highest regard on freedom of speech, freedom of the press and the importance of free and contested elections." (41)
>
> "We desperately want change, reform, democracy, prosperity and modernity, but few of us believe that this will come through the barrels of Western guns." (42)
>
> In Jordan, over 90 percent of university students believe that there is no contradiction between Islamic teachings and democracy or human rights. (43)

Some American pundits have stated their hope that if the Arabs can gain freedom, they will leave behind anti-American political grievances, and they will recognize that America is not after their oil—America just wants their freedom.

> Charles Krauthammer: "When millions of Iraqis risk their lives and then dance with joy at having been initiated into the rituals of democracy, a fact has been created. And the old cliches that America went to Iraq for oil or hegemony begin to look hollow." (44)

We read that demonstrations for freedom have taken place because the U.S. led the way.

Fouad Ajami: "What we are witnessing in the Arab world is similar
to the spring of the European peoples in 1848." (45) "Now the
Arabs, grasping for a new world, and the Americans who have
helped usher in this unprecedented moment, together ride this
storm wave of freedom." (46)

But there are fears. It's not simple. Attaining a democracy is not easy,
and it can still entail serious risks. We hear some hyperbole and wishful
thinking.

Charles Krauthammer: "We are at the dawn of an Arab Spring—
the first bloom of democracy in Iraq, Lebanon, Egypt, Palestine,
and throughout the greater Middle East." (47)

Americans are thinking about democracy, and many Americans
are analyzing our own democracy, what it is, what it means. For any
democracy to work, it requires an *informed citizenry* (a reasonable level
of literacy), *a trust in the opposition* (they will give up power if voted out),
and a *national identity* that transcends allegiance based on kin, tribe,
religion, or ethnic origin. This is difficult in some parts of the Middle
East because many national borders were drawn arbitrarily and incor-
rectly by England and France after they seized control of the region after
World War I, making nations out of people who would not have willingly
been united, and cutting off others who belong. Middle Easterners found
themselves defined for the first time by *geography*. Even now, we cannot
consider the borders in the Middle East as fixed.

The Arabs want democracy as an ideal. It can work in some countries, but the conditions have not been met in others. Reforms such as
pluralism, rule of law, and accountability will come at the expense of the
entrenched elites in every country. The situation is too complicated to
predict with assurance.

"[The call for democracy] has already been happening for many
years through the work of indigenous reformers and democrats
and activists. It is not the American policy of promoting freedom
that is starting to show dividends. . . . What has happened is that
the Americans are finally supporting the democrats rather than
supporting the tyrants, as they did for the last fifty years." (48)

##  ISLAM

Islam in particular elicits vitriolic attacks and impassioned defenses. These are a very few of the comments; for a bigger picture, you can easily find more on this subject. This is, of course, selective.

### Anti-Islam Comments

These are the type of comments that are widely disseminated on the Internet in the Middle East.

> Samuel Huntington: "Some Westerners have argued that the West does not have problems with Islam but only with violent Islamic extremists. . . . Fourteen hundred years of history demonstrate otherwise. . . . The underlying problem for the West is not Islamic fundamentalism. It is Islam." (49)
>
> Franklin Graham: "I believe [Islam is] a very evil and wicked religion." (50) "In most Islamic countries, it is a crime to build a Christian church. . . . Christians are not free to worship Jesus in most Muslim countries. . . .†† The brutal, dehumanizing treatment of women by the Taliban has been well documented . . . the abusive treatment of women in most Islamic countries is nearly as draconian." (51)
>
> Pat Robertson: "These people are crazed fanatics, and I want to say it now: I believe it's motivated by a demonic power, it is satanic and it's time we recognize what we're dealing with." (52)
>
> "The Koran is the doctrinal guideline for the Muslim, therefore what it says explains their beliefs. What it says to me is that a peaceful Muslim hasn't read it! It is one of, if not the most violence-provoking religions on this earth. . . .‡‡ Islam has

---

††Christianity is openly practiced in all Muslim countries except for Saudi Arabia. There are thousands of churches in Muslim countries.

‡‡This kind of argument is essentially pointless. Islam is being judged in the context of our time, not the seventh century. The massacres of Joshua in 1230 B.C. must be understood in the context of their time. The people in ancient times lived in a different world, a world of lawlessness and violence. In truth, Muhammad fought fewer than ten battles in his lifetime, resulting in barely 1,000 casualties on both sides. (53) As in the Bible, every accusation and (selected) quotation can be refuted with the opposite (selected) quotation somewhere, if one keeps looking.

unhidden plans to take over the world by the worst brutality imaginable. . . . Open up your eyes, America and the world—your governments are selling you out to the enemy by denying that he even exists. It is all under the guise of 'multi-cultural-ism.'" (54)

Bill O'Reilly: "Teaching our enemy's religion is like teaching *Mein Kampf.*" (55)

## Defense-of-Islam Comments

"We consider the Sept. 11 . . . criminal act as foreign to our honored culture, our peaceful and tolerant faith and our hospitable way of life. Terrorism cannot be eradicated until the underlying causes are justly addressed." (56)

"Islam has brought comfort and peace of mind to countless millions of men and women. It has given dignity and meaning to drab and impoverished lives. It has taught people of different races to live in brotherhood and people of different creeds to live side by side in reasonable tolerance." (57)

"If Islam were really just the caricature that it is often reduced to, then how would it be so appealing as to become the world's fastest-growing religion? . . . because it also has admirable qualities that anyone who has lived in the Muslim world observes: a profound egalitarianism and a lack of hierarchy that confer dignity and self-respect among believers, greater hospitality than in other societies, an institutionalized system of charity, *Zakat*, to provide for the poor. Many West Africans, for example, see Christianity as corrupt and hierarchical and flock to Islam, which they view as democratic and inclusive." (58)

Since the genocide, Rwandans have converted to Islam in huge numbers. Muslims now make up 14 percent of the 8.2 million people in Africa's most Catholic nation. "We have our own Jihad, and that is our war against ignorance. . . . It is our struggle to heal," said the head mufti of Rwanda. (59) Fundamentalists from outside tried to organize and were rejected. During the genocide, Muslims were among the few Rwandans who protected both neighbors and strangers; the churches were not safe.

The subject of anti-Americanism clearly elicits wide-ranging and conflicting opinions, both in explaining its causes and in advocating its remedies. The issue is growing increasingly politicized. Because much of the mass media blends entertainment with news, in many instances there is little incentive to present thoughtful analyses of events backed by thorough fact checking. The stakes are high; they couldn't be higher. Every American needs to be knowledgeable on this subject and develop his or her own convictions.

## CHAPTER 13

# ARABS AND MUSLIMS IN THE WEST

There has been a sharp rise in both Arab and Muslim immigration to the West, which has affected the host countries and also the societies back home. The trend toward increased emigration, except from Saudi Arabia and the Arabian Gulf states, continues. Muslims and Arabs, however, are entirely different populations. Statistics for both of these groups are variable and estimates vary widely.

## ❈ ARABS IN THE UNITED STATES

There are more than three million people of Arab origin in the United States. Of these, more than half (possibly as many as 70 percent) are Christian. Christians, especially Lebanese and Syrians, got a head start; they began emigrating in the late nineteenth and early twentieth centuries. Arabs who arrived after the 1960s are mostly Muslims. About 65 percent of all the Arab Americans were born in the U.S.

The following is the breakdown of Arabs' countries of origin by percentage:

❋ ❋ ❋ ❋ ❋ ❋ ❋ ❋ ❋ ❋ ❋ ❋ ❋ ❋ ❋ ❋ ❋ ❋ ❋ ❋ ❋ ❋

## COUNTRIES OF ORIGIN, ARAB-AMERICANS, 2006 (1)

| | |
|---|---|
| Lebanon | 32% |
| Iraq | 4% |
| Syria | 10% |
| Egypt | 11% |
| Palestine | 5% |
| Jordan | 4% |
| Morocco | 5% |
| (Other) | 29% |

41 percent of Arab Americans have college degrees (compared to 28 percent in the U.S. population as a whole). (2) (3) There are 72 percent working in professional, managerial, technical, and administrative jobs, and 82 percent are citizens. Arab American women work at the rate of 46 percent (compared to 56 percent in the nation as a whole). (4)

In 2001, 69 percent of the Arab Americans supported an all-out war with countries that support or harbor terrorists. (5) After 9/11, Arab American groups very quickly raised money to donate to the Red Cross and to the victims of the attack. Arab Americans also sponsored blood drives, rallies, and vigils all over the nation.

After Hurricane Katrina in 2005, Muslim groups contributed one million dollars to relief efforts. They also provided hot meals to those in shelters on September 11. (6) (7) When Hurricane Sandy hit in late 2012, the Arab American Association of New York contributed and distributed food, water, and basic goods throughout the New York-New Jersey region. They coordinated donations from Arab American communities across the U.S. (8)

## ❋ MUSLIMS IN THE UNITED STATES AND CANADA

The Muslim population in the United States has increased to roughly five million (estimates range from two and a half million to seven million), and Islam is now the second most commonly practiced religion in America. (9) More than half of all American Muslims live in California, New York, Michigan, Illinois, and New Jersey. (10) In 2011 there were about 3,500 mosques, large and small Islamic centers, and prayer locations (not a large number; compare, for example, to 11,000 places of worship for Jehovah's Witnesses). (11)

In Canada, there were about 1.2 million Muslims in 2011, most of them living in Ontario, Quebec, and British Columbia. (12) In 2010, there were about 200 mosques and Islamic centers. (13)

Among the Muslims in the United States, Arabs constitute about 20 percent, one-third are of South Asian origin (India, Pakistan, Bangladesh), 30 percent are African Americans, and the others are mainly African and East Asian. There are about 15,000 Muslims serving in the U.S. armed forces. (14)

American immigrants of Middle Eastern Muslim ancestry (not just Arabs) are more affluent, better educated, and more likely to be married and have children than the average citizen. In the U.S. 77 percent of the Muslims are active in organizations that help the poor, sick, elderly, and homeless; 69 percent are active in school and youth organizations; and 46 percent belong to a professional organization. (15) They favor tougher laws to prevent terrorism at a rate of 84 percent. (16)

A Gallup study in 2011, "Muslim Americans: Faith, Freedom, and the Future," found that 89 percent of American Muslims opposed violent attacks on individuals, compared with 71 percent of Catholics and Protestants, and 75 percent of Jews. It showed that 65 percent of American Muslims were registered to vote. (17) A Pew poll in 2007 showed that Muslims are decidedly mainstream, largely assimilated, happy with their lives, and moderate on political issues. (18) In late 2011, a Pew poll showed that Muslims are optimistic about life in the U.S. Half of them said American leaders have not done enough to combat Islamist extremism. About 56 percent are satisfied with the way the country is going (compared with 23 percent of the general population). (19)

*The vast majority of American Muslims were appalled by terrorist attacks because all of them have a huge stake in the future welfare of America.* Such attacks also lead to erosion of their civil liberties. Many believe that the mainstream Muslim majority in the U.S. has been silent about extremism and terrorism for too long (they have been afraid of law-enforcement personnel and of reprisals if their identities became known), and they are actively working to bring attention to anything of this sort to government authorities. Like other Americans, Muslims' safety and security depend on combating terrorism. And *every time a terrorist incident occurs, those most vulnerable to unfounded suspicion are the Arabs and Muslims living in the West.* In 2004 the American Muslim Group on Policy was formed, to focus on ways that the Muslim community can provide assistance and help build trust and communication in the nation. Muslim immigrants also want to play an active role in helping to improve the U.S. image in the Muslim world.

## ❋ MUSLIMS IN EUROPE

Statistics for the number of Muslims in Europe are indefinite. Muslims come from numerous countries of origin, and Europe's governments tend to collect fewer religious statistics than the United States does; furthermore, many Muslims are in Europe illegally and are therefore not counted in official estimates. There are 13 to 20 million Muslims in Western Europe, and Islam is the second most commonly practiced religion there. (20) The approximate breakdown for Muslims in Western Europe is shown in the following chart.

### NUMBER OF MUSLIMS IN WESTERN EUROPE 2010 (21)

| | |
|---|---|
| France | 4,700,000 |
| Germany | 4,100,000 |
| U.K. | 2,800,000 |
| Italy | 1,500,000 |
| Spain | 1,000,000 |
| Netherlands | 900,000 |
| Belgium | 630,000 |
| Austria | 500,000 |
| Sweden | 450,000 |
| Switzerland | 430,000 |
| Denmark | 220,000 |
| Norway | 144,000 |
| Portugal | 65,000 |
| Ireland | 43,000 |
| Finland | 42,000 |
| Luxembourg | 11,000 |
| (Australia) | (340,000) (22) |

Unlike the Muslims in the United States and Western Europe, Eastern European Muslims are mostly indigenous; their ancestors converted to Islam while the region was part of the Ottoman Empire. Shown here are the statistics for Muslims in Eastern Europe.

❂ ❂ ❂ ❂ ❂ ❂ ❂ ❂ ❂ ❂ ❂ ❂ ❂ ❂ ❂ ❂ ❂ ❂ ❂ ❂ ❂ ❂ ❂ ❂

## NUMBER OF MUSLIMS IN EASTERN EUROPE, 2010 (23)

| | |
|---|---|
| Russia | 22,000,000* |
| Albania | 2,200,000 |
| Kosovo | 1,600,000 |
| Bosnia | 1,600,000 |
| Bulgaria | 900,000 |
| Macedonia | 700,000 |
| Ukraine | 470,000 |
| Serbia | 310,000 |
| Croatia | 56,000 |
| Slovenia | 49,000 |
| Poland | 27,000 |
| Belarus | 19,000 |
| Moldova | 18,000 |
| Czech Republic | 4,000 |
| Slovakia | 4,800 |

*Muslims constitute 10 to 16 percent of Russia's population. (24)

❂ ❂ ❂ ❂ ❂ ❂ ❂ ❂ ❂ ❂ ❂ ❂ ❂ ❂ ❂ ❂ ❂ ❂ ❂ ❂ ❂ ❂ ❂ ❂

## MOSQUES AND ISLAMIC CENTERS IN WESTERN EUROPE* (25) (26)

| | |
|---|---|
| France | 2,000 |
| United Kingdom | 1,600 |
| Germany | 1,000 |
| Netherlands | 500 |
| Belgium | 350 |
| Italy | 250 |
| Spain | 200 |

*Huge "mega-mosques" are proposed or underway in several cities, including Cologne, Marseille, Stockholm, and Copenhagen. These have been controversial.

Athens is the only European Union capital without an official mosque. One is being discussed, but it is opposed by the Christian Orthodox

Church and some right-wing groups. Minarets were banned in 2009 in Switzerland. (27) Similar bans are proposed in the Netherlands and Italy. A province in Austria requires new buildings to "fit within the overall look and harmony of villages and towns," which effectively bans mosques and minarets. (28) Muslims in Spain would like to recreate the "old city" of Cordoba, once the heart of Andalucia, which would include the right to worship in a cathedral that had originally been a mosque. (29)

Muslim numbers in Europe are increasing—their numbers doubled in the past thirty years. They have not shown an inclination to organize along racial or religious lines—they are too diverse, even with respect to understanding of religion. (30) Muslims are entering Europe at a rate of 1.6 to two million per year. (31) In 2011 they constituted 25 percent of Rotterdam, Marseilles, and Amsterdam; 20 percent of Malmo; 15 percent of Brussels and Birmingham; and 10 percent of London, Paris, Copenhagen, and Vienna. (32)

Muslims in Western Europe originate from both Arab and non-Arab countries. Those in the United Kingdom are primarily from South Asia, in France from North and West Africa, in Germany from Turkey, in Belgium from Morocco, and in the Netherlands from Morocco and Turkey. The mix is slightly different in every country. Europe also receives waves of Muslim refugees periodically; it is affected far more than the U.S. by destabilization in the Muslim world.

There are crucial differences between the Muslim population in Europe and that in the United States:

> U.S. Muslims are well educated and most are professional and fairly affluent. Muslims in Europe are often not well educated and constitute an underclass, working at menial jobs, and they are often marginalized.
>
> U.S. Muslims are viewed as potential citizens. In Europe, they are often seen as immigrants or "guest workers," even after two or more generations.
>
> U.S. Muslims are mostly married, with children. Muslims in Europe are often unmarried and not as committed to their host country. Many Muslims in Europe initially planned to stay only temporarily, then later decided to remain.

U.S. Muslims are more geographically spread out than in any single
country in Europe. Some concentrate in certain areas, but they
are less visible and do not change the nature of cities or regions.
Unlike the U.S., these small, old countries have deep historical,
cultural, religious, and linguistic traditions. It is harder for their
citizens to think of non-Europeans as "belonging."
While earlier immigrants assimilated quite well, younger Muslims
in Europe appear to be less inclined to true assimilation. Without integration, polarization and ghettos can result.

The result of these differences is that Europeans are more likely to
view Muslims as a threat than is generally the case in the United States.
Many of the Muslims in Europe came in the 1950s and 1960s when
there was a severe shortage of workers; most were from Turkey, Algeria,
Morocco, Tunisia, and Pakistan. They stayed and later settled in with
their families. Very quickly, their increasing numbers become a significant
percentage of local populations, whereas in the U.S., Muslims make up
barely 1 percent, if that.

In November 2004, European leaders met at a summit conference to
discuss the level of legal migrants needed to compensate for continuing
domestic labor shortages and Europe's aging population. An EU report
said that the working population in the twenty-five-nation bloc would fall
from 303 million to 297 million by 2020, and to 280 million by 2030. (33)
In fact, however, Muslim birth rates have leveled off* and European birth
rates have increased, both unexpectedly, so the numbers are too low. The
fertility rate in Britain rose from 1.6 to 1.9 in six years; it rose in France
from 1.7 in 1993 to 2.1 in 2007 (despite a steady fall in birthrates among
women not born in France); and it jumped 8 percent in Sweden in 2004
and has remained level. (35) In 2004, the EU expected its population to
decline by 16 million by 2050; now it is projected to increase by 10 million
by 2060, some due to a higher birth rate, some due to immigration. (36)

Muslims have increasing opportunities to acquire citizenship. Because
the vast majority are not radicalized (as was once feared), this settling

---

*In the Netherlands, the fertility rate for Moroccan-born women fell from 4.9 to 2.9
between 1990 and 2005, and for Turkish-born women from 3.2 to 1.9. U.N. data suggests
that all Arab birthrates are dropping fast, including in the Middle East, except for Yemen
and the Palestinian Territories. (34)

in and enfranchisement are already integrating European Muslims into the mainstream and have the potential to produce a moderate type of Euro-Islam. (37)

## ❖ THE IMAGE OF ARABS AND MUSLIMS

Both Arabs and Muslims have been portrayed in Western media and print (especially in cartoons) as excessively wealthy, irrational, sensuous, and violent. The general premise seems to be that "the men seem not to go very far without their scimitars." (38) They are seen as alien and therefore dangerous. If a person in the news is Muslim, this is mentioned, even if national origin is not. There is little counterbalancing information about ordinary people who live family- and work-oriented lives on a modest scale. The media concentrate on reporting the sensational, not the truly typical. This misleading image has persisted for decades in America and in Europe. No real distinction is made between Arabs and Muslims.

According to Dr. Yvonne Haddad, a specialist on Islam in the West, Muslims have an image problem:

> For Muslims . . . discrimination has been aggravated as a con-
> sequence of growing hostility towards Islam in the West, some-
> times called "Islamophobia." Recently, the religion factor has been
> especially significant. The stereotyping that has come from media
> responses to international events usually has repercussions on Mus-
> lims living in minority communities in the West. They become the
> focus of attention and scapegoating. (39)

### In America

Thirty years ago one observer remarked, "The Arabs remain one of the few ethnic groups who can still be slandered with impunity in America." (40) Unfortunately, not only has there been no improvement, the situation has actually gotten worse, in both the quantity and the quality of remarks. Ten years ago there was an almost identical statement, "Arabs are the only really vicious stereotypes acceptable in Hollywood." (41) Hollywood has portrayed the Arabs as everything from violent terrorists and criminals to evil viziers, decadent sheikhs, and smarmy buffoons;

examples include the movies "True Lies," "Executive Decision," "Delta Force," and "Black Sunday." (42) Such stereotypical images are numerous and well documented. This reinforces a fear present among Americans that can only be diminished through information and contact with Arab and Muslim citizens.

Ever since the attacks of September 11, 2001, especially in the first year, Muslims have faced increased discrimination, threats, name-calling, violence, and vandalism (Sikhs have been targeted too). From September 11 to December 6, 2001, the U.S. Equal Employment Opportunity Commission received more than double the number of complaints of discrimination toward Muslims in the workplace compared with the previous year (166 vs. 64). (43) Between 2001 and 2011, there has been a 163 percent rise in workplace complaints. (44) In 2000, the FBI reported 33 anti-Islamic hate crimes across the country; in the four months following September 11, authorities investigated more than 250 incidents. (45) Muslims are 1 percent of the population and victims in 14 percent of religious discrimination cases. (46)

In 2006, a poll jointly sponsored by the *Washington Post* and ABC News found that 46 percent of Americans held a negative view of Islam, compared to 39 percent right after 9/11. (47) It was explained that "conservative and liberal experts said Americans' attitudes about Islam are fueled in part by political statements and media reports that focus almost solely on the actions of Muslim extremists." One in three Americans had heard prejudiced comments about Muslims lately, and one in four admitted to harboring some personal bias against Muslims. Pollster James Zogby said he was not surprised by the results. "The intensity has not abated and remains a vein that's very near the surface, ready to be tapped at any moment.... Radio commentators have been talking about it nonstop." (48) Yet Muslims are the most tolerant of faith groups in the U.S. (49)

In a *Newsweek* poll in 2007, 63 percent of the randomly interviewed Americans said that they believe most American Muslims do not support violence in the name of Islam, but 41 percent said they feel that Islam glorifies suicide. (50)

In 2006, conservatives objected when a newly-elected Muslim congressman, Keith Ellison (D-Minn) wanted to use the Qur'an to take the oath of office. The objection was ignored; there are several precedents of oaths taken on books other than the Bible. Congressman Virgil Goode, Jr. (R-Va) stated, "We need to end the diversity visas policy . . . [we need to] adopt the strict immigration policies that I believe are necessary to preserve the values and beliefs traditional to the United States of America." (51)

In 2005, conservative radio commentator Michael Graham was fired for describing Islam as a "terrorist organization." (52) A high school teacher was fired when she lashed out at a group of students for opening a commemorative speech on the 9/11 attacks with the greeting *Assalamu Alaykum*, Arabic for "Peace be with you." (53) A college student was detained at the Philadelphia airport because he was carrying Arabic flash cards to study for his language course. (54) The television show *All American Muslim* was criticized because it projected a too favorable view.

A school principal, Debbie Almontaser, was fired in New York for not preventing a student from wearing a T-shirt that said "Intifada." She explained that the word is seen by many Arabs as a valid term for popular resistance to oppression, and she had a strong record of interfaith activism. (55) The school offered Arabic-language classes. In this regard, it was reported that "Daniel Pipes, a pro-Israel conservative who created Campus Watch, a web site dedicated to exposing alleged bias in university Middle East studies programs, wrote in the *New York Sun* that the school would cause problems because 'learning Arabic in [and] of itself promotes an Islamic outlook.'" (56)

Muslim charities have had a difficult time. Under the USA Patriot Act, the government is authorized to close down a charity while an investigation is going on, without revealing evidence used to justify seizure of assets or designation as a terrorist supporter. From 9/11, 2001 until 2006, six American Muslim charities sending money to Palestine were closed in this fashion, although the government never found evidence against any employees or board members, or documented a trail to a terrorist organization. In desperation, a group of Muslims started a new charity to try to get money to Palestinian children. Some in this new charity believe that this harassment was a charade to make the American people believe that the government was disrupting terrorist financing. (57). A similar case took place in 2005, when the Senate Finance Committee investigated two dozen Muslim charities, think tanks, and other organizations for two years but found nothing that required additional follow-up. (58)

There is always controversy surrounding the building of mosques. The most famous instance recently has been the proposed Islamic and community center in New York City, which was opposed through blogs, demonstrations, meetings, and very harsh rhetoric, and denounced by many politicians. However, after the congressional election of 2010, it all died down and the center is now in place. (59) In Tennessee, a mosque was opposed with a sign that said "Keep Tennessee Terror Free" and a billboard that read "Defeat Universal Jihad Now." This left the congregation, which has been there thirty years, bewildered by the vitriol. (60) Reverend Pat Robertson said of it, "The next thing you know, they're going to be taking over the city council. They're going to have an ordinance that calls for public prayer five times a day." (61) There has also been opposition to Islamic schools in many states and communities, because they are said to "teach terrorism."

Congressman Peter King held hearings in 2011 to investigate "Muslim radicals" in ordinary communities. He stated that there are "too many mosques" in this country and that most of them are extremist. (62) He asserted that Muslim community leaders have failed to cooperate with law enforcement. (In fact, Muslims are the largest source of tips to authorities tracking terror suspects.) The vast majority of mosques are supported by Muslim Americans, who want to be independent of overseas influences. Mosques do what churches do—they hold worship services, have classes for adults and children, arrange charity, provide counseling, and participate in interfaith programs. (63)

An Interfaith Center in Richmond, Virginia, in order to illustrate to the community the unreasonable fear of Arabs and Muslims, including their language, distributed small signs written in Arabic on buses and at colleges. The signs said "Paper or plastic?" Below them was written, "Misunderstanding can make anything scary" and "What did you think it said?" Some viewers at first thought the FBI should be called in to investigate. (64)

On the plus side (there is a plus side), Senator Richard Durbin held hearings, also in 2011, on violations of the civil rights of Muslims. The *New York Times* lauded these hearings, in light of "the steady stream of more than 800 cases of violence and discrimination suffered by American Muslims at the hands of know-nothing abusers." (65)

In Washington, D.C., the Kennedy Center organized a "Festival of Arab Culture" in 2009, to "provide a counterpoint to the reality of war and violence that many Americans associate with the region." The festival included film, visual arts, literature, poetry, music, and dance. (66)

The U.S. post office issues a stamp for the Eid holiday every year (along with Hanukah and Kwanzaa). In August 2011, I saw a large billboard in New Jersey that said "Ramadan, 1.57 billion celebrating."

Muslims know that there is prejudice against them, and they believe this prejudice is based on a lack of unbiased information about them. Some mosques have open-house receptions, and there are community outreach activities all over the country. The Islamic Society of North America (ISNA) has an informative website.† The Islamic Networks Group (ING) maintains a nationwide speakers' bureau.

## In Europe

Despite efforts by governments and civic leaders, hostility toward Muslims is still problematic across much of the European Union. Muslims are subject to verbal and physical attacks as well as discrimination in employment and housing. European governments have dealt with the Muslim minorities in various ways—considering them as temporary residents, trying to assimilate them, and giving them citizenship while encouraging them to maintain their cultural identity.

A period of heightened worry about terrorism in Europe occurred between 2004 and 2006, when bombs exploded in Madrid and London, a controversial film director was killed in Amsterdam, and angry demonstrations took place against the Danish publication of satirical cartoons about the Prophet Muhammad. As it turned out, the situation calmed down after that.‡

Mass radicalism among Muslims has not taken place. A Gallup poll in 2007 showed that when asked if violent attacks on civilians could be

---

†At the ISNA conference in 2002, someone asked, "What should we do now that the first anniversary of 9/11 is coming up?" The response was, "Don't hide—invite your neighbors to dinner."

‡In 2009, a Europol report showed that more than 99 percent of terrorist attacks in Europe over the last three years were carried out by non-Muslims. (67) In terms of fear and trauma, however, Muslim terrorism is the most effective.

justified, 82 percent of French Muslims and 91 percent of German Muslims said no. Devoutness had no effect on the responses.§

The demographic scenario of increasing numbers of immigrants and decreasing numbers of native Europeans is a trend that persists in the public mind. "Though a steady drumbeat of apocalyptic forecasts continues, such fears are beginning to look misplaced." (69) We have heard from Dr. Bernard Lewis (American) that France will soon be "part of the Maghreb," and that Europe will be Islamic by the end of this century. Commentator Daniel Pipes imagined a scenario that if non-Muslims flee Europe, "grand cathedrals will appear as vestiges of a prior civilization—at least until a Saudi-style regime transforms them into mosques or a Taliban-like regime blows them up." (70)

Fear is mixed with a clash of values. Secular France banned the Hejab hair cover in schools (it also stopped the wearing of large crosses and the yarmulke), and a full cover over the face and body cannot be worn in public or when driving. This ban is being considered in some other countries; it is enforced in some locales and in law courts in Denmark, and in law courts and some schools in the Netherlands. (71) Full cover is banned in Belgium (72), Italy, some parts of Spain (73), and was proposed, (and criticized) in the Netherlands as of early 2013. (74) Fully covered women have been repeatedly refused access to buses in the United Kingdom, simply out of unfounded fear. (75) Some people say that the hair cover, or full face cover, symbolize the oppression of women (if so, it is cultural, not Islamic).¶ It is seen by others as an unfortunate "mark of separation." Bans may be argued as essential because the countries emphasize secularism, such as in Tunisia and Turkey. These issues have not arisen in the

---

§By comparison, a Gallup poll in the U.S. in 2007 showed that 24 percent of randomly selected Americans said such attacks are sometimes (19 percent) or often (5 percent) justified. (68)

¶Ayaan Hirsi Ali, a Somali-origin Dutch politician, has written extensively about her unhappy upbringing, blaming many cultural practices on Islam, confusing the two. She blames Islam for women's status in Somalia, and she even blames it for female circumcision, which was a Nile Valley practice centuries before Islam, and spread to parts of Africa (but not all of the Arab world). It is outlawed in many Muslim countries. She now lives in the U.S.

U.S., probably because of low numbers and because Muslims do not live together as a community in one place where it can become the norm.

It is noteworthy that many Muslim women in Europe and the Middle East welcome the bans on the veil; they see it as a strike against the conservative Muslim right wing. Full cover is only an *interpretation* of the Qur'an, and they believe they should support resistance to any such practices promoted in the name of culture and religion. (76)

Controversies involving Muslims have led to extreme right-wing political movements in nations such as France, Britain, and the Netherlands that now speak against Islam in general, not just its people. One British journalist stated, "Anti-Muslim bigotry [is] the last socially acceptable racism." (77) In 2006, 40 percent of the people in France, Britain, and Russia had a negative view of Islam; the numbers were 36 percent in Germany and 29 percent in Spain. (78) In 2008, a Pew poll showed that 45 percent of Europeans had a negative view. (79)

There is a growth in right-wing, anti-immigrant (mainly anti-Muslim), anti-elite (80) political parties across Europe. Recent regional and parliamentary elections show the following (81):

| 2004 | Belgium, Flemish Block | 24% |
|------|------------------------|------|
| 2005 | Alliance for the Future of Austria | 10.7% |
| 2007 | Denmark, Danish People's Party | 13.9% |
| 2008 | Austria, Freedom Party | 22.9% |
| 2008 | Italy, Northern League | 12.7% |
| 2010 | France, National Front | 12% |
| 2010 | Norway, Progress Party | 22.9% |
| 2010 | Netherlands, Freedom Party | 15.5% |
| 2010 | Sweden, Sweden Democrats | 5.7% |
| 2011 | Finland, True Finns | 19% |

The reason most voters gave for supporting right-wing parties was their perception that immigrants are reluctant to integrate and to adopt local customs. In 2011, surveys showed that the parties in France, the Netherlands, and Finland scored 20 percent or more. (82) The English Defence League, organized in 2009, has staged a series of marches throughout Britain. It was described by M.P. John Cruddas as "the biggest danger to community cohesion in Britain today." (83) A recent poll in

Britain showed that 52 percent of the respondents believe that Muslims create problems in their country. (84) There is, however, some reaction to far-right parties. In Germany, there is talk of banning the far-right National Democratic Party, a move supported by almost 70 percent of the Germans. (85)

The 2011 attack by Anders Breivik in Norway was explicitly motivated by anti-Islamic sentiment as a focal point for a larger worldview. He attacked "liberals" who, in his view, were allowing Muslims to take over Norway (and Europe). (86) Some in the media have called this "Christian terrorism," although others say Breivik cannot be a real Christian based on his actions: "to label Breivik a Christian requires a depraved understanding of what it means to be a Christian." (87) This is *precisely* what many Muslims have been saying about the fanatic terrorists in their society.

In Britain, France, Denmark, and the Netherlands, there are training programs for imams who head up mosques and Islamic centers. To be acceptable to the government, the imams must show that they have had some training in Europe and that they understand local values. (88) Imams have been deported in the past because of radical views. The Islamic Council stated that extremist clerics "tarnish the image of Islam." (89)

In 2009, President Sarkozy of France launched a debate on national identity. (90) It was thought to be unnecessary by 55 percent of the French, and 42 percent said that it went in the wrong direction, focusing on problems caused by Muslims and immigrants, rather than on what it means to be French.

A Gallup poll in 2009 asked Muslims to rate their success in Europe to date, with these results: (91)

|  | Thriving | Struggling | Suffering |
| --- | --- | --- | --- |
| German Muslims | 47% | 48% | 5% |
| French Muslims | 23% | 69% | 8% |
| British Muslims | 7% | 72% | 21% |

My belief is that the Muslims in Europe will have to make an effort to assimilate in order to be successful as citizens. They must make concessions regarding clothing, equality of the sexes, freedom of speech and the press, and violence. Forming "parallel societies" will not bring about the desired result.

## ❊ THE FUTURE OF ISLAM IN THE WEST

Moderate Muslims are speaking out more and more, in the West and in the Middle East. This will lead to an improved, vibrant Muslim community everywhere. If people take to heart the advice to be loyal to both their faith and, if in the West, the country in which they live, this will gradually heal the bruised image that Islam has today. Scholar Tariq Ramadan** has stated, "Loyalty to one's faith and conscience requires firm and honest loyalty to one's country. Sharia [law] requires honest citizenship." (92) In his book, *Western Muslims and the Future of Islam*, Ramadan stated:

> We are currently living through a veritable silent revolution in Muslim communities in the West: more and more young people and intellectuals are actively looking for a way to live in harmony with their faith while participating in the societies that are their societies, whether they like it or not. French, English, German, Canadian, and American Muslims, women as well as men, are constructing a "Muslim personality" that will soon surprise many of their fellow citizens. Far from media attention, going through the risks of a process of maturation that is necessarily slow, they are drawing the shape of European and American Islam: faithful to the principles of Islam, dressed in European and American cultures, and definitively rooted in Western societies. This grassroots movement will soon exert considerable influence over worldwide Islam. (93)

Some neoconservative Americans have called for modernizing Islam, to result in an American Islam committed to American values. It is already here. And it came from inside, not from outside or from U.S. government campaigns. European Islam and American Islam can be models for each other. Muslims are working hard to promote gender equality, for example, and moderates state that inequality is not a firm tenet of Islam any longer but a mark of misguided tradition. In the U.S., a woman has led group prayers, a practice approved by an influential scholar of Islamic law. (94)

---

**Tariq Ramadan was denied entry into the United States in July 2004 and September 2006. When Barack Obama became president, he was allowed in, as there was nothing against him in any records anywhere.

The number of Arabs and Muslims in the West continues to grow. In the U.S., the Muslim population is set to double by 2030. (95) Muslims will go from less than 1 percent of the population to 1.7 percent. (96) Muslims are expected to make up about 8 percent of Europe's population by 2030, up from 6 percent in 2010. (97) There is no need to fear a "Eurabia." (98)

In the United States, there is a heightened interest in the region that is still growing, dating from 9/11. Enrollments in Arabic language, Islamic studies, and Middle East studies have tripled and quadrupled. Students are spending summers and their junior year in Egypt, Morocco, Tunisia, Lebanon, Syria, Jordan, and the United Arab Emirates; Jordan and Dubai are currently becoming popular. (99) Between 2002 and 2007, the number of American students studying in Arabic-speaking countries increased sixfold, from 560 to 3,400. (100) The Department of State offers scholarships through its Critical Language Scholarship Program—since 2006, 12,000 students have applied for 800 scholarships. (101) In 2010, about 35,000 college and university students were studying Arabic. (102) This is an excellent investment in their own and their country's future.

## CHAPTER 14

# THE ARAB COUNTRIES, SIMILARITIES AND DIFFERENCES: THE ARAB COUNTRIES IN AFRICA

Generalizing about Arabs is a little like generalizing about Europeans—they have many traits in common, but regional differences are striking. Arabs are more alike than Europeans, however, because they share the same language and, most important, they believe that they are a cultural unit, as they say "one Arab nation comprised of numerous Arab states." Arab nationalism has a broad appeal, despite shifting political alliances.

The national and social characteristics described here, as well as statistical information, reveal some notable differences among various Arab national groups. The most important single difference that affects foreigners is the distinction between the conservatism of Saudi Arabia (and, to some extent, the rest of the Arabian Peninsula) and the more liberal, or tolerant, ways of life elsewhere.

All of the countries are challenged by the large number of young people in their population (two-thirds are under age thirty in many cases), (1) and their increasing assertiveness. There is a generational shift underway. Among the young in particular, new technology is driving rapid changes in society and political thought. The "Arab Spring" demonstrations for democracy and freedom may be the single most significant event in the region since the majority of Arab states became independent after World War II—it was a breath of fresh air, not just the ideas, but also the positive images of Arabs on television.

It is significant that along with governmental change there appears to be a transition to attitudes that are less pro-American, and American power in the region is perceived as weakening. (2) There are also strong pro-Palestinian sympathies coming to the fore. Arabs from Morocco to the Gulf always mention the Palestine issue as one of their top concerns—it underlies all other issues with the West. Palestine is a pivotal issue in modern Arab nationalism, and the concern is as great as it ever was.

The Arab Labor Organization stated that unemployment in the Middle East was the worst worldwide. The general rate of unemployment exceeds 14 percent, which equates to 17 million persons unemployed in the Arab region. (3) There is an urgent need for reform of education policies and training programs to deal with this. Youth unemployment is 25 percent, the highest in the world. (4) Bureaucracy and corruption must be addressed, to encourage entrepreneurs and to attract foreign investment. But the recent upheavals have set the economies of some countries back even further.

Water resources are a looming problem. The entire Arab world is dry and the supply of water is scant, much of it depending on underground aquifers. As the population increases from its current 360 million to a projected 600 million by 2050, the amount of fresh water available per person will be cut in half, and declining resources will likely lead to political disputes. (5) Several solutions are being tried, including drip irrigation, desalinization, recycling and, in some cases, renting fertile agricultural land in other countries.

There are also dramatic differences among the Arab countries: some are very rich, while others are desperately poor. We hear that the Arabs are awash in oil, but in reality, most Arab countries have far less income than developed economies. Relative prosperity can be seen from averaged per capita income in 2010 (some countries are not listed because of insufficient data).

By way of comparison, the GDP per capita in the US in 2009 was about $46,000.

## NATIONAL INCOME PER CAPITA (6)

|  | $US |
| --- | --- |
| Qatar | 79,426 |
| United Arab Emirates | 58,006 |
| Kuwait | 55,719 |
| Bahrain | 26,664 |
| Saudi Arabia | 24,726 |
| Libya | 17,068 |
| Algeria | 8,320 |
| Tunisia | 7,979 |
| Jordan | 5,956 |
| Egypt | 5,889 |
| Syria | 4,760 |
| Morocco | 4,628 |
| Sudan | 2,387 |
| Yemen | 2,051 |

All Arab countries have experienced a degree of unrest among their people, because of authoritarian governments, corruption, unemployment, high prices, and strained resources. Here is one assessment, an "index of unrest" for the year 2010, before uprisings and protests began on a large scale. It is useful for comparison.

## INDEX OF UNREST* (7)

| 0 = most stable | 100 = least stable |
| --- | --- |
| Yemen | 87 |
| Libya | 70 |
| Egypt | 67 |
| Syria | 67 |
| Iraq | 67 |

*(continued)*

INDEX OF UNREST* (*continued*)

| 0 = most stable | 100 = least stable |
|---|---|
| Oman | 60 |
| Saudi Arabia | 53 |
| Algeria | 52 |
| Jordan | 50 |
| Tunisia | 49 |
| Morocco | 48 |
| Bahrain | 37 |
| Lebanon | 34 |
| UAE | 25 |
| Kuwait | 24 |
| Qatar | 22 |

*Sudan and Palestine were not rated, but the level of unrest is very high in both.

The Arab countries discussed throughout the rest of the chapter are listed in groups: countries in Africa, countries in the center, and countries in the Arabian Peninsula.

The Arab countries in Africa include those of the Maghrib and the Nile Valley.

## ❈ THE MAGHRIB

*The Maghrib (Maghreb)* is a term used for the entire region of North Africa (the adjective form is *Maghribi*). *Maghrib* comes from Arabic and means "The Arab West." Four countries are of concern here: Morocco, Algeria, Tunisia, and Libya.

This region has been inhabited by Berbers (a Caucasian people) for millennia, since at least 3000 B.C., and today Berber is the mother tongue of 12 million people in the Maghrib, most of whom are bilingual in Arabic. Berber nationalism is growing and will be a significant social and political factor in the future, especially in Morocco and Algeria, where a Berber alphabet has been devised, the language has been introduced in schools, and Berber is heard on the radio. Newspapers and magazines have begun appearing, and local music is influenced by Berber tradition, with summer arts festivals taking place in Morocco. Berbers have used the Internet to establish themselves internationally as a distinct cultural group. (1)

The number of speakers per country is as follows:

## NUMBER OF SPEAKERS OF BERBER (2) (3)

| Morocco | 7,500,000 |
|---------|-----------|
| Algeria | 4,000,000 |
| Tunisia | 26,000 |
| Libya | 162,000 |

There are also large numbers of Berber speakers in Mali and Niger.

Arabians and some Arabs arrived in the seventh century, and there were several migrations after that, so that by the twelfth century, about 10 percent of the population were Arab. Many Arabic-speakers came from Spain in the late fifteenth and early sixteenth centuries. Berber ethnicity is present in about 80 percent of the people in Morocco and Algeria, and about 60 percent in Tunisia and Libya. (4) Most Berbers live in rural villages and work the land; a few are nomadic.

Regional Maghribi Arabic dialects are distinctive and almost unintelligible to Arabs in the east; they constitute a separate dialect group called "Western Arabic." The Maghrib has its own special foods, religious practices, style of art and architecture, music, and traditional clothing, with much Berber influence.

## Morocco

Morocco, a monarchy, has been strongly influenced by its proximity to Europe and its colonization by France until independence in 1956. Educated Moroccans are bilingual in Arabic and French, and although a campaign of Moroccanization has been underway, French is still needed for professional and social advancement. Some Spanish is spoken in northern Morocco, and a growing number of Moroccans, particularly younger people with commercial interests, now speak English. Morocco sees itself as moderate and pro-Western, and it has a free-trade agreement with the U.S.

The royal family traces its descent from the Prophet Muhammad, which bolsters its legitimacy (the king's ancestry is inscribed into a pillar in a mosque in Casablanca for all to see). King Hassan II ruled for thirty-eight years before his death in July 1999; his son King Muhammad VI now rules, and he is making efforts toward political and social liberalization.

This calm is jeopardized, however, because although Morocco has maintained a tradition of political moderation, large numbers of the younger generation, especially, are turning toward Islamic radicalism and are playing a bigger role in Islamist militant groups, including in Iraq. (1) There have been incidents of terrorism, mainly directed at tourist sites: bombings occurred in Casablanca in 2003 and 2007, a Moroccan group was responsible for a bombing in Spain in 2004, and there was a bombing in Marrakesh in April 2011.

The government's response has been to crack down but, among other things, it has also instituted mainstream religious training to counteract extremist, puritanical Islam and reemphasize mainstream Sunni Islam. Many of the students in religious training are women, and female religious "guides" perform almost all the functions of a male Imam (prayer leader), except for delivering the Friday sermon. (2) The Ministry of Islamic Affairs is making every effort to promote moderation. However, Islamists won the majority of seats in parlimentary elections in late 2011.

Under the new king, Morocco has made a slow but real transformation from a traditional monarchy to a constitutional monarchy. It has genuine political parties and leaders, as well as a relatively free press (although the most provocative paper, *Le Journal*, (3) was forced to close in 2010). The king has instituted a commission to examine past human-rights abuses that occurred during his father's reign. (4) (5) A referendum was held that gives more powers to elected leaders, and the constitution has been revised. Demonstrations have occurred, repressed sometimes firmly, but the king is containing calls for reform by instituting "change with continuity."* (6)

Educated women in Morocco have been entering the professions for a generation, especially in the urban areas. Half of the students in universities are women; 20 percent of the judges are women. A growing number

---

*The king will cede half his power to the prime minister appointed by the majority party in Parliament, and the constitution assures the rights of women and the Berbers. (7)

of women cover their hair, yet they consider themselves to be modern, educated, and emancipated; they state that they are simply asserting their identity as Muslims. One problem for women is the disparity in pay as compared to men; it is about 40 percent less, according to UNICEF. (8) A national strategy for gender equality was launched in 2006.

Family law is intended to be compatible with both Sharia law and international conventions on human rights. The government first revised the family law code in 2004, and women may initiate divorce, obtain custody of children, and claim an equal share of goods acquired during marriage. The age for marriage was raised to eighteen, and polygamy has been severely restricted. (9) The mayor of Marrakesh is a thirty-three-year-old woman.

There are three distinct social classes: the royal family and a small educated elite, a growing middle class comprised of merchants and professionals, and a lower class that includes more than half of the people. The population was estimated at 32 to 34 million in 2010, with a growth rate that is among the highest in the world. By 2015, 28 percent of the population will be under age fourteen. (10)

The ethnography of Morocco is mixed; most people are mixed Arab and Berber (the king's mother is Berber), and a large number are of sub-Saharan African descent, especially in the southern part of the country. Recently, the Qur'an was translated into the Berber Tamazight language, and there is a Berber research institute.(11)

Tribalism is important in rural parts of the country. Farming remains the occupation of half of the people, but there is a trend toward urbanization, which began early in the twentieth century. Cities have grown quickly, with severe housing shortages and expanding slums. About 40,000 Moroccans migrate abroad each year. The unemployment rate is improving; it was 9 percent in 2010. Currently about 1.7 million men work outside the country, mainly in France and Spain.

Education has increased greatly since Morocco's independence—the literacy rate was up to 56 percent in 2010. It is increasing slowly because many rural children are not in school, despite attendance being free and compulsory. Both French and Arabic are taught in schools, although Arabic is the only official language.

Although about 99 percent of the Moroccans are Muslims, other religions have always been practiced freely. Half of the Jews in the Arab world reside in Morocco, approximately 7,000 (from a high of 350,000 in the 1950s). (12) Morocco's 70,000 Christians are of European origin. The practice of Islam is often mixed with local folk practices, such as the veneration of saints' tombs and their artifacts. Religious brotherhoods, mainly Sufi, are also common.

The Moroccan economy is largely dependent on agriculture, tourism, and phosphate mining (Morocco is the world's largest exporter of phosphates). Fishing is important, as well as the textile industry, which has grown enormously in the last thirty years.

Moroccans are friendly and hospitable and usually very interested in becoming acquainted with foreigners. The elite are at ease with Westerners because of their exposure to French and European cultures. There are at least three study-abroad programs for young Americans learning Arabic in Morocco.

## Algeria

Algeria is a constitutional republic with a democratically elected government, although the military is very influential. Since the early 1990s, there has been a shift from a state capitalist to a free-market economy. There are more than forty political parties (which must be approved by the Ministry of Interior), and the last legislative election was in 2007. President Bouteflika was elected to a third term in 2009. He has pledged further political reforms.

Arabization has been strongly emphasized, partly as a reaction to the Algerians' experience with French colonization and their long, traumatic war; independence was achieved in 1962, at a terrible cost—one million Algerians and 28,000 French dead. (1) Despite the fact that Arabic is the official language of the country, French is still widely used, particularly for professional purposes. Both languages are taught in the schools, but only younger Algerians are truly comfortable with Standard (written) Arabic. Arab nationalism has been promoted through government political campaigns, the news media, and the school curriculum, although it is easing now because the government fears increasing religiosity and Islamism. Many in the younger generation are more religious than their parents. (2) The people are 99 percent Muslim.

Algeria experienced a devastating civil war, starting in 1991, between the government and Islamist activists, the largest group being the Islamic Salvation Front (FIS). The war began after the government cancelled elections in 1992 when FIS was projected to win. Guerrilla warfare began, and throughout the 1990s, there was a rising cycle of violent attacks, many of them random, many in villages, to the point that 300 to 400 people were killed each week. Ultimately the figure reached about 150,000. (3) This was met with severe government retaliation and FIS was banned. The population is polarized between secular and Islamic groups, radicals and moderates. A branch of Al-Qaeda operates in Algeria.

The security situation has improved and the state of emergency, declared in 1992, was lifted in February 2011. There were demonstrations and protests in early 2011, and the government cut taxes and lowered food prices. In April 2011, the president promised to amend the constitution to reinforce representative democracy. (4)

Algeria is the world's largest producer of liquefied natural gas; gas and oil provide 98 percent of the national income. (5) It also has income from mining and agriculture. Partly because of rapid population growth, the people remain poor; 23 percent live below the poverty line. The country faces social problems such as unemployment and rapid urban migration. But the government has a surplus of money because of recent high oil and gas prices, and there is a program underway to liberalize and diversify the economy. In 2010, Algeria began a five-year, $286 billion development program to update the infrastructure and provide jobs. (6) The economy has grown at a rate of 4 percent annually since 2000. (7)

Algeria is immense, the second largest state in Africa, but 85 percent of it is in the Sahara Desert region, and only 3 percent is suitable for agriculture, along the temperate northern coast. The population is 36 million, with a growth rate among the highest in the world. 91 percent of the people live along the coast. 24 percent of the population is under age fifteen, 70 percent are under age thirty, and there is a desperate housing shortage. Schools operate in shifts (attendance has doubled since 1999), (8) and health-care facilities are overburdened. Education is free and compulsory to age sixteen, and the literacy rate is 70 percent and climbing. Because the unemployment rate is about 30 percent, (9) in 2004, two million Algerians were working abroad, mostly in France and Spain. (10)

Many are menial workers, but there is also a brain drain as the educated people leave.

Almost all Algerians are of Berber ethnic origin, but about 70 percent identify themselves as Arabs and only 30 percent as Berbers. Arabic is the native language of 80 percent of the people. Algeria's social classes consist of a small professional and technocratic elite, a growing middle class, and a large number of poor people. A growing number of educated Algerians are entering professional and technical fields. Women comprise 60 percent of university graduates.

Women make up 70 percent of Algeria's lawyers and 60 percent of its judges. (11) They also dominate medicine. They are starting to drive buses and taxis. Women make up an ever-increasing percentage of the work force, now about 35 percent, which is more than twice what it was a generation ago. More women are wearing the Hejab scarf. Many women are delaying marriage, partly because of high unemployment for both men and women.

Outside the cities, family and social traditions are conservative. The government instituted a Family Code in 1984, which restricted women's rights, but the president has stated that it must be amended. If a man chooses to marry a second wife, then the first wife may have grounds to divorce. If a man divorces a woman and is judged to have abused the privilege of the marriage, she may be awarded damages and support if she does not have family support.

Algerians are very accommodating toward foreigners, although a bit reserved. Algeria is a lovely country, with a beautiful coastline, and the Sahara Desert in the south.

## Tunisia

Tunisia is a small but diverse country that gained its independence from France in 1956. From that time until early 2011, it was governed by one secular political party. President Habib Bourguiba, who led the country to independence, was quietly removed by his Prime Minister, Zein al-Abidin Ben Ali, in 1987. Ben Ali became his successor as president, and ruled until he fled the country in 2011 after political protest demonstrations. The Tunisians had a bloodless victory, a "Jasmine Revolution;" and they are proud that theirs was the first of many uprisings in the Arab world.

The new government is being formed, led by the moderate Islamist party, Ennahda, elected in October 2011. There continue to be demonstrations by people who believe that too many officials from the former regime are still in power. They have protested against corruption, graft, economic hardship, and police brutality under the former regime.

Tunisian society is cosmopolitan, at least in the cities, and many Tunisians are well traveled. They are friendly and hospitable to foreign visitors.

The Tunisians are descended from Berber and Arab stock, but all speak Arabic, the official language. Educated people are bilingual in Arabic and French, and many semi-educated people speak some French. French is taught in schools alongside Arabic; there has been a campaign for the Arabization of education.

The Tunisian government has encouraged private enterprise, and about 60 percent of the people are upper or middle class. Tunisia is the most advanced country in the Arab world in terms of women's rights, family planning, and education, and it is considered a model of success in economic reform and family law. At the same time, however, the former Tunisian government was criticized as a violator of human rights because it did not tolerate political dissent. It remains to be seen what the effects of policies of the new government will be.

There has been concern in Tunisia about growing Islamic extremism and, for this reason, beards are banned, and the Hejab headscarf is banned in government buildings and in schools and universities. This could change. After the Islamist party Ennahda was elected, some Tunisians have been concerned that this moderate secular state may eventually be governed by strict Islamists. (1) Ennahda has stated that when it controls the government, it will not impose Sharia law or ban alchohol. (2)

While most women in Tunisia wear Western clothing, some older or traditional women wear loose outer cloaks, which they pull over to partially cover their faces when in public. Women's clothing is modest by Western standards.

The Tunisian economy depends mainly on the large tourism industry, which brings in about half of its annual income and employs 36 percent of the working population; (3) there are many beach resorts and Roman antiquities. Tourism decreased temporarily because of political events, but is recovering rapidly (though it may be affected by ongoing events in Libya). Of the relatively small population of 10.5 million, about a third work in agriculture, which produces 10 percent of the country's earnings. (4) This sector is being reinvigorated by adopting some desert farming practices, such as drip irrigation. The former government encouraged diversification and especially light industry, which has become an important source of employment, and generates 35 percent of the national income. (5) Because of uncertainties, the economy is expected to grow by only 1 or 2 percent in 2011 (compared with 5 percent normally), according to the central bank; it would need to grow at a rate of 7 percent annually to create enough jobs. (6)

Although the government established agricultural cooperatives and production has been rising, people are still leaving the rural areas and moving to the cities, where they join the urban poor, living in crowded conditions. About 700,000 Tunisians work outside the country, mainly in France and, until recently, in Libya. Those returning from Libya are adding to the unemployment problem. The Tunisian interim government has signed an agreement with Qatar for the employment of 22,000 workers and is negotiating job opportunities for 10,000 in Italy, France, Canada, and Australia, as well as other European countries. (7)

The Tunisian government allocates more than 20 percent of its operating budget to primary and secondary education, and 95 percent of eligible children are in primary schools. Unfortunately, a good education doesn't guarantee a job after secondary or university graduation. For the many educated young people, the unemployment rate was 23 percent in 2009. (8) (9) Half of the people of Tunisia are under age twenty-five.

Tunisia has been at the forefront of the Arab nations in its effort to liberalize its society. Tunisian women are certainly among the most liberated in the Arab world; they are well educated and active in the workplace in such fields as education, social services, health care, office administration, and the judicial system. Laws benefiting women were enacted in the 1950s. Women have the same divorce rights as men. Polygamy is outlawed, and the minimum age for a woman's marriage is seventeen. Laws were made in the 1990s that further strengthened women's rights pertaining to custody and financial support. According to the new interim government, "There will be no going back in the democratic revolution of Tunisia for our women; they will be full participants." (10)

Tunisians are 98 percent Muslim. Only about 1,800 native Jews remain, most of them on the southern island of Jerba. The government permits freedom of worship and partially subsidizes the maintenance of synagogues. (11) Islam in Tunisia is mixed with a number of folk practices, such as veneration of saints' tombs and periodic festivals. Tunisia is a popular tourist destination.

## Libya

Libya is much in the news, and the country may well enter into a civil war. The former president Colonel Muammar Qaddhafi, was killed in October 2011 by opposition forces. Now that Qaddhafi is dead, attention has shifted to the nature of the new government, and there is a struggle for power among militias which fought together as opposition but which differ in their goals.

The territories of Tripolitania (capital Tripoli), Cyrenaica (capital Benghazi), and Fezzan were united under Italian colonial rule in 1934. It is not surprising that Cyrenaica, in particular, was the first to break away from Tripoli. The U.N. has recognized the interim government, but due to anti-government violence, the situation is far from stable and the government is not completely in control. It was the instability and prevalence of arms among militia groups that led to the attack on the U.S. consulate in Benghazi in September 2012. Many Libyans expressed their sorrow after this happened, in a demonstration, in the media, and in the social media.

After World War II, full self-rule over Libya was restored to its monarchy in 1949. The monarchy was overthrown in 1969, after which point Libya was governed by a leftist military regime under Qaddhafi, who introduced radical socialist and economic development programs, instituted a strong campaign to educate and politicize the people, and set up programs to spur rapid social change. Because of his support for radical revolutionary and terrorist movements, Libya was viewed as a pariah state by the West.

Before the 1969 revolution, most Libyans outside the cities were farmers or tribal seminomads, who were largely uneducated and lived simply. In 1951 Libya was considered one of the poorest countries in the world. When oil was discovered in 1959, its effect on the economy was immediate. By 1969 the country's revenues were twenty times greater than they had been in 1962. (1) Because of Libyan terrorism and political policies, the country was under U.S. sanctions from 1986 to 2003, and U.N. sanctions from 1992 to 2003. Sanctions by the European Union were imposed in 1992 and were lifted in 2004. (2) Because of the revolution and chaos, the economy for 2011 is projected to fall to 56 percent of its level in 2010. (3)

Oil accounts for 95 percent of Libya's export earnings, (4) so it was a serious setback for the regime when rebels disconnected the last oil pipeline to the only refinery. (5) The country's income is high, but much has been lost because of corruption, waste, arms purchases, and donations to developing countries to increase Qaddafi's influence in Africa and elsewhere. There have been high inflation and increased prices for imports, with a recent decline in the standard of living for those of lower and middle incomes. In 2008, the government announced plans to increase foreign investment in its oil, and also to begin large infrastructure projects such as highways, railways, air, and seaports, telecommunications, public housing, and medical facilities.

Under Qaddafi, Libya was a welfare state, and the people (particularly the middle and lower classes) generally experienced a dramatic rise in their standard of living over four decades, although with shortages of some goods. There have been steady improvements in health and nutrition programs, transportation, communications, and education. Nine years of education is compulsory, and 90 percent of the children are in school; literacy has reached 83 percent among younger Libyans. These social improvements were offset, however, by the repressiveness of Qaddafi's military regime, with its absolute intolerance of dissent.

Libyans are a homogeneous ethnic group; 97 percent are of mixed Berber and Arab descent, and all speak Arabic. Tribalism is an important source of identity (it accounted for much of Qaddafi's support). Although under Qaddafi there were theoretically no social classes because of the government's stated policy of strict egalitarianism and rule "by the people," in reality rule was authoritarian and only a few people are part of the elite upper class. The recent rebellion brought together the Berbers and Arabs, united in opposing Qaddafi, and there is a call for more rights and recognition for Berbers, whose identity was denied under the regime. (6) Qaddafi repressed the Berber language; it is now being taught, and there is a Berber newspaper. (7)

Libya's economic viability is almost entirely dependent on oil; its soil is poor and its natural resources and water are sparse. Less than 10 percent of the land is suitable for agriculture (90 percent is desert), and 75 percent of the country's food is imported. (8) The population is about 6.5 million, and large numbers of foreigners have lived and worked there (approximately 1.5 million in 2010), (9) though most of them have left. Libya badly needs its own trained and skilled workers; at the same time, unemployment is 21 percent. One third of the people are under age fifteen. (10)

Libya has a history of sending university students abroad, especially to the United States and Europe. From a high of 3,000 students studying in the United States in 1978, the current number is about 2,000. These students were unable to receive payments on their government scholarships after the American government froze Libyan assets, but stipends were reinstated a few months later. (11) Some students were threatened with reprisals if they did not participate in pro-Qaddhafi rallies in the U.S. (12) There are about 2,000 Libyan students at British institutions of higher education. (13)

Libyan women constitute 30 percent of the workforce, and they are working in all social, political, and economic occupations, including as ministers, judges, doctors, and lawyers. But the society is conservative and most have more modest jobs, as teachers, secretaries, and nurses. A few have succeeded as business entrepreneurs. (14) Not all are free to work without obstacles such as family objections, and working women are mostly confined to the cities. Qaddhafi, however, encouraged Libyan women to work.

Libyan women were active in the uprising in opposition to Qaddhafi's government in 2011. However, they feel now that they are being sidelined, because only two top jobs (out of about forty) in the eastern Libya interim government went to women. (15)

It was illegal to establish women's rights groups that are independent of the state, and individuals were subject to abuse if they were suspected of sympathizing with opposition groups.

The legal age for marriage for both men and women is twenty years, and the practice of early marriage has declined sharply. Polygamy is legal but uncommon, and it requires legal permission and the first wife's consent. (16) Most domestic law is governed by Sharia law, with some modifications; it remains to be seen if this will change with a new government.

Libyans are 99 percent Muslim. The government promoted Islam mixed with a strong revolutionary message in order to guide social change and control dissent, but it opposed Islamism. Arab nationalism is strong. In the past, Libyans were hesitant to interact with foreigners, but when this may change when the government is modified.

## ❋ THE NILE VALLEY

The two Nile Valley countries are Egypt and Sudan.

## Egypt

Egypt dominated the news while its revolution was occurring in early 2011. After the departure of former president Hosni Mubarak, who ruled from 1981 to 2011, elections were called. A new government was elected in mid-2012, led by an Islamist, Muhammad Morsi. This government was dissolved in June 2013 by the military, led by the defense minister, Abdel Fattah Al-Sisi, after widespread demonstrations by citizens (up to three million in the street in Cairo at one time). *The Islamists were accused of corruption and refusal to allow a role for non-Islamists in government; Morsi and thousands of other Islamists were arrested, and hundreds taken to trial. Al-Sisi resigned his post in order to run for president, and new elections are planned. Demonstrators want economic reform, justice, a civilian government, and a say in managing Egypt's resources. (1) It remains to be seen whether the military will share governing with civilians or other interest groups.

The Islamists' parties have far more strength, cohesion, and political experience than other groups. A poll in April 2011 showed that the largest Islamist party, the Muslim Brotherhood, which ran in elections as the Freedom and Justice Party, was the best organized, with a well known platform. Islamist parties, the Muslim Brotherhood and the hardline Salafists of the Nour party, won 70 percent of the seats in constitutional elections. The secularists were a distant third; their support is largely in the cities. (2)

Part of the reason for the popularity of Islamist groups is that they provide a wide range of social services, such as clinics, job centers, and

*Egyptians resent labeling the overthrow of the government as a "coup," as was widely done in the Western media. They state that it was a "revolution" in accordance with the people's will, and while Morsi was elected, it was not democratic, due to strong and sometimes misleading pressure at the polls.

food banks, not available from the government. But there is a deep division among the people on the role of religion in politics. The three leading candidates for president, all secularists, had high approval ratings as well.

The Egyptian people's top priority has been the need for improving economic conditions. (3) The economy had been projected at 6 percent before the crisis, but in fact fell by 4 percent in 2011. (4) It improved in 2012, reaching a high of 5.2 percent. (5) On the political side, 54 percent of the people want to annul the peace treaty with Israel because of Israel's treatment of the Palestinians. There is also an expectation that Egypt will resume its dominant role in regional politics.

Many social and political adjustments are surely coming in the future; the press is already freer than it was. The younger generation has shown a new assertiveness and lack of fear that will continue, spurred on by easy communications and organization through Internet sites. They have returned to demonstrations several times, to protest the slow pace of change and reforms, including the delayed prosecution of key regime figures. Senior police officers were forced into retirement (5) and there has been talk of constitutional guarantees of civil liberties. The future role of the powerful military, which has been accustomed to virtual autonomy, is also of considerable concern. Military leaders announced in October 2011 that they intend to remain outside civilian government control. (6) But anti-military sentiment lessened when it seemed to be the most immediate viable alternative to Islamism at the present time.

Egypt has by far the largest population of any Arab nation, approximately 80 million in 2009. † As in all Arab countries, the proportion of young people is high—33 percent under age fifteen in 2011 (down from 40 percent in 1990). (7) The population nearly doubled in the past thirty years, but as a result of vigorous government campaigning, the population growth rate decreased to 2 percent in 2011. Because only 3 to 4 percent of Egypt's land is habitable, its population density is among the highest in the world. In Egypt 95 percent of the people live on 5 percent of the land. (8)

Egypt's long history and ancient traditions have resulted in a homogeneous and distinctive society with much about its culture that is unique.

---

†The second largest Arab state is Sudan (when it was one country), with 44 million, a distant second. And most people in South Sudan are not Arabs.

Egyptians all speak Arabic, except for some Nubians in the far south, and English is the most common second language. French is also spoken by many.

About 10 percent of the Egyptians are in the elite upper class, which dominates the country politically and economically. The middle class is expanding; nevertheless, about 55 percent of the people are still peasant farmers, villagers, or among the urban poor.

Because of its long tradition of education for the upper and middle classes, Egypt has an abundance of professionally trained people. At any given time there are about 2.5 million Egyptians working abroad as teachers, doctors, accountants, and laborers. (9) A large number work in the Arabian Peninsula, and many had worked in Libya. Unemployment is 20 percent overall, and in the age group under twenty-five it is officially 25 percent, but it actually runs to 70 percent, a serious and growing problem. 90 percent of the Egyptians between the ages of fifteen and twenty-nine are unemployed, (10) and one of the strident demands in the recent revolution was the creation of jobs.

Intensive agriculture has always been central to the Egyptian economy. A looming problem is water. More water is needed constantly, and the Nile River must be shared with Ethiopia and Sudan; this is being negotiated. (11) As the country loses 60,000 acres of its best farmland yearly to urbanization, the government is in turn reclaiming 200,000 acres of desert each year, and using drip irrigation to conserve water. (12) It is also looking into growing wheat on two million acres straddling the border with Sudan. (13)

The government has promoted industry and manufacturing; the main sources of income are oil (a modest amount), cotton, and other agricultural products. Tourism is the most important of all, and this dropped sharply after the revolution, but it is finally reviving. Egypt's relative poverty makes it heavily dependent on aid from the United States. Once an exporter of food (since ancient times and up to about 1960), Egypt now imports 40 percent of its food and 60 percent of its wheat. (14) Agriculture yields only 20 percent of the national income, and employs 55 percent of the labor force. (15) Egypt's economy grew just 1.2 percent in 2011, down from 5.1 percent in 2010.

Poverty is increasing. Inflation was over 12 percent in April 2011 and food prices increased 20 percent in a year. (16). Wheat prices were up 47 percent in a year. (17) In May 2004, vehement opposition caused the government to reverse its intention to abolish subsidies; it reintroduced vouchers to subsidize twenty-five staple foods. About 40 percent of the people live on less than two dollars a day. (18) Bread riots broke out in the spring of 2008, as prices rose fivefold in private bakeries (not the subsidized government bakeries) and the price of gasoline doubled overnight. (19) There has also been a surge in crime, as the police are less assertive, wary of their reputation for abuses in the past. (20)

The Egyptian government has been socialist since the revolution in 1952, when Gamal Abdel Nasser and other military officers overthrew the monarchy. It was one-party rule, under Nasser, Sadat, and Mubarak, until 2011. When Sadat became president, his "Open Door" policy led to the privatization of many industries, but it also resulted in corruption and the creation of a very wealthy class, which is still in place.

All of the presidents repressed Islamists, although that party gained some representatives in the People's Assembly in later years. Over the years, Islamists (especially the Islamic Group) engaged in terrorist violence against the government and against tourists, and thousands were arrested. They later renounced violence and have held to this.

Health has improved dramatically due to government programs instituted in the 1960s; unfortunately, education has not fared as well. Despite the fact that education is free and compulsory, the rate of literacy is only 66 percent, but it is growing.

Egyptian women have always been at the forefront in women's rights, and have been integrated into the workforce at all levels for a generation. Half the university students are women. Egypt was in fact the first Arab country to admit women to its national university, in 1928, and education is entirely coed. In 1957 two women were the first to serve in an Arab parliament, and in the most recent government, there were 64 seats out of 518 reserved for women in the People's Assembly. About 28 percent of the university professors are women, compared to 24 percent in the United States. (21) (22)

The government has amended women's rights constantly. In 1979 the divorce law was amended regarding women's rights to divorce, alimony, and child custody, but it was declared unconstitutional in 1985. In 2000 the law was again amended, granting women much broader grounds for divorce, although the right to divorce is still gender-biased. (23)

Although virtually no urban women covered their hair in the 1960s, a growing number (over 80 percent) have made the decision to do so. This does not always indicate religiosity; it is also a social trend.

About 91 percent of the Egyptians are Muslims and 9 percent are Christians, mostly Copts (the Coptic Church estimates 15 percent). Islam is Egypt's official religion, but religious tolerance has long been practiced. There has been an upswing in religious clashes, however, and the interim government is cracking down hard. After a Coptic church was wrecked by Islamists in mid-2011, the government arrested 190 people and prohibited demonstrations in front of houses of worship; the military rebuilt the church at the cost of $1 million. Young Muslims have been seen protecting both churches and synagogues. In October 2011, twenty-three Copts were killed in a protest parade. This caused an angry reaction throughout the country. (24) There have been attacks at the rate of about one a month throughout 2012; they are inevitably carried out by extremist groups. Many Egyptians urgently want the new Egypt to be built by Christians and Muslims together.

Egypt has long been a dominant cultural influence in the Arab world—it is the leader of the Arab nations in such fields as filmmaking and literature. At any given time there are about 400 young Americans studying Arabic in Egypt (some left during the revolution and are returning), most of them at the American University in Cairo. It is common for students to want to return to Egypt, and many want to live there. Cairo, home to 14 million people, is a big, hot, crowded, polluted, poor city—still, *to know it is to love it.*

The Egyptian people are known to be especially friendly and good-humored. They are very outgoing toward foreigners.

## Sudan

Sudan is the largest country in Africa, with an area of one million square miles (about one fourth the size of the United States). It is tribal and diverse, with considerable sub-Saharan African influence on its social structure and ethnic composition. Counting southern Sudan, the country has had one of the most ethnically diverse populations in the world, with more than 400 languages, 19 major ethnic groups, and 597 subgroups, most of them in the non-Arab south. (1). It is one of the 25 poorest countries in the world, with 90 percent living below the poverty line. (2)

Sudan has always been divided culturally into two distinct regions, the Arab north and the non-Arab south; the ten provinces in the south make up one third of Sudan's land area. In both areas, most of the people are farmers. The south became independent South Sudan on July 9, 2011, after a referendum was held in which 98.83 percent of the people voted to separate. (3) There were two long and brutal wars between north and south, from Sudan's independence from Britain in 1956 until a peace agreement between the two sides in 2005, which paved the way for the referendum. In South Sudan there is very little infrastructure—roads, schools, health care—and there is a low literacy rate. A new currency has been introduced, and there are plans to build an entirely new capital city. (4)

Unless otherwise specified, "Sudan" will refer to both north and south together before the south's independence.

Unlike most urbanized Arab populations, in Sudan 60 percent of the people live in rural areas and work in agriculture, although in this large country only 7 percent of the land is arable; it depends on the Nile River and its tributaries. The southern region, if developed, has a huge economic potential in its oil and minerals, rare timbers, and abundant water. (5)

Oil was discovered in the south in 1979. Large-scale exports began in 1999 and now make up 60 percent of the country's export earnings; oil will be 98 percent of earnings in South Sudan. (6)(7) Many southerners have resented the disproportionate share of oil money being spent in the north. A report in 2009 suggested that the regime in the north was underreporting oil production to deprive the South of its share of the revenue. (8) Certainly Khartoum, the capital city, is glitzy, with oil money financing big buildings and affluent neighborhoods. These are alongside mud-brick slums and refugee camps, which are mainly on the outskirts of town. In fact, the government razes these shantytowns periodically and moves refugees and the poor further into the desert. (9)

This huge country has a population of only 44 million, over 80 percent living in the north. The population of Khartoum is 6 to 7 million. In

Sudan, 41 percent of the people are age fifteen or younger. (10) The growth rate is 2.5 percent a year, and population will increase 80 percent by 2050, (11) placing huge pressures on education, health, and food resources.

There is a separate conflict in the Darfur region, which is the western one-fifth of the country, population 7.6 million. Nearly 2 million people have been displaced there; the war has caused 200,000 to 400,000 deaths. (12) There are 7,000 peacekeeping troops from the African Union in the area trying to stabilize the situation.

Many parts of South Sudan are isolated, and some do not even have a cash economy. The civil war in the south was one of the worst sustained conflicts since World War II. Large-scale famine and unchecked disease have ravaged the region and still continue; some 2 million are dead and 4 to 5 million displaced from their homes. The total population is about 8 million. (13) The Sudanese government, or groups it tolerated, were repeatedly accused of genocide, human rights abuses, and toleration of slavery, and this has led to a major humanitarian crisis. Thousands of people, including orphaned or abandoned children, live in refugee camps. Many international relief organizations are present, both in the south and among the people in camps around Khartoum.

There are also Arabic-speaking nomads in the south, some of whom were hired by the government during the civil war to serve as mercenaries (Janjaweed). But most were neutral. They also fight among themselves, often about migration routes. Many of them, too, are being served by relief organizations. (14)

In 1993, Sudan was placed on the U.S. list of countries that sponsor international terrorism. The U.S. maintains comprehensive sanctions, imposed in 1997 and 2007. The Sudanese government has been isolated internationally, and its acceptance of separation into north and south is seen by some as a way for the president, Omar Al-Bashir, to bring an end to sanctions and possibly avoid trial in the International Criminal Court for war activities. (15) Sudan is considered one of the world's most corrupt states; corruption is also a serious problem in South Sudan. (16) The U.S. State Department considers Sudan to be a source, transit, and destination country for persons trafficked for forced labor and sexual exploitation. (17)

The northern Sudanese are Arabs (in language, only partially in ethnicity). Tribalism is dominant in the north as well as the south and many men are marked with identifying facial scars, as is common in sub-Saharan Africa. Arabic has been the official language in the country, although only about 60 percent of the people speak it. The northerners are Sunni Muslim. In the south the predominant religions are Christianity, 5 percent, and indigenous animism, 25 percent.

Education has been available to the upper and middle classes for generations in the north, and this group is highly literate, but the literacy rate is only 61 percent for the country as a whole. There is a large pool of well-educated Sudanese professionals but because of low salaries at home, about 1.2 million people work abroad, mainly in the Arabian Peninsula. (18) This has caused a shortage of trained manpower in the country; at the same time, the over-all unemployment rate was 20 percent in 2009.

Education for women has been steadily increasing, but only about 24 percent of Sudanese women work outside the home, mainly as teachers and social workers. Sudanese culture is extremely conservative in its view of women's rights. The birth rate is high, 4.1 children per woman, down from 6.5 in 1960. (19) Women rarely cover their faces, but they all wear a long cloak and voluminous scarves in public.

Since a military coup in 1983, Sudan has had the only avowed Islamist government in the Arab world (Saudi Arabia is conservative but not Islamist), with Islamic law prevailing. Women's rights had been granted after independence from Britain (free consent to marriage, equal rights in divorce, custody of children and financial support), but when the current government in Khartoum came into power, strict Sharia law was enforced and many discriminatory practices were reinstated. Sudanese women in the north now have no legal right to ownership of property or access to land, and cannot manage their assets freely, nor can they obtain bank loans. (20) Except for a small number of liberated, educated young women in the elite class, women are generally separated from men, even at mealtimes. There is a Sudanese Women's Union which works with the government and advocates greater rights for women.

Women once had much greater cultural freedom in the south and were active in public affairs; presumably, these rights will return after South Sudan is fully operational as a nation. In fact, women are seeking 30 percent representation in the new state, at all levels; they constitute 60 percent of the population. (21) In January 2012 tribal violence broke out, affecting about 60,000 people, who are receiving humanitarian assistance. (22)

Sudanese are known throughout the Arab world as friendly, sincere, and generous, and they are proud of this reputation. Their nation is in turmoil and life will be better when political and economic problems are addressed and settled.

CHAPTER 15

# The Arab Countries in the Center

The Levantine region is located in the center of the Arab world, in western Asia.

## The Levant

The *Levant*, a French term, is used to identify the countries of the Eastern Mediterranean: Lebanon, Syria, and Palestine. Also in the region are Jordan and Iraq geographically, although not ethnically.

The Levantine people in Lebanon, Syria, and Palestine are mainly from the same Semitic origin, descended from indigenous inhabitants of the region from Neolithic times. They constitute a linguistic and cultural unit and identify with each other. Jordanians, however, are of Bedouin descent, from the northern Arabian Peninsula (now Saudi Arabia). Many Iraqis are Arabian too, because Iraq was severely depopulated and then repopulated by Bedouin tribes from Arabia. The Arabic spoken in Baghdad is a Bedouin dialect.

The borders in the Levant do not conform to geography or history. They were drawn by Britain and France after World War I, when these countries had mandates over the region.

The acronym UNRWA will be referred to in this section; it stands for the United Nations Relief and Works Agency (for Palestine Refugees in the Near East). UNRWA works in Palestine, Jordan, Lebanon, and Syria.

## Lebanon

Lebanon is a small country, both in size and population, which is a little over four million. It has a diverse geography and a long history of commercial and maritime importance. Its people are descended from the same (non-Arabian) Semitic stock, mainly Phoenician and Canaanite. Religious diversity and social class in Lebanon have been divisive and have created barriers to social integration. All Lebanese feel an intense loyalty to their own clan and religious group. The Lebanese speak Arabic, and educated people also speak French, English, or both.

From 1975 to 1990, Lebanon experienced a disastrous civil war, during which 25 percent of the population was displaced and at least 130,000 people were killed. Religious tensions were part of the cause—the Christians, who represented 25 to 43 percent of the population (estimates vary), have traditionally had more wealth and political power than the more numerous Muslims (about 60 percent), who in turn are divided between Sunnis (about 25 percent) and Shia (about 35 percent). Religion has become a substitute for ethnic affiliation in many cases; it is of overriding importance in defining the Lebanese population. Lebanon has by far the highest number of Christians in the Arab world, divided into many sects. Numbers in Lebanon's religious communities are vague because there has been no official census since 1932, due to the sensitivity of this issue.

A third influential denomination is the Druze religion, which originated in Lebanon in the eleventh century and is derived from Shia Islam; the Druze are classified as Muslim and make up about 5 percent of the population. Altogether, seventeen religious sects are officially recognized, and many government positions are reserved for certain religions. The social and political effects of this mix of religious groups is tumultuous at best; it has affected government stability.

During Lebanon's civil war the factions were religion-based. The Syrian army occupied the country from 1976 to 2008, partly because of the unrest. Syrians were resented by some of the Christians but welcomed by many in other religious groups. Syria (and its ally, Hizbollah) stand accused of assassinating the Lebanese prime minister, Rafik Hariri, in February 2005. Tensions rose again in 2008, and continue today. (1)

Prior to the beginning of the civil war in 1975, the Lebanese government was pro-Western and pro-capitalist, and the country was a leader in service industries such as banking, commerce, and tourism. The Lebanese had the highest standard of living in the Arab world and the most cosmopolitan way of life, at least in Beirut. This is rapidly returning, although the Gulf states are catching up.

Lebanon was created when it was carved out of the region of Greater Syria—"Sham" in Arabic—as a haven for Christians, who had suffered massacres by the Druze and the Turks in the 1860s. This was done through an agreement among Europe's Great Powers and the Ottoman authorities. France drew Lebanon's present borders in 1920. There are 935,000 Syrian refugees in Lebanon, so that they and the Palestinians constitute 25% of its population of 4.5 million. This is a larger proportion than any country in the world.

Social classes are clearly defined in Lebanon, with a small upper class, a sizeable middle class, and a large lower class made up of about half of the people. The lower classes are quite poor, and the majority live in urban areas. Agricultural production is limited by inadequate natural resources, and imports far exceed exports. Unemployment stood at 18 to 20 percent from 2003 to 2008, but it improved in 2009 and 2010, and it currently stands at 9.2 percent. (2) The youth unemployment rate, however, is 21 percent. (3).

There were about 425,000 Palestinian refugees in Lebanon in January 2010, which means that they constitute more than 10 percent of the population. (4) These refugees are considered foreigners and are denied basic rights. They are confined to crowded refugee camps and cannot attend public schools, own property, or make an enforceable will. (5) They engage in menial work and are not allowed to work in professions such as medicine or law. Work restrictions were eased somewhat in 2010.

The concept of giving these refugees citizenship is a controversial issue in Lebanon. They are almost all Sunni Muslims, so if they became citizens, it would affect the religious electoral balance. As a result, their citizenship is opposed by the Christians and Shia. Refugees are the poorest community in Lebanon, as well as the poorest Palestinian refugees except for those in Gaza. (6) Lebanon received about 100,000 Iraqi refugees because of the war there; most are undocumented.

Although Christians ruled Lebanon since its inception, this was challenged by rising Muslim populations, notably Hizbollah*, a Shia party. There was sectarian fighting, notably in 2008 (7). A Sunni leader announced that he would not join the new government (8). Lebanon was without a government for eighteen months in 2007-2008 (9) and for eleven months from March 2013 to February 2014 (10). Government positions are still assigned by religion, with the President a Christian, the Prime Minister Sunni, and the Speaker of Parliament Shia; a religious quota in Parliament results in about half Christian, half Muslim delegates. No census has been taken since 1932, at which time the Christians were a 54% majority, so there is great religious sensitivity, which led to the eight-year civil war from 1975 to 1990. Shia are now the largest group. Sectarian fighting in Syria may well spill over.

The Lebanese people are well traveled and sophisticated, and they are politically oriented and patriotic. Some, mainly Christians, believe that Lebanon should be more Western than Arab and should identify with Europe; others, mainly Muslims, identify with pan-Arab sentiments and want to deemphasize Western influence. The Lebanese have migrated abroad since the late nineteenth century, and more live outside the country than inside. Sustained contacts with these emigrants all over the world has influenced the society and economy.

The Lebanese are highly educated. Free public education has long been available, and the literacy rate is 90 percent. In the mid-nineteenth century, French and American missionaries established schools and universities in Lebanon. The missionaries had a strong influence, and they trained many future leaders and intellectuals of the Arab world.

Urban Lebanese women, especially Christians, are active in the professions, commerce, and social organizations. Women constitute 32 percent of the workforce, one fourth of them in the professional sector. They generally dress in the Western manner and mix freely in society. In contrast, women in rural areas are restricted by the prevailing traditional values. The Hejab headscarf has begun making an appearance.

---

*For a description of Hizbollah's history, see "Hezbollah's Rise Amid Chaos" by Robert F. Worth, *New York Times*, January 15, 2011.

Women were granted the right to vote and run in elections in 1952. They are seriously under-represented in politics, with only 2.8 percent of the government positions. (11) From 1997 to 2000, the government initiated a National Action Plan to improve the status of women, and it has instituted a National Authority on Women's Issues as well. (12) There are active organizations seeking to place more women in leadership positions and replace some Islamic laws with civil ones. Women are still discriminated against in laws concerning family, the right to travel, and the right to work. (13)

Beirut is exceptionally built up and modernized. Situated along the Mediterranean seacoast, it is sometimes called "the Paris of the Middle East." The society in the city is the most liberal in the Arab world; it is luxurious and highly social, with an active nightlife. Many students from Europe and the U.S. have studied at the American University in Beirut, as well as several other universities. Westerners feel comfortable and safe in Lebanon.

## Syria

Since Syria's independence from France in 1946, it had a series of secular, authoritarian governments, culminating in the Assad takeover in 1970. Bashar Al-Assad, president since his father's death in 2000, heads a repressive state with curtailed rights of assembly and expression.

Syria is currently in a state of armed rebellion against the government, after protests (nonviolent at first) beginning in March 2011. Opposition groups include some who aspire to democracy, but there are also many Islamist (including Jihadist) groups. Violence has been widespread and the government has responded with brutality. Government buildings have been bombed and soldiers killed, and retaliations have included attacks on entire towns and neighborhoods, with large areas completely devastated. Repeated international protests to the Syrian government have had no effect. The final shape of a resolution is unclear as of early 2013.

There are now 2.5 million Syrian refugees, mainly in Lebanon, Turkey, and Jordan; the rate of departure is 2,000 per day. (1) Aid organizations cannot meet the needs, and winter weather makes conditions worse. (2) About 100,000 have declared asylum in Europe.

A major concern is that Syrian violence and factionalism could spread to neighboring countries—Lebanon, Iraq, and Jordan. Local groups could attract support from, for example, Saudi Arabia and Turkey (Sunnis) and Iran (Shia). The regime has support from minority groups (mainly Christians and Shia), who fear for their safety if a Sunni Islamist government is formed. It is even possible that Syria could break up as a cohesive state; the borders are less than one hundred years old. The Kurds could also break away.

The U.S. has had economic sanctions against Syria since 2004 and imposed personal sanctions against President Assad in May 2011 on the grounds of human rights abuses. In November 2011, the Arab League expelled Syria." (3)

Syria's population of 22 million is diverse—about 90 percent Muslims, 7 percent Christians, and 3 percent Druze. The Alawites (a variation of Shiism) are 12 percent of the population but have controlled the government since 1970. The upper and middle classes are 35 percent of the population. Health care is widely available, and expenditure on education doubled between 2000 and 2005. (4) Syria has attained universal primary education and literacy is 84 percent.

The Syrian government has long attempted to control Islamists. In 1982 an Islamist threat was harshly put down in Hama, during which 10,000 to 20,000 civilians died. Islamism is again on the rise. Many Syrians fear political Islam and the religious revival, and they do not want to lose the secular nature of their government, regardless of what may happen in the future. If the current government falls, it will very likely be replaced by one based on religion. One reporter gave this assessment before the uprisings: "There would be little public regret if the regime did just fall apart. Yet few in the opposition really want it that way. They fear that with ethnic and sectarian tensions, civil war—even another Iraq—could occur." (5) Many analysts believe that without the current government there may be Sunni-Shia clashes throughout the wider region.

Syria still claims the Golan region, occupied by Israel since 1967. In late 2012, Israel announced that it will build a separation wall there. Because of the Golan occupation, Syria will not open talks with Israel.

Agricultural production is an important factor in Syria's economy, as are oil, phosphates, and textiles. Land reform and the establishment of agricultural cooperatives have led to improvements in the lives of small farmers, who are about a third of the population. The unemployment rate was 8.5 percent in 2011, down from 20 percent in 2005. (6) The public sector employs about 73 percent of the workforce. (7)

There were 540,000 Palestinian refugees in the country in early 2014. They are allowed to work, own a house, and study in Syrian secondary schools and universities. They have full access to government services. (8) Nevertheless, about half live at or below the poverty line. They are assisted by the U.N. organizations UNICEF and UNWRA. Despite the turmoil in Syria, it also hosts about one million Iraqi refugees, (9) some of whom have begun to return home because it is safer there. The U.N. supports about 40 percent of them. (10)

Syrian women in the upper class have been well educated for a long time and have been working, primarily in education and medicine; they hold over 35 percent of positions in the national university system. They represent 39 percent of the workforce, but only 9 percent have a university-level education and work at that level. Many work in agriculture or in menial jobs. Women have about 10 percent of the positions in government.

Despite these numbers, women do not have equality in the legal system, which is a combination of civil and Sharia law. The most prominent advocate for women is the Syrian Women's Observatory, founded in 2005. It spreads knowledge about rights, including online, and recently succeeded in making the government drop a proposed "personal status law" (Islamic domestic law) that it judged as a violation of women's rights. Islamist sentiment is present in the society, and while traditionally Syria has a good reputation for women's rights within the Arab world, the annual World Economic Forum Gender Gap Index shows that the status of women has worsened in recent years. (11)

Syrians are friendly and welcoming to Westerners. There were several study-abroad programs for students learning Arabic. In the past decade, there had been about two hundred Western students living in Damascus at any given time, about fifty of them American. They returned home telling of how friendly and nice the Syrians are toward them, and many hope to find a way to return.

## Palestinian Territories

The presence of conflict dominates the narrative of Palestine. Conflict affects every aspect of life and government activity. This section is a description of the situation as it pertains to Palestine. It is not an analysis of the overall Israel–Palestine issue.

The Palestinian Territories (Palestine) include three regions: the West Bank, East Jerusalem, and Gaza, which is under separate governance. The Palestine Authority governs the West Bank and (theoretically) East Jerusalem, which is slated to become the capital of Palestine. Hamas governs Gaza. Hamas (the Islamic Resistance Movement) was elected democratically in 2006, but it has not been recognized by the U.S. or Israel, because it denies Israel's right to exist. One reason Hamas was elected is because of its extensive social and charity work over the years, such as providing medical centers, food banks, summer camps, schools, and sometimes direct financial aid to families. (1) Many of these services are run by other Islamic charities as well. Some facilities are supported by supplemental money from international donors.

There is constant talk about making Palestine an independent state and joining the West Bank and Gaza into a contiguous whole, with borders yet to be determined. A "land swap" is envisioned, with Israel keeping some land on the West Bank (there were 500,000 settlers there in 2011) (2) in exchange for other land elsewhere, but this has to be negotiated. Israel currently controls 60 percent of the West Bank. The simplest step would be to return to borders that were in place before the 1967 war, but that is now impossible because of the settlements. It is the preference of the U.S. government to use those borders as a starting point for negotiations between Israel and Palestine, when discussing a land swap. This is envisioned as part of the peace process, which has been under discussion for decades. The U.S. has been involved in peacemaking efforts from the beginning, but it is not viewed as an "honest broker" and has lost credibility among many Arabs.†

In September 2011, the Palestinians petitioned the U.N. for recognition as a state and membership in the U.N. The U.S. has opposed this. As of this writing, the issue is with the Security Council, and unsettled. Palestine recently became a member of UNESCO.

The Palestinians point to Israel's confiscations of their land, the expansion of settlements, humiliating checkpoints, home demolitions (more than 24,000 from 1967 to 2011), open-ended detentions, extrajudicial killings, and thousands of dead civilians. (4) Additional statistics (from September 2000 to February 2011): 1,000 Israelis and 6,500 Palestinians killed, including 124 Israeli children and 1,400 Palestinian children killed; 9,000 Israelis and 45,000 Palestinians injured; 1 Israeli (released in October 2011) and 5,500 Palestinians held prisoner; and unemployment rates of 6.4 percent in Israel, 16.5 percent in the West Bank, and 40 percent in Gaza. (5)

The Israelis have grievances in turn. They state that because of terrorism, their security is not guaranteed, so they cannot withdraw the military forces occupying the West Bank.

The total population of Palestine is a little over four million: 2.5 million in the West Bank, 1.6 million in Gaza, and 250,000 in East Jerusalem, plus about 3 million refugees outside of Palestine (in camps in Lebanon, Syria, and Jordan). In total, some 4.8 million Palestinians, inside and outside the country, now have refugee status and are registered with UNRWA. (6) Palestine wants a Right of Return for all Palestinians; i.e., all Palestinians abroad would be able to come back. It is a doubtful concession to expect because of the balance of population compared with Israel. Other difficult issues include recognition and security for Israel, trade and travel agreements, withdrawal of Israeli forces, the demilitarization of Palestine, the status of Jerusalem, and whether there can be a "two-state solution." The last issue questions whether Palestine and Israel can

---

†In February 2011 the U.S. voted against a U.N. Security Council Resolution calling the Israeli settlements in the West bank "illegal." The vote was 14 to 1. The American president had previously referred to the settlements as illegal, but backed down. (3)

be recognized as separate states, or whether the Arabs will be absorbed into a Greater Israel.

There have been constant clashes along Palestine's borders, and both sides point to provocations. Israel has built a steel-concrete barrier wall (the Wall) to separate it from nearly all the Palestinians, 450 miles long; it intends this as a permanent border. It swallowed up 733 square kilometers of land, or 13 percent of the West Bank. The wall is intended to protect settlers, who are also connected to Jerusalem via special highways (they don't go through checkpoints). The wall surrounds many Palestinian towns and cuts them off from their fields. There were also 267,000 settlers in East Jerusalem in 2011 (Jerusalem is divided, and East Jerusalem is considered Arab, slated to become the capital of Palestine), which will greatly complicate any future agreement. (7) In August 2011, the Israeli government announced approval of 1,600 more housing units in East Jerusalem; it now controls one third of this part of the city. Settlement-building involves demolitions of Arab homes; at least 60,000 Palestinians are at risk of having their homes destroyed because they are located in violation of Israel's zoning laws. (8)

The Palestinians live in great poverty, especially in the densely crowded Gaza refugee camp where many fled from other parts of Palestine. 1.6 million people are living in an area roughly twice the size of Washington, D.C. Gaza is one of the most crowded places in the world, with 8,666 individuals per square mile in 2009. (9) The people's movement and imports have been severely restricted. The revolutionary government in Egypt opened the corridor on its border with Gaza in May 2011, to alleviate shortages.

On May 15, 2011, Palestinians clashed with Israeli forces on the borders of Lebanon, Syria, Gaza, and the West Bank to protest their situation and to mark the anniversary of the founding of Israel in 1949. (10) This mass civil disobedience copied the uprisings elsewhere in the Arab countries at the time. They again demonstrated at the border with Syria on June 5, the anniversary of the 1967 war, and some were killed.

Palestine received 400 million dollars from the U.S. in 2010, for humanitarian and development assistance, as well as 100 million dollars to train police.‡ U.S. funding is usually through non-governmental

---

‡In contrast, Israel receives $3 billion annually from the U.S., and aid will continue at that level through 2018. Altogether, from 1949 through 2010 Israel has received at least $109 billion. (11)

organizations (NGOs), for projects such as improved water access, health care, education, and vocational training. (12) Some funding has gone to the Palestinian Authority to strengthen it against competing political parties, particularly Hamas. But in late 2012, the Palestinian Authority and Hamas began talks, and relations may improve. The U.S. also partially funds U.N. agencies such as UNRWA, and it gave $61.5 million in emergency aid after Israel's assault on Gaza in late 2008 through early 2009. (13) Similarly, aid was provided after the extreme damage to West Bank towns (especially Jenin and Nablus) from an Israeli strike in April 2002, after the second Intifada.

But enough about the conflict. Let's take a look at the Palestinians themselves.

Palestinians are among the most homogeneous in the Arab world, in that 98 percent are Sunni Muslim and 2 percent are Christian (down from about 8 percent in 1949). The 52,000 Christians (estimates range from 50,000 to 90,000) in the three regions of Palestine are concentrated in East Jerusalem (2.5 percent, down from 51 percent in 1947), Bethlehem, and Ramallah. They belong to many different sects. In 2004, they were estimated at 360,000. (14) Christians have 8 percent representation in the Palestinian Legislative Council. (15) The majority of Palestinian Christians live abroad, in the Americas and in Arab countries.

Palestine's economy is not self-sustaining, due to lack of access to land in Israeli-controlled areas, import and export restrictions, and little private sector growth. (16) There was a downturn for a decade, but since 2008, the Palestinian Authority has implemented a successful campaign of institutional reforms that increased both security and economic performance. The entire country relies heavily on donor aid from the U.S., the European Union, Japan, and other nations, which reached a total of more than 3 billion dollars in 2010. (17) This aid has been much reduced because of Palestine's bid to be recognized as a sovereign state by the United Nations, and because of unity negotiations with Hamas. (18)

The West Bank economy depends on agriculture, 12 percent; industry, 2 percent; and services, 65 percent (as of 2008). The Gaza economy was agriculture, 12 percent (only 29 percent of the land is arable); industry, 5 percent; and services, 83 percent. Gaza's exports of agricultural produce are frequently disrupted and cannot be relied upon. The economy of East

Jerusalem is not under Palestinian control; there is widespread poverty, and the Wall obstructs the movement of goods and labor.

The population growth rate is high, overall about 3 percent per year. In the West Bank, 36 percent of the population is under age fifteen, as are 44 percent in Gaza. Unemployment was 16.5 percent in the West Bank in 2010, and 40 percent in Gaza. (19) In the West Bank, 46 percent of the people lived below the poverty line in 2009; the number was 70 percent in Gaza.

Education is good, although it is subject to disruptions because of events. Literacy is 98 percent, the highest in the Arab world. There are fifteen colleges and universities.

Health care is a problem, however, because of inadequate hospitals and medical personnel, a lack of specialists, and a lack of investment. Some Palestinians have access to medical care in Israel, and there have been training programs for doctors and nurses there. (20) The World Bank estimates that over half of the Palestinians lack reliable provisions of food, and 11 percent of the children are malnourished, an increase of 40 percent between 2000 and 2010. (21)

Palestinian women have many advocacy groups, and their legal status is improving. Recent legislation accords them equality before the law, but there are still discriminatory laws in effect regarding marriage, divorce, custody, and inheritance, left over from Jordanian and Egyptian law in the West Bank and Gaza respectively. Women are marginally represented among judges and police. The recent Palestinian Labor Law and Social Status Law are mostly gender-sensitive, specifying equal rights for women. Few women own property, much of the reason being poverty. A child whose mother holds a Jerusalem residency permit has difficulty going to school there if their father is from elsewhere, because marriage does not entitle a spouse to a permit from the Israelis. The third draft constitution of March 2003 states that Palestinians will not be subject to "any discrimination on the basis of race, sex, color, religion, political convictions, or disability." (22)

In the West Bank, women average 3 children each, and in Gaza, 4.7 children. Only 10 percent of the women are in the workforce, although among those with thirteen or more years' schooling, 56 percent are employed. But women reportedly earn only 65 percent of men's wages in the West Bank and 77 percent in Gaza.

A surprising number of foreign students are in the Jerusalem and West Bank area learning Arabic. They report making good friends and finding acceptance, including a welcome for Americans.

## Jordan

Jordan is a relatively new nation. It was created under a British mandate after the end of World War I, as a kingdom to be ruled by the Hashemites.§ Jordan became independent of Britain in 1946. Its borders are artificial—Jordan was essentially made up of the leftovers when the borders of adjoining nations were determined by the British (for their own interests). Jordan ceded the West Bank (of the Jordan River, occupied by Israel since 1967) to the Palestinian Authority in 1988.

Over half of Jordan's 6.5 million people are Palestinians, most of whom arrived after the wars of 1948 and 1967. Many of these Palestinians are well educated and many are wealthy. They have been granted Jordanian citizenship and have the same political and economic rights as Jordanians do. Two million are refugees; they live in thirteen refugee camps, ten of which are administered by UNRWA. Jordan went through a traumatic civil war in 1970, when Palestinians attempted (unsuccessfully) to take over the government. Jordan also hosts about 500,000 Iraqi refugees, (1) and it had 575,000 Syrian refugees as of early 2014 (2).

*In Jordan, there is a significant distinction between Palestinians* (who identify more readily with Lebanese and Syrians) *and Jordanians.* The Palestinian dialect is predominant in the urban centers, but elsewhere the Jordanians speak their own dialect, close to the Bedouin and Peninsular dialects. The Jordanian Arabic dialect has been encouraged and promoted in television programs. Most Jordanians speak English, but there is an effort at language planning, to strengthen the use of Arabic rather than foreign languages. (3)

About 10 percent of the Jordanians are Bedouins. By now, only about 1 percent of Bedouins (6,000) are nomadic. The Badia Project has been instituted to help them care for the environment and for their animals, in the hope that they can maintain their lifestyle. Many settled Bedouins

---

§Hashemites are originally from the Hejaz region of western Saudi Arabia, where they fought with the British against the Turks in the Arab Revolt during World War I.

work in the tourism industry. (4) Jordanians (not Palestinians) hold most of the administrative posts in the country.

After the death of King Hussein in 1999, his son Abdullah assumed the throne. The Jordanian government is viewed as moderate and pro-Western. Jordan and the U.S. work together in counter-terrorism, and have done so for thirty years. (5)

Most Jordanians are Sunni Muslim, but 6 percent of the population is Christian (400,000 people). Religion has not been a divisive factor in the society. King Abdullah is a leading proponent of moderate Islam, and he has called for the "quiet majority" of Muslims to "take back our religion from the vocal, violent, and ignorant extremists." (6) He has initiated a legal and scholarly effort to undermine clerics who issue religious rulings that justify violence.

Jordan is a constitutional monarchy, with a parliament. The latest parliamentary elections were held in 2010. Twelve seats are reserved for women (20 percent of the positions are reserved for women at the municipal level). (7) But the government has pushed economic liberal-ization harder than democratic improvements, and the electoral system favors tribal candidates who support the government. (8) There was only a 53 percent turnout at the last election and many were cynical about the results, because it was boycotted by the Islamist parties. The vast major-ity of those elected were pro-government; although seventeen candidates were from opposition parties. (9)

The Islamists won a majority in Parliament in 1989, and about one fourth of the seats in 2003. After their boycott in 2010, their influence is uncertain; they want the current parliament dissolved. And despite the government's pro-Western policies, it still has to contend with the atti-tudes that were recorded in the results of a Pew Global Attitudes Project poll in April–May 2011, in which a large majority of the people viewed the U.S. unfavorably because of "a perception that the U.S. acts unilater-ally, opposition to the war on terror, and fears of America as a military threat." (10) 87 percent of those who took the poll stated that they want the U.S. out of Afghanistan.

When uprisings were breaking out all over the Arab world in early 2011, Jordanians demonstrated too, and these acts were repressed with force. They did not call for the downfall of the monarchy, but they were protesting government corruption, rising prices, rampant poverty, and high unemployment. The king formed a National Dialogue Commission with a reform mandate, including discussion of controversial social issues. (11) He shuffled the cabinet, and in October 2011 he also acceded to the demand that future governments be based on a parliamentary majority, not appointed by the king. (12) The Prime Minister will be elected by Parliament. A Cabinet that dissolves Parliament must also resign. (13)

Jordan has one of the smallest economies in the Arab world. It is poor in natural resources, and despite numerous economic initiatives, the nation is heavily dependent on foreign aid. There are worsening water shortages. Only 6 percent of the land is arable, and 3 percent of the population are farmers. The economy is based on tourism, industry, agriculture, and exports such as uranium and oil shale. Tourism is variable, always subject to a downturn when there is unrest in the region. Most people have experienced a decrease in income. Approximately 14 percent of the people live below the poverty line. (14) However, rapid privatization of previously state-owned industries and liberalization of the economy is spurring unprecedented growth in Jordan's urban centers, such as Amman and Aqaba. (15)

Jordan's location between Israel and Iraq is a disadvantage, and it has suffered because of both neighbors. Before the Gulf War of 1991, 75 percent of its trade was with Iraq (1 billion dollars per year); this was reduced to one quarter of that amount. (16) Some 380,000 Jordanians returned from jobs in the Arabian Gulf at the time of the first Gulf war, and unemployment rose to 30 percent. The second Gulf War caused an even greater crisis in the energy supply situation, as oil had been imported (below market cost) from Iraq; it is far more expensive now. Jordan joined the World Trade Organization in 2000 and entered into a Jordan-U.S. Free Trade Agreement in 2001. It has more free trade agreements than any other Arab country.

Jordan's educational system is excellent, and 6.4 percent of the government's total expenditure is spent on education. (17) The literacy rate was 92 percent in 2010. There is also an excellent nationwide health program.

Jordanian women are well educated and working in a wide array of fields; about 27 percent are in the workforce. Queen Rania is championing the cause of women's rights. Sharia law, combined with civil law, is used in the country.

Jordanians are very personable, warm, and welcoming. They enjoy friendships with foreigners. Many American students choose to study in Jordan, and even more travel there. They are unanimous in their praise of the country and people.

## Iraq

Iraq (Mesopotamia) has a proud history and was the home of five magnificent ancient civilizations. But time after time, Iraq was beset by invasions and conquests. Iraq is underpopulated, considering its antiquity and fertility, with 30 million people; this is the consequence of repeated wars and devastation. Iraq's location has always made it a strategic battlefield for the region.

Only 75 percent of the Iraqis are Arabs, and 20 percent are Kurds, who are bilingual in Kurdish and Arabic. ¶ The remainder are comprised of small ethnic groups, such as Turkomans, Assyrians, and Armenians. Arabic is the official language, and English is widely spoken.

In Iraq 97 percent are Muslim, of whom 60 percent are Shia. The remaining 3 percent are Christians and other minorities, such as Mandeans and Chaldeans. Iraq has been strongly influenced by its Islamic heritage because several sites sacred to Shia Muslims are located there and have long been the object of religious pilgrimages.

Iraq's revolutionary socialist government was established after the Hashemite monarchy was overthrown in 1958, and there have been four coups since then. The Ba'ath political party took power in 1968, and Saddam Hussein was president from 1979 to 2003.

Iraq has been hard-hit by two wars, ten years apart (not to mention an eight-year war with Iran prior to these two). The first phase was Gulf War I, after Iraq's invasion of Kuwait.** This was followed by an international embargo imposed in 1991 (referred to by Iraqis and other Arabs as "the American sanctions"). In ten years the sale of oil went from generating

---

¶Kurds are not Arabs or Semitic; they are ethnically Aryan, related to the Persians.
**The territory of Kuwait was once Iraq's nineteenth province, until the British bestowed Kuwait on the current ruling family. The Arab nationalist version of events is: "British imperialism gave us Kuwait and in the view of the Arab nationalists, American imperialism made sure we still have Kuwait, in the face of Iraqi attempts to undo British conniving." (1)

95 percent of the foreign earnings to 10 percent. Social services declined drastically, and money that was intended for food and medicine in the oil-for-food program was mostly diverted to government loyalists. By 2001 an estimated 800,000 to 1.2 million people had died because of the embargo, half a million of them children under the age of five. (2) Because of scarcities, the people became more dependent on the government for necessities, including drinking water.

Then came Gulf War II, the American invasion of March 2003. The chaotic results are well known, and they continue. Even as 8 million Iraqis voted and exuberantly demonstrated their love of freedom and democracy in the elections of January 2005, at the same time 92 percent of them wanted the Americans out. The current government is Shia, with Nouri Al-Maliki as president. Strong sectarian and ethnic tensions are present—among Sunnis, Shia, and Kurds. It remains to be seen whether the government can hold the country together.

Iraq was created in 1918 from three separate Ottoman provinces, Sunni, Shia, and Kurdish, by the British when they had a mandate over the region. The boundaries were based on "consultation with the tribes, consideration of Britain's need for oil, and her own idiosyncratic geopolitical beliefs." (3) In 1921 the British selected a Hashemite king, Faisal (a Sunni), who ruled until a bloody military coup in 1958. Iraq needs a period of calm to build up its institutions and economy, but it is doubtful that this will occur.

39 percent of the Iraqis are under age fifteen. In 2003 about 25 percent of the children were malnourished, which was up 73 percent from 1991. Infant mortality more than doubled between the late 1980s and early 2000s; by 2001 it was about 133 per thousand births (as compared with 4 to 5 in Western Europe and 6.7 in the U.S.). (4) A United Nations report stated, "The country's fall on the UNDP Human Development Index from 96 to 127 reflects one of the most rapid declines in human welfare in recent history." (5) A UNICEF report stated that in mid-2005, 4,000 children under the age of five died every day. (6) In 2007, 23 percent of the population was living on less than two dollars per day.

The situation had improved by 2010; at that time the infant mortality rate was thirty-five per thousand births. (7) About 7 percent of the children were reported as malnourished in 2009. (8) But there are severe problems with water, sewage, and electricity, which affects the standard of living. A World Health Organization survey found that 17 percent of Iraqis over eighteen suffer from mental disorders such as depression, phobias, post-traumatic stress disorder, and anxiety. (9)

In February 2011 the Iraqis staged a "Day of Rage," copying uprisings in other Arab countries at the time. They were protesting the government's failure to create jobs; the failure to provide public services such as clean water, electricity, and health services; and the rampant corruption. The government dealt with the protesters harshly, and over twenty were killed and scores injured. (10)

Education has been hard hit. Enrollment in primary schools dropped from 100 percent in 1980 to 85 percent in 1996, and 76 percent in 2003. It was 85 percent in 2007, and the government's target is 100 percent enrollment by 2015. (11) Once, 92 percent of the population was literate; in 2011 the rate was 74 percent. (12)

Only 12 percent of Iraq's land is cultivated, and efforts have long been underway to reclaim more. (It was irrigated and fertile in ancient times.) About 30 percent of the Iraqis work in agriculture.

In the mid-twentieth century, Iraqi women were among the most liberated in the Middle East, and they were thoroughly integrated into the workface, many as professionals. Within a span of twenty years, thousands of women became lawyers, physicians, professors, engineers, scientists, and writers. In 1959, Iraq became the first country in the Middle East to have a female minister and four female judges. The 1959 Code of Personal Status gave women equal political and economic rights and extensive legal protections, so they were full participants in society. (13) The ruling Ba'ath party was secular, and it promulgated laws specifically aimed at improving women's status. It set up the General Federation of Iraqi Women, which coordinated more than 250 urban and rural centers for job training, education, and social programs. Women were granted equal opportunities in the civil service sector, as well as maternity leave and freedom from harassment in the workplace.

Unfortunately, the impressive progress toward women's rights was completely wiped out by the two Gulf Wars. After the first Gulf War, Saddam decided to embrace Islamic and tribal traditions as a political tool in order to consolidate power. (14) Many steps toward women's advancement were reversed—there were changes to the personal status laws and the legal code. (15) As the economy grew worse under the sanctions, women were pushed out of the labor force to ensure employment for men. All state ministries were required to enforce restrictions on women working. Freedom to travel abroad was restricted, and coeducational secondary schools were changed to single-sex only.

In 2005 a new constitution was voted in, with a return to Sharia law in its most conservative interpretation. Women clearly lost ground—the constitution reinstates ancient punishments, forced marriage, and one-sided divorce. Women were discouraged from driving, and most spent their time at home, fearing attacks or kidnapping. Some receive death threats because of their sect or careers. (16)

Shia predominate in the National Assembly. A quota of seats on the Supreme Court, which would weigh the constitutionality of all laws, was set aside for Muslim clerics, but this was suspended because of opposition from women's groups. (17) Women have 25 percent of the seats in the parliament (they lobbied for 40 percent). Islamism has been growing along with anti-American sentiment since the Gulf War. (18) One woman summarized, "We are suffering right now. *The war took all our rights.* We're not free because of terrorism." (19)

In northern Iraq, Kurdish women are even more restricted; they may face abuse in the street if they are not wearing a Hejab. The Human Rights Ministry says that factors that give men authority to oppress women include poverty, lack of education, and traditional customs. (20) The regional government's human-rights minister is trying to sponsor laws to make women more equal to men, promote education about human rights issues, and assert that transgressions against women are not according to Islam. (21)

There are between 750,000 and one million widows in Iraq, and a survey found that three fourths of them are not receiving pensions, because there are simply too many. (22) A women's political party, comprised of twelve women, has a platform built on women's rights and a jobs program for widows, who suffer poverty and unemployment. (23) It is common to see widows begging.

Iraqi women emphasize that they are not trying to replicate Western-style liberation of women. They want rights in the constitution and, more important, they want them applied. In their view, application within the context of Islam is fine, but they seek more liberal interpretations of Sharia law. One political analyst said in 2010, "Iraq is formally advanced, with many female M.P.'s and ministers. But this is only a false bright image. In reality, Iraq is left behind other countries." (24)

By 2010, things were easing up somewhat. Women do not have to wear a Hejab, and many are starting to drive again.

There are about 4.5 million orphans in Iraq. (25) This constitutes the greatest orphan crisis in the history of any Middle East country. There are organizations working with them, as well as mosques and churches, (26) but it is estimated that half a million are on the streets, uncared for and begging or being exploited. The first conference on orphans was held in Baghdad in 2009, (27) and work is also being done by the Iraqi Orphan Foundation. (28) Iraq hosts 220,000 Syrian refugees.

Estimates of Iraqi civilian deaths range from 111,000 (29) to 864,000 (30) to 1,455,000 (31). These are defined as violent deaths caused by the U.S. invasion of 2003, but criteria vary greatly.

Until recently, most Iraqis were determinedly secular. There was little sectarian tension; in fact, people frequently married across Sunni-Shia lines. Now it is doubtful that Iraq will ever again have a secular government. Most Westerners would prefer to see a system that separates church and state. Unfortunately, this has become difficult for Americans to promote when the current trend in the U.S. appears to be mixing faith and government.

We read (unrealistically) optimistic scenarios for Iraq in the future, after the Americans left.†† But without a strong American presence, civil war is ever more likely.

Baghdad is still a beautiful city, with its parks and its broad boulevards, illuminated against the Tigris River at night. It was designed in the eighth century, had a million inhabitants by the tenth century, and was the very heart of Islamic civilization during its Golden Age from the eighth to the thirteenth centuries. There are still traces of the inner city's circular, geometric plan.

Iraq once had one of the highest living standards in the Middle East. It had an educated populace, a relatively small population, and plenty of money. Iraq was filled with universities, museums, libraries, and art galleries. It was a cosmopolitan center of culture, art, and intellect. No longer.

---

†† "Just as significantly, Iraq remains an ally of the United States, an enemy of Al-Qaeda and a force for relative good in the Middle East. . . . The Arab Spring, in short, is making the invasion of Iraq look more worthy—and necessary—than it did a year ago [2010]." (32)

## CHAPTER 16

# THE ARAB COUNTRIES IN THE ARABIAN PENINSULA

The Arabian Peninsula is the homeland of the Semitic Arabian people, in the true ethnic sense. This region has had the least contact with foreigners and is the most conservative in its traditions. In the Peninsula (called Al-Jazeera in Arabic), by law the men wear the long robe and head cloth ("the national dress") on official occasions and at work. Women wear long dresses and add a covering cloak when in public. Veiling (full face cover) is common in this region, but it is not universal. Veiling is required by law only in Saudi Arabia.

The Peninsula can be divided into three distinct regions: Saudi Arabia, Yemen, and the Arabian Gulf states. Saudi Arabia is rich (although less so than before), Yemen is poor, and the Arabian Gulf states are fabulously rich, their societies changing very quickly. Most foreigners particularly love the Gulf states: the people are friendly and hospitable, and although the cities are flamboyantly sleek and modern, with every convenience, there remains a desert-Arab charm and simplicity of values that permeates everything. Many foreigners who come to the Gulf for work quickly try to extend their stay as long as possible.

## ❈ SAUDI ARABIA

Saudi Arabia has always been prominent in the news because of its wealth, its size, and its location. It is a relatively new nation, contains mostly desert, and has a population of 26 million (up from 6 million in 1970). The population growth rate was 1.5 percent in 2001 (down from 6 percent in 1980), (1) and 30 percent of the people are under age fifteen.

Prior to unification in 1935 by King Abdel-Aziz Ibn Saud, the region that is now Saudi Arabia was loosely governed and inhabited by numerous Bedouin tribes. The Hashemites controlled the west coast region (Hejaz), with its port of Jeddah and its holy cities, Mecca and Medina. Ibn Saud conquered the region in 1924 (as well as other areas in the 1920s), and his descendants still rule. Also included in the new nation are the central highlands (the Najd) and the Eastern Province, on the oil coast. Saudi Arabia has evolved into a viable nation since its official founding in 1932, and most of the people say they have a Saudi identity.

Two important elements influence Saudi society: the fact that Arabia was the birthplace of Islam, and the discovery of oil in 1938, which led to sudden wealth. Religiosity, conservatism, wealth, and foreign workers—all of these factors are present in Saudi Arabia and result in ever-changing attitudes and social policies.

Muslim pilgrimages to the holy cities of Mecca and Medina, throughout the year and especially at the annual Hajj Pilgrimage season, are a significant source of income and prestige for the nation; one of the king's titles is "Keeper of the Two Holy Mosques." During the Hajj (in the twelfth Islamic month every year), the entire country is filled with pilgrims, two million from all over the world. There are special airports, camping areas, and health facilities. Saudi Arabia is often referred to as the Holy Land; its Islamic history is central to its identity.

Saudi Arabia is the world's leading producer and exporter of oil, which accounts for 90 percent of its export earnings. Although oil was first produced in 1938, the real effects of wealth were not felt until the 1960s and 1970s. The Saudis' immense wealth has made them influential in the Muslim world, and they are in the forefront of efforts to promote conservative Islam. The proposals of modernizers inside Saudi Arabia are constantly countered by demands from the religious authorities, with whom the government is allied.

Until the 1960s, most of the population was nomadic or seminomadic. Because of rapid economic and urban growth, more than 95 percent of the population is now settled and the people are 82 percent urbanized. Some cities and oases have densities of more than 2,600 people per square mile. Arable land is scarce. Saudi Arabia tapped aquifers and became self-sufficient in wheat in the 1980s, even exporting some. But they are phasing out the program because it uses too much water. (2) Now they have started searching for farmland in countries like Pakistan and Sudan, with the goal of growing crops to be shipped home. (3)

In 2010 there were more than 6 million foreign workers in the Kingdom. (4) This compares with a Saudi workforce of 7.3 million. (5) In 2010, a new law was passed to require foreign workers to wait two years before transferring sponsorship to a new employer; this was done to stabilize the job market. (6) The country's goal is to reduce the number of foreigners to less than 20 percent of the population, or two million, by 2013, but this seems unrealistic, in that much of the youth population lacks the education and technical skills needed by the private sector. (7) The plan is to replace foreigners with Saudis, especially in management positions.

Young university graduates, who were once assured of good positions, are finding that jobs and upward mobility are far less certain because of the number seeking jobs. National income has fallen since the heyday of the 1970s. Unemployment was 11 percent in 2010, and 25 percent for ages fifteen to twenty-four. (8) Every year 200,000 people enter the Saudi workforce. Per capita income in 2010 was a relatively modest $25,000. (9)

The government continues to pursue economic reform and diversification, and to promote foreign investment. King Abdullah has boosted spending on job training and education as part of his reform program. In 2009 he opened the King Abdullah University of Science and Technology, Saudi Arabia's first coeducational university; all religious and ethnic groups are welcome. (10) A record number of Saudi students are studying in the U.S., about 11,000. (11) The government of Saudi Arabia is establishing six "economic cities" in different regions of the country. (12)

King Abdullah is becoming known as a reformer, and he would like to move his reforms even faster. He initiated an Inter-Faith Dialogue in 2008 to encourage religious tolerance on a global level, "the spread of moderation that embodies the Islamic concept of tolerance." (13) In February 2009 he reshuffled the cabinet to increase the number of moderates holding ministerial and judicial positions, and he appointed the first female to the cabinet, Nora al-Faiz, who is the deputy minister of women's education. (14) Saudi Arabia's top religious leadership, the Council of Senior Ulema, issued a fatwa in 2010 denouncing terrorism *and those who finance it*. Much private Saudi money has gone to terrorist groups. (15)

Health and education facilities are both excellent, and they have been supported lavishly. Life expectancy was age forty in 1955; it was age seventy-four in 2011. The entire country is well provided with schools, universities, hospitals, and primary care centers. About 65 percent of the doctors and nurses are foreign. Literacy is 85.5 percent, compared with less than 3 percent in the early 1960s. In universities, 60 percent of the students are women. (16) There is a new women's university, Princess Noura Bint Abdul Rahman University in Riyadh. It is directed by a woman, Her Highness Dr. Hoda Bint Mohamed Al-Ameel.

Saudi Arabia is a welfare state. The government subsidizes food, water, electricity, and other consumer products, and it provides interest-free loans. The government plans to cut subsidies and increase taxes, but with the recent rise in oil prices, it can move more slowly.

In this austere Sunni Wahhabi country, there are two to three million Shia, who make up 8 to 15 percent of the population, and 40 to 50 percent of the population of the Eastern Province. (17) (18) This is a highly sensitive issue, and a census has never been taken. The Shia have had limited employment opportunities; they are rarely accepted into national-security positions, such as the military and the Ministry of Interior. The number of Shia admitted to universities is also restricted, as are the construction of Shia mosques and schools; most are built with private money. No Shia elite has developed.

Many of the skilled and semi-skilled Saudi employees working in the oil industry are Shia, because the oil wealth is in the Eastern Province. In 1979, the Shia rioted, demanding a more equitable share of the money. In 2003, the government initiated a "national dialogue" to give a hearing to minority religious groups. This was after the Shia improved their image with their enthusiastic defense of Saudi Arabia during the Iraqi invasion of Kuwait. (19)

*There is no freedom of religion in Saudi Arabia.* The government prohibits public practice of non-Muslim religions, and there are no non-Muslim places of worship; Christians and others usually meet in private homes.

Saudi Arabia is absolutely unique in the Muslim world in this respect. *Thousands of foreigners who have worked in Saudi Arabia unfortunately assume that all Arab and Muslim governments act the same way.* When you read accounts of events, attitudes toward non-Muslims, treatment of women and the like, keep in mind that if they occurred in Saudi Arabia, they are the exception, not the rule. The Saudi government has always kept tight social control; the press is itself tightly controlled, although these restrictions are being lessened by the Internet and social media.

Alcohol, pork products, "pornography" (pictures of nude paintings or statues, photos of women wearing little clothing, non-Muslim religious pictures), and religious artifacts such as Bibles, crosses, or statues of Buddha are all forbidden. Print materials from abroad are subject to censorship. Even Muslims from other countries need time to adjust to the harsh social control.

Saudi Arabia has by far the most severe restrictions on women in the Middle East, if not the world.* Women are fully veiled in public, in a long black cloak (an *Abaya*). They may not travel alone, leave the country, or take a job without permission from male relatives, and they may not drive cars. Many Muslims from Arab countries and elsewhere find these rules outrageous. Due to protests in June 2011, the government is now considering lifting the ban on driving; when one woman was arrested for driving, the outcry included 30,000 responses. Some women defiantly drove in Riyadh in June 2011, in front of police, who avoided a confrontation. The real problem is the Wahhabi religious authorities. (20) The government is taking steps to increase women's rights, but slowly. In December 2001, women were issued separate identification cards, so now they have a fully legal identity. (21) In 2008, a government decree was issued that allows women to stay in a hotel or rent an apartment alone. (22)

Few women work outside the home (about 17 percent), although they make up more than half of the university graduates. (23) Women who do work usually enter the workforce as professionals: scientists, medical personnel, teachers and professors, and managers in "women's banks." They do not work side-by-side with men, with the exception of some

---

*The Taliban in Afghanistan would institute even more restrictions on women if they took control in Afghanistan.

hospitals. Women now comprise 48 percent of Saudi teachers and 40 percent of Saudi doctors. (24)

The government plans to promote women's employment to replace some foreign workers. As they diversify away from oil, it makes little sense to have almost half of their population staying at home instead of working and contributing. Dr. Maha Almuneef, one of six women appointed in 2009 to the king's Consultative Council (Shura), said, "The King and the political system are saying that the time has come. There are small steps now. There are giant steps coming." (25) Dr. Hanan al-Ahmady, who heads the women's department at the Institute of Public Administration added, "You have to prove that participating in public affairs and taking leadership positions doesn't jeopardize Islamic values and Saudi identity." (26) Many women do not work publicly but own their own businesses, often computing companies and retail stores.

During the uprisings in Arab countries in early 2011, there were modest incidents in some cities, predominantly staged by Shia demonstrators. Other demonstrations, which were minor by comparison, focused on labor and infrastructure complaints, and the government defused the situation by allocating $93 billion for social, educational, and housing aid, on top of the normal budget, and for government-sector jobs and services. (27) Any demonstrations were met with a strong police presence and some arrests. It is noteworthy that groups of women also appeared, calling for release of their imprisoned relatives. (28)

The image of Saudi Arabia to a visitor is one of modern cities with high-rise buildings, huge freeways, luxury shopping malls thronged with people, and fast-food shops, mixed with vistas of the desert, tents, and camels. Saudis like Western consumer goods, and their life continues to change quickly. They are reserved, so they are not quick to welcome foreigners into their private lives, but when they do, they are very generous and hospitable.

## ❀ YEMEN

Yemen, long isolated from outside contact and influences, is one of the most colorful and tradition-oriented countries in the Arab world. It was called "Arabia Felix" by the Romans and was known as the main source of incense.

Social practices in Yemen have changed relatively slowly since modernization programs were introduced in the late 1960s. Much of the country is rugged and mountainous, and outside of the cities it is a land of tribes and guns. Many of Yemen's 24 million people live in some 150,000 remote villages; (1) only 32 percent of the people are in urban areas. Yemen's architecture is traditional and distinctive, mainly stone-mud high-rise buildings decorated with white geometric designs. It is the poorest country in the Arab world, but it is spectacularly beautiful, with its mountains, valleys, and terraced hillsides. Unlike the rest of the Peninsula, Yemen has a temperate climate.

For three hundred years, from the eighteenth century to 1990, Yemen was divided into two separate nations, North Yemen and South Yemen (formerly Aden). The king of North Yemen was deposed in 1962; the current regime has been in power since 1976. Aden became independent of Britain in 1967 and was ruled by pro-Soviet Marxists beginning in 1971. In 1990 the two countries united under a broadly socialist government. Since the union, numerous clashes have occurred, including a civil war in mid-1994, when the south tried to break away from the dominant north. Another region is the arid Hadramaut, the long coast along the southern rim of the Arabian Peninsula. It still produces incense.

In 1993 Yemen conducted the only fully free elections ever held in the Arabian Peninsula. President Ali Abdullah Saleh was elected, for a term of seven years, after which he retained power. The last Parliamentary elections were held in 2003; those scheduled for 2009 and early 2014 were postponed.

Beginning in January 2011, there were repeated massive demonstrations against the government, which responded with force, killing hundreds. The protesters' complaints include high unemployment, poor economic conditions, and corruption, and this escalated to calls for the president's removal. In June 2011 the presidential compound was shelled and the president injured. He went to Saudi Arabia for treatment, but returned some months later and resisted giving up power. In late 2011 he agreed to step down and place power with his vice president, Abed Rabbo Mansour Hadi, who established a unity government after elections in 2012 (Saleh still has considerable influence). A goal is to work toward a democracy and a new constitution. But Yemen remains deeply divided, by

Islamists, loyalists to the former regime, the military, and various militias, and violence continues. In collaboration with the Yemeni government, the U.S. has used drone airstrikes against some militants affiliated with Al-Qaeda, especially in the south. Yemen may well be headed toward more chaos, as Al-Qaeda affiliates repeatedly attack the army. A food shortage has developed in the country.

The Yemeni government has long been under pressure to assert control over terrorism; a notable event was the bombing of the *U.S.S. Cole* in 2000. Government control is limited though—there are thousands of miles of unpatrolled coast, and another thousand miles of wide-open frontier. (2) Yemen has been listed as a haven for terrorists, and Al-Qaeda has a strong presence there, especially in the southern areas where the government has little authority. In late 2009 the government deported many foreign Muslims, closed down religious schools, and started a public campaign against extremism, (3) although extremism continues to be strong.

In the north, the most notable division is between Sunni Muslims and the Zaidi (Shia) sect, which dates to the thirteenth century; each group has well-defined geographic boundaries. Shia make up about 36 percent of the population, compared with 63 percent Sunnis. (4)

Yemenis speak Arabic, including some unusual, isolated dialects in remote areas, and educated Yemenis speak English. Traditional Yemeni men wear distinctive dress, a sarong-like skirt and a wide belt in which they place the traditional dagger (*jambiyya*). Traditional women are completely covered in a black cloak.

The climate of Yemen has made intensive agriculture possible, much of it on terraced land, but only 2.9 percent of the land is arable. Cotton and coffee are sources of revenue. In fact, the first coffee in Europe was imported from Yemen, probably through the port of Mocha. Traditional skills include construction and stonemasonry, carpentry, and metalworking. Before the first Gulf War of 1991, many thousands of Yemenis worked abroad, and their wages strengthened the nation's economy. After the war, however, Saudi Arabia expelled 800,000 Yemenis because the Yemeni government supported Iraq, with serious economic consequences—income fell by one fourth. Today, unemployment is estimated at 35 percent, and 45 percent of the people live in poverty. (5)

The former South Yemen has a semi-arid climate, and the people have traditionally been fishermen and merchants (in the coastal area), as well as farmers and herders. The south's geographical location has been advantageous for commerce with countries of the Indian Ocean.

Yemen's great hope for the future was once oil, first exported in 1993. In 2000, oil constituted nearly 97 percent of total exports; in 2011, the percentage dropped to 60 percent. (6) Oil resources are declining and two major fields will be drained in ten years. (7) The government began a program to diversify the economy in 2006. In 2009 Yemen exported its first liquefied natural gas as part of this diversification effort. (8) About 1.3 million Yemenis work abroad, and in 2010 they sent home 1.5 billion dollars, up from 1.3 billion dollars in 2009. (9) This constitutes an important part of Yemen's economy, accounting for 5.2 percent of its GDP. Yemen also depends on foreign aid.

Yemen faces a problem of inadequate water, especially in the capital city of Sanaa, which may run dry by 2015. (10) Groundwater is becoming less, and the rural economy could disappear within a generation. (11) Yemen's water comes 99 percent from illegal wells (not government-controlled), and the water is seriously mismanaged. Yemen cannot afford desalinization, and other methods have not been successful. The price of trucked water, which 70 percent of the people in Sanaa rely upon, has tripled since 2005. (12)

Productivity and prosperity are also affected by the social custom, mostly among men, of chewing a leaf called *Qat*, which produces a feeling of mild euphoria. *Qat* is chewed every day, beginning in the early afternoon. Unfortunately, much fertile land is devoted to growing this plant and it consumes more than half of Yemen's scarce water. (13)

Health programs are growing; nonetheless, Yemen's health facilities are among the least developed in the Arab world. Infant mortality is still very high, 55 per thousand births, and life expectancy is only age sixty-four. In general, sanitation is poor and awareness of general health practices low. Health care is also hampered by a severe shortage of qualified practitioners, particularly in rural areas, and 58 percent of the children are malnourished. (14)

Yemen also faces a severe problem in its population growth. It was estimated at 2.6 percent per year in 2011, and the fertility rate is 4.6

children per woman. (15) The population tripled since 1980, and it will triple again by 2060. Fully 43 percent of the people are under age fifteen. Yemen also hosts more than 250,000 Somali refugees, as well as 350,000 internal refugees fleeing from fighting in the north. (16)

Education is improving. It accounted for 33 percent of the government's expenditure in 2011. Attendance at elementary school is 62 percent, and fewer girls are enrolled than boys. (17) Total literacy is 33 percent, but literacy for ages fifteen to twenty-four is 50 percent. The government maintains an adult education program.

Traditional women in north Yemen are fully veiled in public and many are uneducated. Only 7 percent over-all work outside the home for pay; of those, 21 percent of the working women have secondary degrees and 48 percent have a university degree. (18) Younger women, especially if unmarried, are interested in pursuing a career and want equality with men. They also want political participation (19). In former South Yemen, women were granted equal status under the then-Marxist government and they were recruited into many work fields. Women in southern Yemen are more integrated into society than in any other Arabian Peninsula country.

There are good-quality programs in place for foreign students to study Arabic, but this has been drastically affected by the protests. Westerners find Yemen to be fascinating and charming.

Yemenis are admired for their industriousness and skills. They are friendly and very accommodating to foreigners.

## ❀ THE ARABIAN GULF STATES (PERSIAN GULF)

The five Arabian Gulf states—Kuwait, Bahrain, Qatar, the United Arab Emirates (UAE), and Oman—are situated along the eastern coast of the Arabian Peninsula. Most were under British administration until 1971.

These countries, as well as Saudi Arabia, are joined in the Gulf Cooperative Council (GCC), which promotes economic integration in the region. Income is high and population is low, but the latter is rapidly increasing. Citizens pay no income taxes or import taxes, and for citizens corporate taxes are non-existent or very low. Most countries can afford to generously subsidize many of the people's living costs.

This is a dramatic change from the poverty of the past. The traditional sources of income had been trade, herding, fishing, pearling, and piracy. Everything has been turned upside down in the last fifty to sixty years.

Although this is the most conservative region of the Arab world (along with Saudi Arabia), women serve as ministers in the governments. This is the situation in 2011:

❖ ❖ ❖ ❖ ❖ ❖ ❖ ❖ ❖ ❖ ❖ ❖ ❖ ❖ ❖ ❖ ❖ ❖ ❖ ❖ ❖ ❖ ❖ ❖

## WOMEN'S MINISTERS IN GOVERNMENTS (1)

| Kuwait | 1 woman and 23 men |
|--------|--------------------|
| Bahrain | 2 women and 24 men |
| Qatar | 1 woman and 20 men |
| UAE | 2 women and 21 men |
| Oman | 2 women and 36 men |

Many American and British universities are opening branches in the Gulf states: in Abu Dhabi, Dubai, Sharjah and Ras Al-Khaymah in the UAE; and in Kuwait, Bahrain, Qatar, and Oman. (1)

## Kuwait

Although Kuwait is small, it is an important country, mostly because of its vast oil wealth, which is the basis of its economic and political influence among the Arab states. It gained its independence from Britain in 1961 and has since been ruled by the Al Sabah royal family. Kuwait has had a National Assembly and parliamentary elections off and on since 1962, most recently in 2009. Power lies in the hands of the ruler, the Emir, Shaikh Sabah Al-Ahmad Al Sabah, who has suspended the Assembly numerous times over the years. Islamists won more than half of the fifty seats in the National Assembly in 2008, which was then dissolved and new elections called. (1) In 2009 elections, four women won seats in the Assembly; women were first allowed to run for office in 2006. (2) At this time, the parliament is one of the strongest in the Gulf.

In November 2011, protesters stormed the parliament, angered at allegations of high-level corruption; these grievances have been present for years. The ruler ordered tighter security in the nation and threatened arrests. (3)

There are about 2.5 million people in Kuwait, of whom the majority are non-Kuwaitis. Until the first Gulf War in 1991, about 450,000 Palestinians lived in Kuwait, but at that time they were expelled, so there are fewer than 40,000 Palestinians in Kuwait today. Many expatriates are from the U.S., Britain, and South Asia. Kuwaitis make up about 45 percent percent of the population in the country, and other Arabs about 35 percent. (4) The government has prioritized replacing foreign workers with Kuwaitis in professional and managerial jobs.

In many ways Kuwaiti society is like other Gulf states and Saudi Arabia: it is tribal, religious, and conservative. About 65 percent of the Kuwaitis are Sunni, and 35 percent are Shia. Their practice of Islam is not as austere as that in Saudi Arabia.

The dominant fact of life in Kuwait is the government's enormous oil-based wealth; oil sales are 95 percent of government income. (5) Kuwait has the reputation of being the shrewdest and most sophisticated of the major Arab overseas investors, and per capita income is one of the highest in the world. Production of oil began in 1946, and within fifteen years poverty was virtually eradicated. (6) Like Saudi Arabia, Kuwait is a welfare state.

Another factor that will dominate Kuwaiti affairs for many years is the Iraqi invasion of 1990, followed by the first Gulf War. Although the economic effects have largely been overcome, the psychological consequences will be felt for a generation.

Kuwait cooperated with the U.S. in the second Gulf War, and when the U.S. invaded Iraq in 2003, Kuwait was the main staging area for military preparations. At one point in early 2005, there were 30,000 American military personnel in the country. It is likely that more U.S. troops will be in Kuwait after American withdrawal from Iraq. (7) The Kuwaitis are the most pro-American in the Arab world; they still feel gratitude for their liberation. Even they have been shaken by recent events (Palestine, Iraq, Afghanistan), however, and many are beginning to reconsider their unqualified political support.

Progress in health, education, infrastructure, and economic development has completely changed the Kuwaiti way of life in the last sixty years. Kuwait City is modern and filled with malls, high-rise buildings, and expensive compounds. The people are 98 percent urbanized. The literacy rate is now 95 percent. Health care is superb. Kuwaitis have everything money can buy.

Virtually all water comes from seawater desalinization plants, an expenditure impossible for governments with less money and more people. The government encourages large families, and the birth rate is 2.6 children per woman; 26 percent of the population is under age fourteen.

Women in Kuwait are the most emancipated in the Gulf region. (8) They are generally veiled in public, although this is easing up. Many are active in education and commerce. They are not prohibited from working in the same environment as men. Women currently receive two-thirds of the bachelor's degrees granted each year. About half of them work.

Kuwaiti women can travel, drive, or work without male permission, and they can hold senior government positions. They may work at night, which was previously forbidden. (9) They attained the right to vote in 2005. They are, however, restrained by Islamic law, although some issues are governed by civil or administrative courts.

Kuwaitis are cordial to foreigners, although they prefer private and family social circles.

## Bahrain

Bahrain, which is an island in the Arabian Gulf, dominated the news in early 2011 because of a Shia uprising that demanded a new constitution, release of Shia prisoners, and an end to discrimination by the Sunni government. The uprising was put down by force, with the assistance of the Saudi Arabian military. The state of emergency was lifted in June 2011, and most foreign troops withdrew. (1)

In March, the royal family promised a National Dialogue with the opposition to implement political reforms. The assembly convened in the summer; the government allowed the opposition only five out of the assembly's 300 seats. Most of the opposition walked out when some items were omitted from the agenda (such as reforming parliamentary districts) and the assembly recommended increased powers to the hard-line Prime Minister. Many workers have not been rehired by the government, and many political prisoners remain in jail. Tensions are still present between the Sunni government and the Shia majority. (2)

Bahrain got very bad press when, in September 2011, it handed down harsh jail sentences to twenty doctors and nurses who had aided injured protesters. (3) In November an independent commission reported that human rights abuses occurred during suppression of the uprisings earlier in the year. (4) There are calls to reinstate workers removed from government and university jobs. Some call for a constitutional monarchy.

Bahrain's Muslims are 70 percent Shia, 30 percent Sunni. It is noteworthy that in the elections of 2006 and 2010, the Shia candidates were elected as a majority in the Chamber of Deputies. (5) In the total population of Bahrain, 81 percent are Muslim and 9 percent are Christian; 10 percent are other religions.

Bahrain is the most modernized of the Gulf states. It was the first to produce oil, and its production and refining bring in about 70 percent of the nation's income, but supplies are declining. In response, Bahrain has worked to create one of the most diversified economies in the Gulf region. Its other industries now include dry-dock ship services, aluminum production, and light engineering. Bahrain's development as a major financial center has been the most widely heralded aspect of its diversification effort; it also has excellent tourist facilities. Bahrain entered into a Free Trade Agreement with the U.S. in 2006. (6) It is the headquarters of the U.S. Navy's Fifth Fleet.

Bahrain imports almost all its food; agriculture represents less than 1 percent of its income. The land is almost entirely desert, and the people traditionally made their living from the sea.

Bahrain's population is 1.2 million. It is 89 percent urbanized, which makes it one of the most densely populated countries in the Middle East; most of the people live in two principal cities—Manama (the capital) and Riffa. In 2010, the number of foreigners was greater than the number of citizens: 54 percent. This has brought calls for limiting the influx of foreigners, who are mostly from South and East Asia (84 percent), as well as from the U.S. and Britain. (7) Unemployment among the young is far higher than the official overall 3.7 percent unemployment rate, and it is also higher among the Shia. In 2010, the Ministry of Labor undertook a "university graduates project" to help these graduates find work, and it also is attempting to improve the quality of job vacancies for all of the unemployed. (8)

Bahrain was a British protectorate from 1861 until its independence in 1971. It was ruled by a Sunni emir, now king, and it elected its first parliament in 1973. In 1975 the National Assembly attempted to legislate the end of the Al Khalifa's rule and also to expel the U.S. Navy. The emir dissolved the National Assembly, and in 1992 he appointed a Consultative Council (Shura), which has forty members. There have been incidents since the 1990s stemming from the disaffection of the Shia majority.

In February 2002, the current ruler, Shaikh Hamad, pronounced Bahrain a constitutional monarchy (rather than a heredity emirate) and changed his status from emir to king. The first elections in nearly thirty years were held at that time, with women being allowed to vote and run for office.

Bahrain's small size and population have contributed to its rapid modernization. Life expectancy is age seventy-eight. Literacy is 91 percent. Bahrain is working to establish itself as a center for higher education, and it has two universities. With the events in early 2011, Bahrain lost some of its luster as a center for promoting arts and culture, and some international events were moved elsewhere. International image is important to Bahrain's economy, and it has been damaged. (9)

Bahraini men generally wear a robe and head cover. Women may appear in a black cloak, but it is common to see foreign as well as local women wearing modern (but modest) clothing as well. (10)

Bahraini women, many of whom are well educated, constitute about 29 percent of the workforce, up from 17 percent in 1991.

Bahrain is a favorite tourist destination in the Gulf. It is connected to the mainland by a causeway to Saudi Arabia. It is relatively liberal and has an active nightlife.

## Qatar

Qatar (pronounced KA-tar) is a small peninsula, fabulously rich in both oil and gas; it is one of the richest countries in the world. The population is 96 percent urbanized, and 80 percent of the people live in the capital city, Doha. Since the discovery of oil in 1949, Qatar's population has exploded: 100,000 in 1970, 350,000 in 1991, and 840,000 in 2011. But these numbers are high because 60 percent of the residents are foreigners, who comprise 80 to 90 percent of the workforce. There are about 300,000 native Qatari citizens.

Until the discovery of oil, the Qatari people were engaged in fishing, pearling, and trading, many living in dire poverty. The ruling family signed a treaty with Britain in 1868, and it was a British protectorate from 1916 until it gained independence in 1971. The constitution was overwhelmingly approved by referendum in 2003. Qatar is an emirate with no legislative body yet, but elections for a Consultative Council are scheduled for 2012. The emir has an Advisory Council, and in May 2011 the fourth municipal elections were held. (1)

Oil, gas, and derivative products bring in 85 percent of export earnings, and in 2010 Qatar had the world's highest GDP per capita; the economy grew by 19.4 percent. (2) In November 2011 the government announced pay and benefits hikes of 60 percent for public employees and up to 120 percent for some military officers. (3)

Although only a little over 1 percent of the land is arable, Qatar produces half of the vegetables it consumes, in open fields and greenhouses. Many people maintain large herds of goats, sheep, camels, and cattle in the desert, and fishing is still a mainstay.

Health programs are numerous and lavishly funded, and life expectancy is now age seventy-six. Qatar had a phenomenal population growth rate of over 6 percent annually between 1990 and 1998, and the government encourages large families. 23 percent of the people are under age fourteen. (4) The average is 2.4 children per woman.

Qatar is pushing education strongly. Through the Qatar Foundation, an initiative sponsored by the ruler's wife, Sheikha Mozah bint Nasser Al-Missned, Qatar hosts several American universities and many training institutes, so that fewer of its students have to study abroad. Literacy is 89 percent. Unemployment is only 0.5 percent.

The population of Qatar is 80 percent Muslim, 6 percent Christian, and 14 percent other religions. Of the Muslims, 86 percent are Sunni and 14 percent Shia. There has been no sectarian tension.

Qatar is comparatively liberal, certainly in comparison with Saudi Arabia. Women can drive, and many are well educated. They make up about 36 percent of the workforce. Most families have no need for a second income. Women usually cover in a black cloak when in public, but they are free to dress otherwise. Women first voted in 1999 and can run for elective office. There is a strong emphasis on equality and human rights, and there is a National Human Rights Committee. This does not pertain to Third-World laborers, however, who have little protection and poor living conditions.

The ruler increased freedom of the press in 1998, ending censorship, and has generously funded the extremely successful Al-Jazeera satellite television channel. The government does not regulate its content.

Qatar has strong military ties with the U.S. It is the location of the Central Command's Forward Headquarters and the Combined Air Operations Center.

The social organization in Qatar is still tribal and strongly family-centered; many people live in compounds that hold several related families. Qataris are friendly to foreigners, who enjoy the country and the society.

## The United Arab Emirates (UAE)

The United Arab Emirates is a federation of small territories that was created as an independent nation in 1971–1972 by uniting seven of the Trucial States (so called by the British, to replace the infamous name "Pirate Coast"). The combined population is 5 million. UAE citizens comprise about 20 percent of the population and the rest are foreign workers, and 40 percent of them live in Abu Dhabi. Dubai is the largest city in the Emirates, with a population of 1.7 million. The country is 88 percent urbanized.

Abu Dhabi is by far the largest of the former territories, comprising 87 percent of the UAE's total area. Abu Dhabi is the capital city, and Dubai is the main port and has become a prosperous commercial center for the whole Gulf region. Dubai created the Dubai International Financial Centre, intended to become a regional center on a par with New York and London. (1) It is also known for some whimsical expenditures, such as an indoor ski slope and the tall Burj Al-Arab tower.

Abu Dhabi began oil production in 1962, Dubai in 1969, and Sharjah in 1973. Life has been transformed since then: former fishing villages are now modern cities filled with high-rise buildings and superhighways. The other four small emirates (Ajman, Umm Al-Qaiwain, Ras Al-Khaimah, and Fujairah), each with a small population, have no oil and are changing more slowly. Still, the entire country has been transformed.

Per capita income is the second highest in the Gulf, after Qatar. Oil and natural gas account for more than 85 percent of the government's revenues, but it is diversifying the economy too, into construction, manufacturing (metals and textiles), and a large services sector. Previously, people made their living from fishing, pearling, oasis-farming, and animal herding. Abu Dhabi and Dubai are the only emirates that contribute to the UAE's finances. (2) Despite the prosperity, nearly 20 percent of the citizens are below the poverty line. (3) All the emirates earn income through the sale of exotic postage stamps.

Ambitious programs have been established in education, health, and agricultural production. Literacy is 90 percent, and life expectancy is age seventy-five. (4) The growth rate is 3.2 percent annually, with an average of 2.4 children per woman. (5) The society is still traditional and conservative, although the legal system is quite liberal, using secular law for all civil and commercial matters, Islamic law only for family and religious issues. The UAE's moderate foreign policy has made it a leader in the region.

Women in the UAE are veiled in public and most participate little in public life, but this will change with the next generation because women's education through university is strongly encouraged by the government; 70 percent of eligible women attend university. Statistics for women are impressive. (6) Women are currently 38 percent of the workforce and constitute 65 percent of the teachers and 15 percent of the professorial staff at UAE University. There are four women in the UAE Cabinet, the largest number in the Arab world. There is a female judge, and two women are ambassadors (to Sweden and Spain). Women make up 66 percent of the government workforce and hold 30 percent of the senior jobs. Women have joined the Armed Forces, the police, and the customs agency. The Businesswomen's Council has 12,000 members, managing 11,000 investments. Women make up 37.5 percent of the workforce in the banking sector.

Despite these numbers, women still do not have the right to vote, although pressure is definitely growing. It is a precedent that Kuwaiti women, after protests, gained the right to vote in 2005 and Saudi women were granted the vote in 2011. UAE women point out that they are the only Arab country without this right.

There are many universities in the UAE, including American and British institutions; it seems that everyone is getting on the bandwagon. There is the American University of Sharjah, and branches of other universities in Abu Dhabi and Dubai. The average length of schooling in the UAE is thirteen years, higher than elsewhere in the Arab world. The UAE is working to create more opportunities for its nationals to enter private-sector employment. Unemployment is just 2.4 percent. A controversial issue at present is how to balance teaching in Arabic and English; Arabic is the heritage but 30 percent of the university's budget is used for remedial English courses—English is essential for technical subjects. (7)

The UAE is known for tolerance; there are thirty-one churches in the country, as well as Hindu and Sikh temples. The constitution guarantees equal rights, and many Hindus and Sikhs have moved there to escape persecution elsewhere. (8) The country is 80 percent Sunni Muslim, 16 percent Shia, and 4 percent Christian and Hindu.

About one hundred Emirati activists and intellectuals made a petition in March 2011 that called for political reform, including the establishment of a parliament and the expansion of the electorate. In April, four activists were arrested for these criticisms of the government. All seven emirates are ruled autocratically.

During the world economic downturn of 2009–2010, Dubai was hard hit by depressed real estate prices, and it lacked sufficient cash to meet debt obligations. In December 2009 Dubai received a $10 billion loan from Abu Dhabi, and the economy is expected to continue a slow rebound. (9)

The UAE depends heavily on foreign workers, who comprise 99 percent of the work force, two thirds of them from South Asia. (10) After a walkout staged by thousands of laborers in Dubai in 2006, the government has regulated mid-day breaks (because of the heat), and improved health benefits and living conditions. The Labor Ministry even paid back wages when companies did not. The government is working to upgrade labor standards. (11)

The UAE has been a major contributor of emergency relief to regions in need, especially in Africa. The Abu Dhabi Fund for Development was established in 1971 and has since provided $45 billion in aid. (12)

Western foreigners enjoy living in the UAE, and many have been there for many years.

## Oman

Oman is situated in the southeast corner of the Arabian Peninsula, in a very strategic location at the entrance to the Arabian Gulf. It is larger than the other Gulf countries, but not as rich. Oman is ruled by a sultan and is a monarchy.

Oman's population is about three million, of whom 20 percent are foreigners (over half of them from southern India). The Omani citizens are 85 percent Arabians, and the rest are of Zanzibari, Baluchi, or of South Asian and African origin. (1) The people are 75 percent Ibadhi Muslim (a sect that is neither Sunni nor Shia), and 25 percent other Muslim or Hindu. Almost everyone speaks Arabic; some non-Arabic Semitic languages are still spoken in the far south. Tribalism is the main source of identity for the Omani people.

Oman has had ties with Britain since 1891, although it was not formally a protectorate. The British came in because of piracy, and they were a strong presence until 1971.

The discovery of oil in 1967 exacerbated the people's impatience with the old sultan, who was reactionary and oppressive: and the Omani people were beset with poverty, disease, illiteracy, and social restrictions, including a prohibition against smoking and against travel inside the country. All this had caused 600,000 people to go into exile. In 1970 the sultan was deposed by his British-educated son Qaboos, who still rules and is popular. He began the extensive modernization of the country.

Oman has seen dramatic changes in health, education, and commercial development. Electricity, telephones, radio, television, public education, roads, hospitals, public health programs—all are new since 1970. The U.N. Development Program (UNDP) listed Oman as the most-improved nation over the last forty years from among 135 countries worldwide. (2)

Oman does not have extensive oil reserves like its Gulf neighbors, and supplies are dwindling—oil accounted for 70 percent of export earnings in 2005. (3) There was a drop to 51 percent of revenues from oil in early 2009. (4) Unlike elsewhere in the Gulf, about 30 percent of the people work in oasis agriculture and in fishing; Oman is only 73 percent urbanized. Although Oman has a considerable amount of potentially arable land, it lacks manpower and water. In some remote interior areas, the people have little contact with the rest of the country. Agriculture accounts for only 1 percent of the country's exports.

The sultan has instituted a development plan called "Vision 2020" that calls for diversification of the economy by the year 2020, two years before oil resources are estimated to run out. (5) The key ideas are diversification, industrialization, and privatization. (6) There is much ongoing domestic and foreign investment in the non-oil sector; industry is the cornerstone, and private-sector participation is encouraged. Tourism is also being promoted. Oman entered a free-trade agreement with the U.S. in January 2009.

The government has given high priority to education, to develop a domestic workforce, essential for Oman's economic and social progress. Sultan Qaboos University was opened in 1996, and there are many colleges of technology, science, finance, and nursing. Scholarships are also awarded for study abroad. In 2004, 70 percent of the university students were women, and 23 percent of the women are in the workforce. Literacy is 87 percent (up from 18 percent in 1970), and the expected length of schooling is twelve years. Unemployment was 15 percent in 2004 (latest figures).

Because of improved health care, Oman's growth rate has been truly amazing. The population tripled between 1965 and 1990, and it is increasing about 2 percent per year (down from 5.3 percent in 1980). Thirty-one percent of the population is under age fourteen. The average is 2.8 children per woman (down from 7.8 in 1987). Life expectancy is seventy-four years. Health care is free.

The sultan rules alone, with an appointed advisory cabinet and an elected advisory council, and there are no political parties. Two women were elected to seats in 2003. (7) There is also a Consultative Council, established in 1981, which is advisory, with members appointed from the government, the private sector, and regional interests (including nine women). (8) The country has three female ministers, and two women ambassadors (to the Netherlands and the U.S.). (9)

During the uprisings across the Arab world in early 2011, some Omanis also demonstrated, and there was a month-long sit-in on the Globe Roundabout, which was finally cleared by force. Protesters were demanding economic benefits, an end to corruption, and greater political rights. The sultan pledged to create more government jobs and implement economic and political reforms. (10) There are also activists who want a rule of law, freedom of speech, and political institutions such as a functioning legislature. (11)

Elections were held in October 2011 for the Consultative Council, and there was a record turnout. One woman was elected, out of the seventy-seven members.

Oman is a delightful country for foreigners, and the people are warm and welcoming.

# CONCLUSION

The more you socialize and interact with Arabs, the sooner you will abandon your stereotyped impressions of them. Individuals behave differently, but patterns emerge if you look for them. Soon you will be able to understand and even predict actions and reactions, some of which may be different from what you expected. Your task is to become aware of how and why things happen in order to feel comfortable with new social patterns as soon as possible.

Arab culture is complex but not unfathomable or totally exotic; many people find it similar to life in the Mediterranean area and Latin America.* Arabs are demonstrative, emotional, and full of zest for life, while at the same time bound by stringent rules and social expectations. Westerners need not feel obliged to imitate Arabs in order to be accepted. All that is necessary for harmonious relations is to be nonjudgmental and to avoid any actions that are insulting or shocking. Westerners, especially Americans, are accustomed to being open and up-front with beliefs and feelings. This forthrightness needs to be tempered when operating in the tradition-bound culture of the Middle East.

Arabs are accustomed to dealing with foreigners and expect them to behave and dress differently and to have different ideas from themselves. Foreigners are forgiven a great deal; even conservative people make allowances, particularly when they trust your motives. The essential thing is to

---

*This is due, in part, to the fact that the Arabs ruled Spain for the seven centuries preceding the discovery of the New World.

make a sincere, well-meaning effort to adapt and understand. This attitude is readily apparent and will go a long way in helping you form comfortable work relations and friendships. Perhaps you will find yourself on good enough terms with an Arab friend to ask for constructive criticism from time to time. If you do, tactful hints will be offered—listen for them.

Most Arabs are genuinely interested in foreigners and enjoy talking to and developing friendships with them. But their attitude toward Westerners is a mixture of awe, goodwill, and puzzled wariness. They admire Westerners' education and expertise, and most of them have heard favorable reports from others who have visited Western countries. Many Arabs express the hope that they can visit or study in the West, and in some countries, travel and immigration to Western countries are popular.

At the same time Arabs feel that Western societies are too liberal in many ways and that Westerners are not careful enough about their personal and social appearance. Arabs have a great deal of pride and are easily hurt; thus, they are sensitive to any display of arrogance by Westerners and to implied criticisms. They also disapprove of and resent Western political policies in the Arab world.

Moving to an Arab country or interacting with Arabs need not be a source of anxiety. If you use common sense, make an effort to be considerate, and apply your knowledge of Arab customs and traditions, it will be easy to conduct yourself in a way which reflects creditably on your background and home country. At the same time, you will have a rich and rewarding experience.

# The Arabic Language

Learning Arabic is indispensable for gaining a real insight into Arab society and culture. If you intend to study Arabic, you should choose the type that suits your own needs best.

Arabs associate foreign learners of Arabic with scholars, who (in the past) have tended to concentrate on Classical Arabic, so if you ask an Arab to give you lessons in Arabic, he or she will usually want to start with the alphabet and emphasize reading. If your interest is mainly in learning spoken Arabic, you will have to make that clear from the outset.

When you speak Arabic, you will find that your use of even the simplest phrases, no matter how poorly pronounced, will produce an immediate smile and comment of appreciation. I have had literally hundreds of occasions on which my willingness to converse in Arabic led to a delightful experience. A typical example occurred once when I was shopping in a small town in Lebanon and spent about half an hour chatting with the owner of one of the shops. When I was about to leave, he insisted on giving me a small brass camel, "because you speak Arabic."

Arabs are flattered by your efforts to learn their language (although they are convinced that no foreigner can ever master it), and they will do everything to encourage you. Even just a little Arabic is a useful tool for forming friendships and demonstrating goodwill.

## ❈ Colloquial Arabic Dialects

The Arabic dialects fall into five geographical categories:

| Category | Dialects | Native or Other Language Influence |
|---|---|---|
| 1. North African (Western Arabic) | Moroccan Algerian Tunisian Libyan Mauretanian | Berber |
| 2. Egyptian/Sudanese | Egyptian Sudanese | Turkish, Coptic, Nilotic |
| 3. Levantine | Lebanese Syrian Palestinian | Local Semitic languages (Aramaic, Phoenician, Canaanite) |
| 4. Arabian Peninsular | Jordanian Saudi Yemeni Kuwaiti Bahraini Qatari Emirates (Emirati) Omani | Farsi (in the Gulf states), Bedouin dialects, South Arabian languages |
| 5. Iraqi* | Iraqi | Local Semitic languages (Assyrian, Chaldean) Farsi, Turkish |

*Iraqi is essentially a non-urban dialect, with three distinct varieties, similar to both Jordanian and Kuwaiti Arabic.

Speakers of dialects in two of the categories—Egyptian/Sudanese and Levantine—have relatively little difficulty being understood. The North African, Iraqi, and Arabian Peninsular dialects, however, are relatively difficult for other Arabs to understand.

The most noticeable differences among dialects occur in the vocabulary, although there are grammatical discrepancies too. These variations should be taken into account when you are choosing a dialect to study, since it is almost useless to study a dialect different from the one spoken in the country to which you are going.

Simple words and phrases, such as greetings, vary widely, while technical and erudite words are usually the same. Educated Arabs get around this problem by using classical words, but a foreigner is more likely to experience each dialect as a different language. The following are examples of differences among dialects.

## SLIGHTLY DIFFERENT

|  | Egyptian | Saudi | Moroccan |
|---|---|---|---|
| paper | wara'a | waraga | werqa |

|  | Jordanian | Moroccan | Egyptian |
|---|---|---|---|
| beautiful | jameela | jmila | gameela |

|  | Saudi | Tunisian | Lebanese |
|---|---|---|---|
| heavy | tageel | thaqeel | ti'eel |

## COMPLETELY DIFFERENT

|  | Lebanese | Egyptian | Iraqi | Tunisian |
|---|---|---|---|---|
| How are you? | keefak? | izzayyak? | shlownak? | shniyya hwalik? |

|  | Moroccan | Egyptian | Jordanian | Saudi |
|---|---|---|---|---|
| now | daba | dilwa'ti | halla' | daheen |

|  | Lebanese | Kuwaiti | Moroccan | Egyptian |
|---|---|---|---|---|
| good | mneeh | zayn | mezyan | kwayyis |

## Attitudes Toward Dialects

Arabs tend to regard their own dialect as the purest and the closest to Classical Arabic; I have heard this claim vigorously defended from Morocco to Iraq. In fact, though, where one dialect is closer to the Classical with respect to one feature, another dialect is closer with respect to another. No dialect can be successfully defended as pure except possibly the Najdi dialect spoken in central Arabia, which has been the most isolated from non-Arabic influences.

Arabs view the Bedouin dialects as semiclassical and therefore admirable, although a bit archaic. Most Arabs find the Egyptian dialect to be the most pleasing to listen to because the pronunciation is "light." Eastern

Arabs tend to look down on western Arabic (North African) because of their difficulty in understanding the dialect (which they attribute, wrongly, to Berber usages). Most of the differences between western and eastern Arabic stem from changes in pronunciation and word stress.

Because all Arabs view their local dialect as the best, they are quick to advise a foreigner that theirs is the most useful, but usefulness depends entirely on where you are in the Arab world.

## ✸ THE STRUCTURE OF ARABIC

The structure of Arabic is like that of all Semitic languages. Its most striking feature is the way words are formed, which is called the "root and pattern" system. A root is a set of three consonants that carry the meaning of the word. The vowels in a word form patterns and, depending on how they are intermixed with the consonants, determine the part of speech of a word. The consonants and vowels have different functions in a word, and together their combinations yield a rich vocabulary. Here are some examples from Classical Arabic, distinguishing roots and patterns (patterns may contain affixes—additional syllables added at the beginning, in the middle, or at the end of words).

|            |              | **Meaning**                          |
|------------|--------------|--------------------------------------|
| Roots:     | k-t-b        | writing                              |
|            | r-k-b        | riding                               |
| Patterns:  | -a-(a)-a (i) | (completed action, past tense)       |
|            | -aa-i-       | agent (one who does an action)       |
|            | ma—a-        | place (where the action is done)     |
| Words:     | kataba       | he wrote                             |
|            | rakiba       | he rode                              |
|            | kaatib       | writer, clerk                        |
|            | raakib       | rider                                |
|            | maktab       | (place for writing) office, desk     |
|            | markab       | (place for riding) boat              |
|            | markaba      | vehicle                              |

As you learn vocabulary, you will notice that words that have the same core meaning come in varying patterns, but almost all can be reduced to a three-consonant base. For example, other words that share the consonants *k-t-b* are

| | |
|---|---|
| kitaab | book |
| kitaaba | writing |
| maktaba | library, bookstore |
| maktuub | letter, something written, fate |

Personal names in Arabic usually have a meaning. Below is a group of names from the same three-consonant base, *h-m-d*, which means "to praise":

| | |
|---|---|
| Muhammad | Hamdy |
| Mahmoud | Hammady |
| Hameed | Hamoud |
| Hamed | Ahmed |

You can see why foreigners find Arabic names confusing.

Arabic pronunciation makes use of many sounds that do not occur in English, mostly consonants produced far back in the mouth and throat. Some of these consonants show up in the English spelling of words, such as *gh* (Baghdad), *kh* (Khartoum), *q* (Qatar), and *dh* (Riyadh). In Classical Arabic there are twenty-eight consonants, three long vowels, and three short vowels. In the Arabic dialects, some consonants have been dropped or merged with others, and some consonants and vowels have been added—features which distinguish one dialect from another.

## ❧ TRANSCRIPTION

There are varying spellings for Arabic words, because some of the sounds do not exist in English, and because words can be transcribed according to different phonetic systems. There is technically a correct way to spell every word, but complete accuracy often makes the words hard to read. Conventions have grown up around spelling common Arabic words.

*Any of these spellings is acceptable.* The column marked Accurate is the closest to actual Arabic pronunciation.

*Note:* North African words, especially names, are written according to the French system, so they do not look like words transcribed into English.

| English | French | Accurate | Other |
|---------|--------|----------|-------|
| Mohammad | | Muhammad | Mohamed Mohammed |
| Hussein | Hocine | Husayn | Hussain Huseen |
| Al-Hussein | Lahoussine | Al-Husayn | El-Hussain |
| Shukry | Choucri | Shukri | |
| Sharif | Cherif | Shariif | Shareef |
| Koran | Coran | Qur'aan | Qur'an |
| Abdel-Hakim | Abdelhakime | Abd al-Hakiim | Abdul-Hakim |
| Abdel-Rahman | Abderahmane | Abd ar-Rahmaan | Abdul-Rahman |
| Saladin | | Salaah ad-diin | Salahedin |
| Ayesha | Aicha | Aa'isha | Aisha, Aysha |
| Suleiman | Slimane | Sulaymaan | Sulayman |
| Gamal, Jamal | | Gamaal, Jamaal | |
| Said | | Sa'iid | Saeed, Sayeed |
| Qaddhafi | | Al-Qadhdhaafi | Qaddafi Qaddafy Gaddafy |

The consonant sounds are quite consistent (except for dialect variation, as in the example *Gamal, Jamal*). The short (single) vowels (not the long doubled vowels) have great variation and usually do not affect the meaning of the word, so they have many spellings. The more common a word is, the more variations you are likely to see.

## ❖ ARABIC WRITING

The Arabic alphabet has twenty-eight letters and is written from right to left. Numerals, however, are written from left to right. Most letters connect with the preceding and following letters in the same word. Sometimes two or three sounds are written using the same letter; in this case they are differentiated from each other by the arrangement of dots, for example:

|   |   |   |   |   |   |
|---|---|---|---|---|---|
| b | ب | r | ر | s | س |
| t | ت | z | ز | sh | ش |
| th | ث | | | | |

Because consonants carry the meaning of words, the Arabic alphabet (like all Semitic alphabets) includes only the consonants and the long vowels (for example, *aa*, which is a different vowel from *a* and is held longer when pronounced). The short vowels do not appear in the alphabet, but the Arab reader knows what they are and can pronounce the words correctly because these vowels come in predictable patterns. Additional signs (diacritical marks) mark short vowels, doubled consonants, and the like, but these are used only in texts for beginners— and are always included in the text of the Qur'an in order to assure correct reading.

The numerals in Arabic are very easy to learn. We refer to our own numbers as "Arabic numerals" because the system of using one symbol for 0 through 9 and adding new place values for tens, hundreds, and so forth, was borrowed from the Arabs to replace the Roman numeral system. Nevertheless, although their numerals are used the same way as ours, they are not alike (note especially their numbers 5 and 6, which look like our 0 and 7).

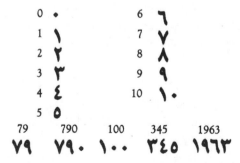

There are several styles of handwriting, and in each the shapes of the individual letters are slightly different. The difference between North

African or western script, for instance, and eastern script is especially noticeable.

## ❊ CALLIGRAPHY AS AN ART FORM

Decorative calligraphy, as you might guess, is one of the highest artistic expressions of Arab culture. Most letters of the alphabet are full of flowing curves, so an artist can easily form them into elaborate designs. Calligraphy usually depicts Qur'anic quotations or favorite proverbs, and the patterns are often beautifully balanced and intricate. Calligraphic designs are widely used to decorate mosques, monuments, books, and household items such as brass trays.

Calligraphy and arabesque geometric designs have developed because of the Islamic injunction against paintings and statues in places of worship. This emphasis is very evident in Islamic architecture.

## ❊ SOCIAL GREETINGS

Arabs use many beautiful, elaborate greetings and blessings—and in every type of situation. Most of these expressions are predictable—each situation calls for its own statements and responses. Situational expressions exist in English, but they are few, such as "How are you?"/"Fine," "Thank you"/"You're welcome," and "Have a nice day." In Arabic there are at least thirty situations that call for predetermined expressions. Although these are burdensome for a student of Arabic to memorize, it is comforting to know that you can feel secure about what to say in almost every social context.

There are formulas for greetings in the morning and evening, for meeting after a long absence, for meeting for the first time, and for welcoming someone who has returned from a trip. There are formulas for acknowledging accomplishments, purchases, marriage, or death and for expressing good wishes when someone is engaged in a task, or has just had a haircut! All of these situations have required responses, and they are beautiful in delivery and usually religious in content. Some examples follow.

| English (Statement/Response) | Arabic Translation (Statement/Response) |
|---|---|
| Good morning./Good morning. | Morning of goodness./Morning of light. |
| Good-bye./Good-bye. | [Go] with safety./May God make you safe. |
| Happy to see you back./Thanks. | Thank God for your safety./May God make you safe. |
| (Said when someone is working) | God give you strength./ God strengthen you. |
| (Said when discussing future plans) | May our Lord make it easy. |
| Good night./Good night. | May you reach morning in goodness./And may you be of the same group. |
| I'm taking a trip. What can I bring you?/What would you like? | Your safety. |
| I have news. Guess what I heard. | [May it be] good, God willing. |

Conversational ritual expressions are much used in Arabic. Sometimes a ritual exchange of formalities can last five or ten minutes, particularly among older and more traditional people.

The Arabs have the charming custom of addressing strangers with kinship terms, which connotes respect and goodwill at the same time. One Western writer was struck by the use of these terms with strangers in Yemeni society (they are as widely used elsewhere).

"Brother, how can I help you?"

"Take this taxi, my sisters, I'll find another."

"My mother, it's the best that I can do."

"You're right, uncle." (1)

Ritualistic statements are required by etiquette in many situations. Meeting someone's small child calls for praise carefully mixed with blessings; for example, "May God keep him" or "[This is] what God wills." Such statements reassure the parents that you are not envious (you certainly would not add, "I wish I had a child like this!"). Blessings should also be used when seeing something of value, such as a new car or a new house. When someone purchases something, even a rather small item, the usual word is *Mabrook*, which is translated "Congratulations" but literally means "Blessed." Some of the most common phrases are given here.

| English | Arabic |
|---|---|
| Hello./Hello. | *Marhaba./Marhabtayn.* |
| Good morning./Good morning. | *Sabah alkhayr./Sabah annoor.* |
| Peace be upon you./ And upon you peace. | *Assalamu 'alaykum./Wa 'alaykum assalam.* |
| Good-bye./Good-bye. ([Go] with safety./May God make you safe.) | *Ma'a ssalama./Allah yisallimak.* |
| Thank you./You're welcome. | *Shukran./'Afwan.* |
| Congratulations./Thank you. (Blessed./May God bless you.) | *Mabrook./Allah yibarik feek.* |
| Welcome./Thanks. (Welcome./ Welcome to you.) | *Ahlan wa sahlan./Ahlan beek.* |
| If God wills. | *Inshallah.* (Said when speaking of a future event) |
| What God wills. | *Mashallah.* (Said when seeing a child or complimenting someone's health) |
| Thanks be to God. | *Alhamdu lillah.* |
| Thanks be to God for your safety. | *Hamdillah 'ala ssalama.* (Said when someone returns from a trip or recovers from an illness) |

Some Arabic expressions sound much too elaborate to be used comfortably in English. There is no need to use them exactly in translation if you are speaking English, as long as you express good wishes.

# NOTES

## A Message from the Author

1. Bruce Feiler. 2011. *Generation Freedom*. New York: Harper Collins Publishers, 119.
2. Al-Quds Al-Arabi (newspaper), June, 1999.
3. "Mullah Omar in his own words." 2001. *The Guardian*, 26 September.
4. Hovik Abrahayan. 2010. "Hovic Abrahayan: Terrorism Is an Evil That Threatens All Humanity." PanArmenian Network. 29 March. (*www.panarmenian.net*).
5. Yu Bin. 2001. "Clash of the Uncivilized—Extremism Mars World Stage." Pacific News Service, 14 April.
6. Marwan Bishara. 2006. "Israel's State-Sponsored Terror." *The Nation*, 13 July. Alternet. (*www.alternet.org*).

## Preface

1. David Fromkin. 1989. *A Peace to End All Peace*. New York: Henry Holt, 306.
2. Charles Krauthammer. 2006. "'Munich,' the Travesty." *Washington Post*, 13 January.
3. Terry Lacey. 2009. "Muslim Population Current Estimate: 1.8 Billion, Christians 2.2 Billion—Only 20% of Muslims Live in the Middle East/North Africa Combined." Pew Forum on Religion and Public Life. 10 September. *(www.waryatv.com)*.
4. John L. Esposito. 2004. "Preface." *The Islamic World: Past and Present*. Cary, N.C.: Oxford University Press USA.
5. Raphael Patai. 2002. *The Arab Mind* (1973; reprint). Long Island: The Hatherleigh Press.
6. Ralph Peters. 2003. *The Tragedy of the Arabs*. Word Gems. March 30. *(www.word-gems.com)*.

## Introduction: Patterns of Change

1. Nadim Kawatch. 2010. "Arab World Needs to Rise to the Literacy Challenge." Emirates 24/7 News. 28 July. *(www.emirates247.com)*.
2. "Arab World." 2011. Wikipedia, February.
3. *Ibid*.
4. "School Enrollment, Tertiary. 2008. " Index Mundi (from UNESCO data). *(www.indexmundi.com)*.
5. Elizabeth Fernea. 2000. "Islamic Feminism Finds a Different Voice." *Foreign Service Journal*, (May), 30.

6. "Labor Participation Rate, Female." 2010. The World Bank World Development Indicators. *(http://data.worldbank.org).*

7. "Egypt," "Kuwait," Morocco," "Saudi Arabia." 2011. Index Mundi. *(www.indexmundi. com).*

8. Martin Walker. 2009. "The World's New Numbers." *The Wilson Quarterly,* (Spring), 26.

9. "Middle East Population Set to Double." 2002. *Popline.* Population Institute, 25 April. *(www.populationinstitute.org).*

10. *Arab Human Development Report 2009. op. cit.*

11. Robin Wright. 2011. "The Struggle Within Islam." *Smithsonian,* (September), 113.

12. "Growing Urbanization." *Human Development Report 1999.* U.N. Development Programme. *(www.hdr.undp.org).*

13. *World Urbanization Prospects, 2009 Revision.* August, 2011. U.N. Dept. of Economic and Social Affairs. *(http://esa.un.org).*

14. *Ibid.*

15. Maricelle Ruiz, ed. 2006. "The United Arab Emirates Tops the List of Internet Use in the Middle East." Internet Business Law Services, 31 May. *(https://ibls.com).*

16. "Internet Users per 1,000 People." 2004. *Human Development Report 2004.* U.N. Development Programme. *(www.hdr.undp.org).*

17. Colum Lynch. 2005. "Report Urges Arab Governments to Share Power." *Washington Post,* 5 April.

18. David K. Willis. 1984. "The Impact of Islam." *Christian Science Monitor,* weekly international edition. 18–24 August.

19. Ahmad S. Mousalli. 1999. *Moderate and Radical Islamic Fundamentalism.* Gainesville: University Press of Florida, 181–86.

20. Benazir Bhutto. 1998. "Politics and the Modern Woman." In *Liberal Islam: A Sourcebook,* edited by Charles Kurzman. New York: Oxford University Press, 107.

21. Muhammad Sayyid Qutb. 1979. "The Role of Religion in Education." In *Aims and Objectives of Islamic Education,* edited by S. N. Al-Attas. Jeddah: King Abdulaziz University, 60.

22. Osman Bakar. 1999. *The History and Philosophy of Islamic Science.* Cambridge, U.K.: Islamic Texts Society, 214.

# Chapter 1

1. "Population Density per Square Mile of Countries." 2009. *(www.infoplease.com).*

2. "Background Note: Egypt." 2010. U.S. Department of State, 10 November.

3. Desmond Stuart. 1972. *The Arab World.* New York: Time Life Books, 9–10.

4. Halim Barakat. 1993. *The Arab World: Society, Culture, and the State.* Berkeley: University of California Press, 21.

5. "Unmarried Childbearing." 2008. Centers for Disease Control and Prevention. *(www.cdc.gov).*

# Chapter 2

1. Recorded December, 2004 in Doha, Qatar.

2. David Shipler. 1986. *Arab and Jew, Wounded Spirits in a Promised Land.* New York: Penguin Books, 387.

3. Ghada Karmi. 2002. *In Search of Fatima: A Palestinian Story.* London: Verso, 181.

## Chapter 3

1. George N. Atiyeh. 1977. *Arab and American Cultures.* Washington, D.C.: American Enterprise Institute for Public Policy Research, 179.
2. T. E. Lawrence. 1926. *The Seven Pillars of Wisdom.* New York: Doubleday, 24.

## Chapter 4

1. Edward T. Hall. 1966. *The Hidden Dimension.* New York: Doubleday, 15.
2. "Hussein Trial Court to Be Disbanded." 2011. *Washington Post,* 5 May.

## Chapter 5

1. Nicholas D. Kristof. 2009. "Islam, Virgins, and Grapes." *New York Times,* 23 April.
2. Neil MacFarquhar. 2007. "New Translation Prompts Debate on Islamic Verse." *New York Times,* 23 March.
3. "Poll: Islamic Women Liked as Leaders." 2006. United Press International. 30 March. *(www.upi.com).*
4. Eman Mohammed. 2008. "Arab First Ladies Speak Up for Women." *Gulf News,* 12 November.
5. Helena Smith. 2009. "The First Ladies of the Arab World Blaze a Trail for Women's Rights." *The Observer* (U.K.), 8 March.
6. Jonathan Simmons. 2011. "Lebanon's First Lady to Arab World: Make Women's Rights a Priority." *Daily Star* (Beirut), 1 February. *(www.dailystar.com.lb).*
7. Nora Boustany. 2006. "U.N. Cites Arab World's 'Empty Gestures' on Women." *Washington Post,* 8 December.
8. Aida F. Akl. 2011. "Will Women Benefit from Middle East Revolution?" *Arab News,* 29 March. *(www.voanews.com).*
9. Mona Lisa Mouallem. 2011. "Will the Revolutions Help or Hurt Women? A Country-by-Country Look." Global Public Square. CNN World. 16 March. *(http://globalpublicsquare.blogs.cnn.com).*
10. Jane Martinson. 2011. "The Fight for Women's Rights in the Middle East." *The Guardian* (U.K.), 11 March.
11. "Hijab by Country." 2011. Wikipedia.
12. Julia Choucair. 2004. "Dates of Women's Suffrage and Current Ministerial Positions Held by Women in Arab Countries." Carnegie Endowment for International Peace. *(http://ceip/org).*
13. "Women in National Parliaments, Situation as of 31 March 2011." Inter-Parliamentary Union. *(www.ipu.org).*
14. Alaa Al Aswany. 2011. *On the State of Egypt.* New York: Vintage Books, 87.
15. *"Al Azhar confirms HIJAB is not part of the religion."* 2012. World Muslim Congress. 23 May. *(http://worldmuslimcongress.blogspot.com).*
16. Thomas Omstad. 2005. "The Casbah Connection." *U.S. News and World Report,* 9 May, 28.

17. Karen Armstrong. 1992. *Muhammad: A Biography of the Prophet.* San Francisco: HarperSanFrancisco, 198.
18. *Ibid.,* 199.
19. Megan Stack. 2005. "The Many Layers of the Veil." *Los Angeles Times*, 12 January.
20. Bernard Lewis. 2002. "Targeted by a History of Hatred." *Washington Post*, 10 September.
21. Halim Barakat. 1993. *The Arab World: Society, Culture and State.* Berkeley: University of California Press, 113.
22. Donna Lee Bowen and Evelyn A. Early, eds. 1993. *Everyday Life in the Muslim Middle East.* Bloomington: Indiana University Press, 77.
23. "Quotation of the Day." 2005. *New York Times*, 13 April.

## Chapter 6

1. Kathy Lally. 2011. "Egypt Calls." *Washington Post,* 1 May.
2. Aida Hasan. 1999. "Arab Culture and Identity: Arab Food and Hospitality." Suite University Online. *(www.suite101.com).*

## Chapter 8

1. Thomas Collelo, ed. *Syria: A Country Study*. 1988. Washington, D.C.: Department of the Army, 81–82.
2. Alean Al-Krenawi and John R. Graham. 2003. "Principles of Social Work Practice in the Muslim Arab World." *Arab Studies Quarterly* 25, 4 (Fall), 85.
3. "Fatima Urges Protection of Arab Family." 1999. *UAE Interact.* Ministry of Information and Culture. *(www.uaeinteract.com).*
4. Hanan Hamamy. 2003. "Consanguineous Marriages in the Arab World." National Centre for Diabetes, Endocrinology and Genetics, Amman, Jordan. July. *(www.ambassadors.net).*
5. *Ibid.*
6. David Brown. 2006. "Global Study Examines Toll of Genetic Defects." *Washington Post,* 30 January.

## Chapter 9

1. "Takbir." 2011. Wikipedia.
2. Robin Wright. 2009. "Islam's Soft Revolution." *Time,* 30 March, 38.
3. *Syria: Country Study Guide.* 2007. Washington, D.C.: International Business Publications, USA.
4. Mustafa Akyol. 2006. "Sexism Deleted in Turkey." *Washington Post*, 16 July.
5. Michelle Boorstein. 2010. "For Critics of Islam, 'Sharia' Is a Loaded Word." *Washington Post*, 27 August.
6. Omar Sacirbey. 2006. "Did Muhammad Really Say That? Muslims Re-Examine the Words of the Prophet in Today's Light." *Washington Post*, 5 August.
7. Boorstein, *op. cit.*
8. *Ibid.*

9. Abraham H. Foxman. 2011. "The New Shape of Anti-Muslim Hatred." *Washington Post*, 30 July.

10. Omar Sacirbey. 2011. "Islamic Law Ban in State Courts Petitioned by Muslims." *Huffington Post*, 13 September.

11. Andrea Elliott. 2011. "The Man Behind the Anti-Shariah Movement." *New York Times*, 30 July.

12. *Ibid.*

## Chapter 10

1. Mounir Al-Ba'albaki. 2004. *Al-Mawrid: A Modern English-Arabic Dictionary.* Beirut: Dar El-Ilm lil-Malayen, 101–12.

2. Andrew Hammond. 2007. *Popular Culture in the Arab World.* Cairo: American University in Cairo Press, 56 (quoting Sheikh Abdel-Nasser al-Jabri of Lebanon).

3. Leslie J. McLoughlin. 1982. *Colloquial Arabic (Levantine).* London: Routledge and Kegan Paul, 2–3.

4. Helen Altman Klein and Gilbert Kuperman. 2008. "Through an Arab Cultural Lens." *The Military Review*, (May–June). 103.

## Chapter 11

1. Daniel Pipes. 2003. *Militant Islam Reaches America.* New York: W.W. Norton & Co., 247–48.

2. Mark Clayton. 2004. "How Are Mosques Fighting Terror?" *Christian Science Monitor*, 12 August.

3. Steve Emerson. 2002. *American Jihad: The Terrorists Living Among Us.* New York: Free Press, 41.

4. Eric Bochlert. 2002. "Terrorists Under the Bed." *Salon*, 5 March. *(www.salon.com).*

5. Mark Potok. 2008. "Hate Rises." *Washington Post*, 9 March.

6. "Terrorism: Is Anders Breivik a Christian?" 2011. *The Week*, 12 August.

7. Andrew Sullivan. 2011. "Breivik: A Living Definition of Christianism." *Daily Beast*, 25 July.

8. Kathleen Parker. 2010. "What Americans Can Do to Discourage Future McVeighs." *Washington Post*, 18 April.

9. *Ibid.*

10. Mark Potok. 2010. "Rage on the Right." *Intelligence Report*, 137 (Spring).

11. Baram, *op. cit.*

12. *Ibid.*

13. Southern Poverty Law Center. 2012. Quoted in *The Week*, March 23, 18. *(http://theweek.com).*

14. Andrea Elliott. 2007. "Where Boys Grow Up to Be Jihadis." *New York Times Magazine*, 27 November.

15. Robert A. Pape. 2005. *Dying to Win: The Strategic Logic of Suicide Terrorism.* New York: Random House, 23.

16. Sarah Kershaw. 2010. "The Terrorist Mind: An Update." *New York Times*, 10 January.

17. Terry McDermott. 2011. "Counting Muslim Terrorists and Coming Up Short." (A review of *The Missing Martyrs* by Charles Kurzman, published by Oxford University.) *Washington Post*, 21 August.
18. Pape, *op. cit.*, 104.
19. Lesley Hazelton. 2009. *After the Prophet*. New York: Anchor Books, 108.
20. Mary Habeck. 2006. "Knowing the Enemy." Essay for *Book Talk*. 17 November, 4.
21. Guy Raz. 2006. "The War on the Word 'Jihad.'" *All Things Considered*. National Public Radio, 31 October.
22. Abdul Wahab Bashir. 2002. "Scholars Define Terrorism, Call for Joint Action to Defend Islam." *Arab News*, 12 January.
23. Karen Armstrong. 1992. *Muhammad: A Biography of the Prophet*. San Francisco: HarperSanFrancisco, 168.
24. Riad Saloojie. 2000. "The Nature of Islam." *The Globe and Mail* (Canada), 16 January.
25. Waleed Ziad. 2005. "Jihad's Fresh Face." *New York Times*, 16 September.
26. Habeck, *op. cit.*
27. Katherine Zoepf. 2008. "Deprogramming Jihadists." *New York Times*, 9 November.
28. Jessica Stern. 2010. "5 Myths About Who Becomes a Terrorist." *Washington Post*, 10 January.
29. *Ibid.*
30. David Ignatius. 2005. "Taking Back Islam." *Washington Post*, 18 September.
31. Amanda Ripley. 2008. "Reverse Radicalism." *Time*, 24 March.
32. Michael Scheuer. 2004. *Imperial Hubris: Why the West Is Losing the War on Terror*. Washington D.C.: Brassey's Inc., 17.
33. Frederick Kunkle. 2011. "Are Good Works Good Politics?" *Washington Post*, 9 April.
34. Erica Simmons. 1990. "A Passion for Justice." *New Internationalist*, 210 (August), 9.
35. Robin Wright. 2006. "Inside the Mind of Hezbollah." *Washington Post*, 16 July.
36. "Worldwide Suicide Rates." 2005. Suicide and Mental Health Association International. February. *(www.suicideandmentalhealthassociationinternational.org)*.
37. Alaa Al-Aswani. 2011. *On the State of Egypt*. New York: Vintage Books, 88.
38. Jackie Spinner. 2005. "An Attack Burns Anguish into Kurdish Region." *Washington Post*, 6 February.
39. "Islam, Jihad, and Terrorism." 2004. Institute of Islamic Information and Education, 14 October. *(www.iiie.net)*.
40. Jonathan Steele. 2003. "Terrorism Is Not an Enemy State that Can Be Defeated." *The Guardian* (U.K.), 23 November.
41. Abdeslam Maghraoui. 2006. *American Foreign Policy and Islamic Renewal*. United States Institute of Peace, Special Report, July. *(www.usip.org)*.
42. *Ibid.*
43. "Tariq Ramadan." 2011. Wikipedia.
44. Jonathan Laurence. 2007. "The Prophet of Moderation: Tariq Ramadan's Quest to Reclaim Islam." *New York Times*, 18 June.
45. "Amr Khaled." 2011. Wikipedia.
46. Samantha M. Shapiro. 2006. "Ministering To the Upwardly Mobile Muslim." *New York Times Magazine*, 30 April.
47. Laurence, *op. cit.*

48. Robert F. Worth. 2009. "Preaching Moderate Islam and Becoming a TV Star." *New York Times*, 3 January.

49. Kevin Sullivan. 2007. "Younger Muslims Tune In to Upbeat Religious Message." *Washington Post*, 2 December.

50. Jeffrey Fleishman. 2010."Egypt's Provocative Voice of Moderate Islam." *Los Angeles Times*, 6 August.

51. "About Free Muslims Coalition." 2011. Free Muslims Coalition, 30 May. (*www .freemuslims.org*).

52. "Report Instances of Extremism or Support of Terrorism." 2005. Free Muslims Coalition. (*www.freemuslims.org*).

53. Ignatius, *op. cit.*

54. David Ignatius. 2010. "Saudis Act Aggressively to Denounce Terrorism." *Washington Post*, 13 June.

55. Fareed Zakaria. 2010. "The Jihad Against the Jihadis." *Newsweek*, 22 February.

## Chapter 12

1. "Arab Spring Fails to Improve U.S. Image." 2011. Pew Research Center Publications. 17 May. (*http://pewresearch.org*).

2. "U.S. Policies Worsen Arab Attitudes." 2011. *The Layalina Review*. July 28. (*http://www.layalina.tv*).

3. Jean-Pierre Filiu. 2011. *The Arab Revolution*. London: C Hurst and Co., Ltd., 125.

4. "U.S. Needs to Go Goodwill Hunting." 2005. *Washington Post*, 30 September.

5. Glenn Kessler and Robin Wright. 2005. "Report: U.S. Image in Bad Shape." *Washington Post*, 24 September.

6. "Transcript of bin Ladin's speech." 2004. *Al-Jazeera*. 30 October. (*www.aljazeera .net*).

7. *Ibid.*

8. *Hurricane Sandy*. 2012. Admin Blog, Arab American Association of New York, 9 November. (*www.arabamericanny.org*)

9. "Poll Data: Arabs Doubt U.S." 2007. Layalina Productions, Inc., April 13–26. (*www. layalina.tv*).

10. John L. Esposito and Dalia Mogahed. 2008. "Muslim True/False," *Los Angeles Times*, 2 April.

11. Sheldon Richman. 2002. "Another Frankenstein's Monster." *Commentaries*. The Future of Freedom Foundation, 27 December. (*www.fff.org*).

12. Rashid Khalidi. 2004. *Resurrecting Empire: Western Footprints and America's Perilous Path in the Middle East*. Boston: Beacon Press, xii.

13. Ghannoushi, *op. cit.*

14. Craig Whitlock and Greg Miller. 2011. "U.S. Creating a Ring of Secret Drone Bases." *Washington Post*, 21 September.

15. "CIA Insider: The Threat We Refuse to Get." 2004. *The Washington Post*, 11 July.

16. Scott McConnell. 2001. "Why Many Arabs Hate America." Media Monitors Network, 12 September. (*www.mediamonitors.net*).

17. Richard Stengel. 2006. "One Thing We Need to Do." *Time*, 11 September.

18.  "Complete Text of President Bush's National Address." 2001. *Globe and Mail* (Canada), 12 September.

19.  M. Shahid Alam. 2004. "The Clash Thesis: A Failing Ideology." Common Dreams News Center. *(www.commondreams.org)*.

20.  *Ibid.*

21.  Gilbert P. Blythe. 2003. "We Are All Jews Now." *The Last Ditch.* WTM Enterprises, 19 October. *(www.thornwalker.com)*.

22.  William J. Bennett and Alan M. Dershowitz. 2006. "A Failure of the Press." *Washington Post*, 23 February.

23.  Glenn Beck. 2009. "Remember Why We Were Attacked on Sept. 11." Fox News, 11 September. *(www.foxnews.com)*.

24.  Rudolph Giuliani. 2007. Republican Debate. 24 November.

25.  Philip Kennicott. 2004. "An About-Face on America." *Washington Post,* 24 August.

26.  Ralph Peters. 2002. *Beyond Terror.* Mechanicsburg PA: Stackpole Books, 35.

27.  Michael Holzman. 2003. "Washington's Sour Sales Pitch." *New York Times*, 4 October.

28.  Philip Seib. 2011. "Obama Tries Again in the Arab World." Scrollpost, 13 May. *(http://scrollpost.com)*.

29.  "U.S. Public Diplomacy in the Middle East on a New Course." 2009. Layalina Productions, Inc., December 18–31. *(www.layalina.tv)*.

30.  Saul Hudson. 2005. "U.S. Halts Arabic Magazine Meant to Boost U.S. Image." Reuters, 22 December. *(www.alertnet.org)*.

31.  Joe Conason. 2010. "Why Nobody Watches Our Arab TV Channel." *Salon,* 12 May. *(www.salon.com)*.

32.  Barry Rubin. 2002. "The Real Roots of Arab Anti-Americanism." *Foreign Affairs*, (November/December), 80.

33.  Lee Smith. 2004. "Democracy Inaction: Understanding Arab Anti-Americanism." *Slate* 23 (April). *(www.slate.msn.com)*.

34.  Bernard Lewis. 1990. "The Roots of Muslim Rage." *The Atlantic Monthly* (September), 56.

35.  Bernard Lewis. 2002. "Targeted by a History of Hatred." *Washington Post*, 10 September.

36.  Samuel P. Huntington. 1993. "The Clash of Civilizations." *Foreign Affairs* 72, 3 (Summer), 31–32.

37.  Samuel P. Huntington. 1996. *The Clash of Civilizations and the Remaking of World Order.* New York: Simon and Schuster, 211.

38.  Robin Wright. 2011. "The Struggle Within Islam." *Smithsonian* (September), 104–114.

39.  Seib, *op. cit.*

40.  Khaled Dawood. 2004. "Arab Opinions." *Al-Ahram Weekly*, 30 July. *(www.ahram.org.eg)*.

41.  "Views of Changing World." 2003. Pew Global Attitudes Project, June. *(www.people-press.org)*.

42.  Rami Khouri. 2003. "For Arabs, A Cruel Echo of History." *The Daily Star* (Beirut), 21 March. *(www.dailystar.com.lb)*.

43. Abdel Mahdi Abdallah. 2003. "Causes of Anti-Americanism in the Arab World: A Socio-Political Perspective." *Middle East Review of International Affairs* 7, 4 (December), 68.

44. Charles Krauthammer. 2005. "Why It Deserves the Hype." *Time*, 14 February, 80.

45. Fouad Ajami. 2005. "Bush Country." *The Daily Star* (Beirut), 23 May. *(www.dailystar.com.lb)*.

46. Fouad Ajami. 2005. "The Meaning of Lebanon." The Foundation for the Defense of Democracy, 1 May. *(www.defenddemocracy.org)*.

47. Charles Krauthammer. 2005. "Syria and the New Axis of Evil." *Washington Post*, 1 April.

48. "Unprecedented Opportunity." The Center for Public Integrity, interview with Rami Khoury. 16 March. *(www.publicintegrity.org)*.

49. Huntington, "The Clash of Civilizations," *op. cit.*, 209, 217.

50. Nicholas Kristof. 2002. "Bigotry in Islam and Here." *New York Times*, 9 July.

51. Franklin Graham. 2001. "My View of Islam." *Covenant News*, 9 December. *(www.covenantnews.com)*.

52. "Islam is Violent." 2008. Jesus-is-Lord, November 29. *(www.jesus-is-lord.com)*.

53. Alexander Kronemer. 2002. "Understanding Muhammad." *Christian Science Monitor*, 9 December.

54. "Islam Comes to Take Over Your Country." Jesus-is-Lord, no date. *(www.jesus-is-lord.com)*.

55. "A Conservative Christian Group Sues the U.N.C. for Assigning a Book on Islam." 2002. Democracy Now, 8 August. *(www.democracynow.org)*.

56. Nassir M. Al-Ajmi. 2003. "Heart-to-Heart Talk—A Friend to Friend Discussion." The Ladah Foundation. 23 October. *(www.ladah.org)*.

57. Ian Buruma. 2004. "Lost in Translation." *The New Yorker*, June, 186.

58. Kristof, *op. cit.*

59. Rodrique Ngawi. 2002. "Rwanda Turns to Islam after Genocide." *Times Daily*, 7 November. *(www.timesdaily.com)*.

## Chapter 13

1. "Demographics." 2003. Arab American Institute. *(www.aaiusa.org)*.

2. *Ibid.*

3. Gennaro Armas. 2005. "Census Bureau Says People of Arab Descent Doing Well in the United States." *Detroit Free Press*, 9 March.

4. Helen Samhan. 2001. "Arab Americans," Arab American Institute. *(www.aaiusa.org)*.

5. Ray Hanania. 2005. "Failure to Understand Arab-Muslim Issues Exposes Nation to Attacks." 11 March. *(www.hananiacreators/blogspot.com)*.

6. Daniel Williams. 2005. "Unveiling Islam: Author Challenges Orthodox Precepts." *Washington Post*, 7 March.

7. Alan Cooperman and Mary Beth Sheridan. 2005. "Muslims to Provide Food on Sept. 11." *Washington Post*, 9 September.

8. *Hurricane Sandy*. 2012. Admin Blog, Arab American Association of New York, 9 November. *(www.arabamericanny.org)*.

9. Jonah Blank. 1998. "The Muslim Mainstream." *U.S. News and World Report*, 20 July, 22.

10. D'Vera Cohn. 2001. "Statistics Portray Settled, Affluent Mideast Community." *Washington Post*, 20 November.

11. Abdel Malik Mujahid. 2001. "Muslims in America: Profile 2001." SoundVision. *(www.soundvision.com)*.

12. "Muslim Population in Canada to Double by 2017." 2009. Madinat Al Muslimeen, 10 March. *(http://jannah.org)*.

13. "Mosques and Islamic Centers in Canada." 2010. Islamic Supreme Council, 20 January. *(www.islamicsupremecouncil.com/canada.htm)*.

14. Mike Barber. 2001. "Muslims in the U.S. Military Are as Loyal as Any, Chaplain Says." *Seattle Post-Intelligencer*, 19 October.

15. John Zogby. 2001. "American Muslim Poll, November-December 2001." Washington, D.C.: Zogby International. *(www.amperspective.com)*.

16. Virginia Culver. 2002. "Many American Muslims Well-Off, College Educated, Poll Shows." *Denver Post*, 18 January.

17. Jane Lampman. 2002. "Muslim in America." *Christian Science Monitor*, 10 January.

18. "Muslim Americans: Middle Class and Mostly Mainstream." 2007. Pew Research Center, 22 May. *(http://people-press.org)*.

19. Carol Morello. 2011. "In Poll, Muslims Largely Upbeat About Life in U.S." Washington Post, 30 August.

20. "Islam in Europe." 2011. Wikipedia.

21. *Ibid.*

22. "Islam in Australia." 2011. Wikipedia.

23. Housain Kettani. 2009. *Muslim Population in Europe.* Proceedings of the 2009 International Conference on Social Sciences and Humanities, 9–11 October. Table 4, "Muslim Population in Northeastern Europe in 2010," "Table 4.1, "Muslim Population in Southwestern Europe in 2010."

24. Steven Lee Myers. 2005 "Growth of Islam in Russia Brings Soviet Response." *New York Times*, 22 November.

25. Molly Moore. 2007. "In a Europe Torn Over Mosques, A City Offers Accommodation." *Washington Post*, 9 December.

26. Soeren Kern. 2010. "Europe's Mosque Wars," Pundicity. 18 August. *(http://kern.pundicity.com)*.

27. *Ibid.*

28. *Ibid.*

29. *Ibid.*

30. Adrian Michaels. 2009. "The EU Is Facing an Era of Vast Social Change, Reports Adrian Michaels, and Few Politicians Are Taking Notice." *The Telegraph* (U.K.), 8 August.

31. *Ibid.*

32. Malise Ruthven. 2009. "The Big Muslim Problem!" *The New York Review*, 17 December.

33. Omer Taspinar. 2003. "Europe's Muslim Street." *Foreign Policy* 135, (March-April), 77.

34. "Population Trends in Europe and Their Sensitivity to Policy Measures." 2004. Committee on Migration, Refugees and Population. *(http://assembly.coe.int)*.

35. Martin Walker. 2009. "The World's New Numbers." *The Wilson Quarterly*, (Spring), 26.

36. *Ibid.*, 27.

37. "EU Opens Debate on Economic Migration." 2005. EurActiv. 14 January. *(www.euractiv.com)*.

38. Scott Timberg. 2007."Middle East through Western Eyes." *Los Angeles Times*, 7 September.

39. Yvonne Haddad and Jane Smith. 2002. *Muslim Minorities in the West: Visible and Invisible.* New York: Altamira Press, xii.

40. Shelley Slade. 1981. "The Image of the Arab in America: Analysis of a Poll of American Attitudes." *Middle East Journal* 35, 2 (Spring), 143.

41. Brian Whitaker. 2000. "Why the Rules of Racism Are Different for Arabs." *The Guardian* (U.K.), 18 August.

42. William Booth. 2007. "Cast of Villains." *Washington Post*, 23 June.

43. Kerstin Grimsley. 2001. "More Arabs, Muslims Allege Bias on the Job." *Washington Post*, 12 February.

44. Michelle Boorstein and Felicia Sonmez. 2011. "Familiar Sparring in Hearing on Civil Rights of Muslims." *Washington Post,* 30 March.

45. Alan Cooperman. 2002. "September 11 Backlash Murders and the State of Hate." *Washington Post*, 20 January.

46. "The Truth About American Muslims." 2011. *New York Times*, 1 April.

47. Claudia Deane and Darryl Fears. 2006. "Negative Perception of Islam Increasing." *Washington Post*, 9 March.

48. *Ibid.*

49. Musaji, *op. cit.*

50. "Polls Point to American–Muslim Rift." 2007. Layalina Productions, Inc., July 20–August 2. *(www.layalina.tv)*.

51. Zachary A. Goldfarb. 2006. "Va. Lawmaker's Remarks on Muslims Criticized." *Washington Post*, 21 December.

52. Paul Farhi. 2005. "Talk Show Host Graham Fired By WMAL Over Islam Remarks." *Washington Post*, 23 August.

53. Ernesto Londono. 2006. "Teacher Charged After Uproar Over Arabic." *Washington Post*, 13 September.

54. Jon Hurdle. 2010. "Arabic Flashcards Land Student in U.S. Detention." Reuters. 10 February.

55. Robin Shulman 2007. "In New York, a Word Starts a Fire." *Washington Post*, 24 August.

56. *Ibid.*

57. Laila Al-Marayati and Basil Abdelkarim. 2006. "The Crime of Being a Muslim Charity." *Washington Post*, 11 March.

58. Mary Beth Sheridan. 2005. "U.S. Muslim Groups Cleared." *Washington Post*, 18 November.

59. Margot Adler. 2011. "Developer: Plans For N.Y. Mosque Moving Forward." *All Things Considered.* National Public Radio, 5 May.

60. Annie Gowen. 2010. "Nowhere Near Ground Zero, but No More Welcome." *Washington Post*, 23 August.

61. "Intolerance." 2010. *The New Yorker*, 20 September, 47.

62. "The Truth About American Muslims," *op. cit.*

63. Edward E. Curtis IV. 2010. "5 Myths About Mosques in America." *Washington Post*, 29 August.

64. "Paper or Plastic?—A More Perfect Union Project." 2010. Flikr, 6 April. *(www.flikr .com)*.

65. "The Truth About American Muslims," *op. cit.*

66. Jacqueline Trescott. 2006. "Kennedy Center Plans Festival as Olive Branch to Arab Culture." *Washington Post*, 28 April.

67. "More than 99% of Terrorism Is Not Islamic." 2010. Disclose TV, 7 October. *(www.disclose.tv)*.

68. Glenn Greenwald. 2007. "Large Number of Americans Favor Violent Attacks Against Civilians." *Salon*, 23 May. *(www.salon.com)*.

69. Doug Bandew. 2009. "Maybe Europe Isn't Lost to Islamic Terrorism." Cato @ Liberty, 26 July. *(www.cato-at-liberty.org)*.

70. Walker, *op. cit.*

71. "Islamic Dress in Europe." 2011. Wikipedia.

72. Edward Cody. 2010. "Belgium Approves Ban on Full-Face Veils in Public." *Washington Post*, 30 April.

73. "Court Upholds Spanish City's Ban on Face-Covering Islamic Veils in Municipal Buildings." 2011. Associated Press. *Washington Post World*. 9 June. *(www .washingtonpost.com/world)*.

74. Masra, Aabeda. 2012. *"Dutch government moves closer to banning the niqab and burqa."* CAIR Chicago. 31 January. *(www.cairchicago.org)*.

75. "Muslim Women Wearing Veil 'Refused Bus Ride' in London." 2010. BBC News, 23 July.

76. Mona Eltahawy. 2010. "Rending the Veil—With Little Help." *Washington Post*, 18 July.

77. Seamus Milne. 2010. "This Tide of Anti-Muslim Hatred Is a Threat to Us All." *The Guardian* (U.K.), 25 February.

78. Delphine Schrank. 2006. "Survey Details 'Deep' Divide between Muslims, Westerners." *Washington Post*, 23 June.

79. Tariq Ramadan. 2008 "Anti-Muslim Bias Taints 'Tolerant' Europe." Topix, 10 December. *(www.topix.com)*.

80. Christopher Caldwell, 2011, "Europe's Arizona Problem," *New York Times*, June 11.

81. Anthony Faiola. 2010. "Anti-Muslim Feelings Propel Right Wing." *Washington Post*, 26 October.

82. Caldwell, *op. cit.*

83. Lauren Collins. 2011. "England, Their England." *The New Yorker*, 4 July.

84. *Ibid.*

85. Tristana Moore. 2011. "After Norway, Will Germany Ban a Far-Right Political Party?" *Time World*, 10 August. *(www.time.com)*.

86. Abraham H. Foxman. 2011. "The New Shape of Anti-Muslim Hatred." *Washington Post*, 30 July.

87. Amy Sullivan. 2011. "Articles of Faith: The Conservative Double Standard on Christian Terrorism." *Time Swampland*, 29 July. *(http://swampland.time.com)*.

88. Yvonne Yazbeck Haddad and Michael J. Balz. 2008. "Taming the Imams: European Governments and Islamic Preachers since 9/11." *Islam and Christian-Muslim Relations*, 19, 2, (April), 215.

89. "Denmark Imposes Restrictions on Imams." 2004. Islam Online, 18 February. *(www.islamonline.net)*.

90. Edward Cody. 2009 "Tensions Grow for Muslims as French Debate National Identity." *Washington Post*, 19 December.

91. Laurie Goodstein. 2009. "Poll Finds U.S. Muslims Thriving, but Not Content." *New York Times*, 2 March.

92. Sarah Wildman. 2003. "Third Way Speaks to Europe's Young Muslims." *International Reporting Project.* Johns Hopkins School of Advanced International Studies, (Spring). *(www.journalismfellowships.org)*.

93. Tariq Ramadan. 2004. *Western Muslims and the Future of Islam*. Oxford: Oxford University Press, 6.

94. Martin A. Lee. 2004. "Not a Prayer." *Harper's Magazine*, (June), 79.

95. Michelle Vu. 2011. "Muslim Population to Double in U.S. by 2030, Report Projects." *Free Republic*, 29 January.

96. Laurie Goodstein. 2011. "Forecast Sees Muslim Population Leveling Off." *New York Times*, 27 January.

97. Vu, *op. cit.*

98. Goodstein, "Forecast," *op. cit.*

99. Milia Fisher and Sara Birkenthal. 2011. "Jordan Becoming Choice Destination for Arabic-Language Study." *Jordan Times*, 5 August.

100. Jennifer Conlin. 2010. "Life Lessons in the Mideast." *New York Times*, 8 August.

101. *Ibid*.

102. "New MLA Survey Report Finds That the Study of Languages Other Than English Is Growing and Diversifying at U.S. Colleges and Universities." 2010. Modern Language Association, 8 December. *(www.mla.org)*.

## Chapter 14

### The Arab Countries: Similiarities and Differences

1. Michael Schuman. 2011. "Seeking Growth After the Arab Spring." *Time*, 22 August.

2. David Ignatius. 2010. "The Mideast's Generational Shift," *Washington Post*, 28 November.

3. "Unemployment in the Arab World." 2008. Layalina Productions, Inc., July 18–31. *(www.layalina.tv)*.

4. Schuman, *op. cit.*

5. Egypt GDP Growth Rate. 2012. Trading Economics, Central Bank of Egypt. *(www.tradingeconomics.com)*

6. Andrew Martin. 2008. "Mideast Facing Choice Between Crops and Water." *New York Times*, 21 July.

7. "Leading Indicators of Revolt in the Middle East and Northern Africa: Corruption, Unemployment and Percentage of Household Money Spent on Food." 2011. "Arab League Index of Unrest." *The Big Picture.* Ritholtz, February. *(www.ritholtz.com)*.

## The Arab Countries in Africa

### The Maghrib

1. Andrew Hammond. 2007. *Popular Culture in the Arab World.* Cairo: American University in Cairo Press, 37.
2. "Berber Languages." 2005. *Columbia Encyclopedia,* 6th ed. *(www.bartleby.com).*
3. "Berber Languages." 2004. Wikipedia. *(www.en.wikipedia.org).*
4. "The Amazigh (Berber)." 2011. Phoenician International Research Center. *(www. phoenicia.org).*

### Morocco

1. Andrea Elliott. 2007. "Where Boys Grow Up to Be Jihadis." *New York Times Magazine,* 25 September.
2. Tim McGirk. 2008. "Morocco's Gentle War on Terror." *Time,* 6 August.
3. Jane Kramer. 2006. "The Crusader," *The New Yorker,* 16 October.
4. Anne Applebaum. 2009. "In Morocco, an Alternative to Iran." *Washington Post,* 30 June.
5. Emma Schwartz. 2008. "Giving Voice to a Long-Repressed People." *U.S. News & World Report,* 24–31 March, 29.
6. Nadim Audi. 2011. "Offering Slow, Small Changes, Morocco's King Stays in Power." *New York Times,* 10 July.
7. Ahmed Charai and Joseph Braude. 2011. "All Hail the (Democratic) King." *New York Times,* 11 July.
8. "Moroccan Women and Gender Inequality in the Workplace." 2010. European Professional Women's Network, 27 April. *(www.EuropeanPWN.net).*
9. Stephanie Willman Bordat and Saida Kouzzi. 2004. "The Challenge of Implementing Morocco's New Personal Status Law." Global Rights. *(www.globalrights.org).*
10. "Morocco Age Structure." 2010. Index Mundi. *(www indexmundi.com).*
11. Schwartz, *op. cit.*
12. "History of the Jews in Morocco." 2011. Wikipedia, 29 April.

### Algeria

1. "Historical Ties Leave Trying Legacy." 1993. *Christian Science Monitor,* 27 January.
2. Michael Slackman. 2008. "In Algeria, a Tug of War for Young Minds." *New York Times,* 23 June.
3. Craig Smith. 2004. "Voices of the Dead Echo Across Algeria." *New York Times,* 18 April.
4. "Algeria." 2011. *The World Factbook.* Central Intelligence Agency.
5. "Economy of Algeria." 2011. Wikipedia.
6. "Algeria," *op. cit.*
7. "Economy of Algeria," *op. cit.*
8. "Background Note: Algeria." 2011. U.S. Department of State, 17 February.
9. *Ibid.*
10. "Algeria Election: Reluctant Youth." 2005. *Arab-American Journal,* 23 December. *(www.arabamerican.com).*

11. Michael Slackman. 2007. "A Quiet Revolution in Algeria: Gains by Women." *New York Times*, 26 May.

**Tunisia**

1. Scott Sayare. 2011. "Tunisia is Uneasy Over Party of Islamists." *New York Times*, 15 May.
2. "Post-Revolutionary Tunisia: Moving Ahead." 2011. *The Economist*, 16 July.
3. "Tourism in Tunisia." 2011. Focus Multimedia. *(www.focusmm.com)*.
4. "Tunisia." 2011. *The World Factbook*. Central Intelligence Agency.
5. *Ibid.*
6. "Tunisian Economy to Grow 1–2 Pct in 2011: Cenbank." 2011. Reuters, 30 April. *(http://af.reuters.com)*.
7. "Tunisia: Minister, Jobs Abroad for 35,000 Tunisians by 2013." 2011. Ansamed, 23 May. *(www.ansamed.info)*.
8. Rania Abouzeid. 2011. "After the Revolution: Young Tunisians Are Still Looking for Work." *Time*, 7 February.
9. Schumpeter. 2011. "Young, Jobless and Looking for Trouble." *The Economist*, 3 February.
10. Jeffrey Goldberg. 2011. "Danger, Falling Tyrants." *The Atlantic*, June, 50.
11. "Tunisia: International Religious Freedom Report 2003." 2003. Bureau of Democracy, Human Rights and Labor. U.S. Department of State, 18 December.

**Libya**

1. J. A. Allen. 1981. *Libya: The Experience of Oil*. Boulder, CO: Westview Press, 22.
2. "Libya." 2011. *The World Factbook*. Central Intelligence Agency.
3. "Libya's Well-Oiled Revolution." 2011. *Time*, 7 November.
4. "Background Note: Libya." 2010. U.S. Department of State, 17 November.
5. "War in Libya: Closing in on Tripoli." 2011. *The Economist*, 16 July.
6. Borzou Daragahi. 2011. "Libya's Fed-up Berbers Aiming for Equality." *Los Angeles Times*, 17 July.
7. C. J. Chivers. 2011. "Amid a Berber Reawakening in Libya, Fears of Revenge." *New York Times*, 9 August.
8. "Background Note: Libya," *op. cit.*
9. David Goodman. 2011. "United States and Other Nations Step Up Libyan Evacuations." *New York Times*, 23 February.
10. "Libya's Well-Oiled Revolution," *op. cit.*
11. Nicholas K. Geranios. 2011. "Libya Ends College Funding for 2,000 U.S. Students." Associated Press, 13 May.
12. "Libyan Students in U.S. Blackmailed into Attending Pro-Qaddafi Rallies." 2011. *The Arab-American News*, 18 February. *(www.arabamericannews.com)*.
13. William Green. 2011. "Libyan Students Worth More Than 160 Million Pounds to UK Universities." Journal Live, 4 March. *(http://blogs.journallive.co.uk)*.
14. Rana Jawad. 2008. "Women's Lib Takes Off in Libya." BBC News, 29 April. *(http://newsvote.bbc.co.uk)*.
15. Kareem Fahim. 2011. "Libya Revolt Leaves Women, Who Led It, on Sidelines." *New York Times*, May 20.

16. "Gender Equality and Social Institutions in Libya." 2006. Social Institutions and Gender Index. *(http://genderindex.org).*

**The Nile Valley**
1. "The Egyptian Revolution." 2011. Wikipedia.
2. Jack Shenker. 2011. "Egypt Election Results Put Muslim Brotherhood Ahead." *The Guardian* (UK), 30 November.
3. David D. Kirkpatrick and Mona El-Naggar. 2011. "Poll Finds Egyptians Full of Hope About Future." *New York Times*, 26 April.
4. Tarek El-Tablawy. 2011. "Egyptian Food Prices Have Risen 20 Percent In The Last Year." Huffpost Business, *The Huffington Post*, 10 May.
5. Egypt GDP Growth Rate. 2012. Trading Economics, Central Bank of Egypt. *(www.tradingeconomics.com).*
6. David D. Kirkpatrick. 2011. "Egypt's Military Expands Power, Raising Alarms." *New York Times*, 14 October.
7. "Egypt: Population under Age 15." 2011. Human Development Report. UNDP. Globalis - Egypt.
8. "Fertilizer Use by Crop in Egypt." 1998. National Resources Management and Environmental Development. FAO Corporate Document Repository. *(www.fao.org).*
9. "Egypt." 2005. *Encarta Online Encyclopedia.* Microsoft Corp. *(www.encarta.msn.com).*
10. Lisa Hymas. 2011. "Egypt Has a Population Crisis as Well as a Democracy Crisis." *Grist*, 5 February. *(www.grist.org).*
11. Jeffrey Fleishman and Kath Linthicum. 2010. "Demands on the Nile Imperil Egypt's Lifeline." *Los Angeles Times*, 12 September.
12. Andrew Martin. 2008. "Mideast Facing Choice Between Crops and Water." *New York Times*, 21 July.
13. *Ibid.*
14. "What Lies Behind Egypt's Problems?" 2011. Bill Totten's Weblog, 4 February. *(http://billtotten.blogspot.com).*
15. "Fertilizer use by crop in Egypt," *op. cit.*
16. El-Tablawy, *op. cit.*
17. "Making Egypt More Food Secure: Short-Term and Long-Term U.S. Actions." 2011. Center for American Progress. *(www.americanprogress.org).*
18. *Ibid.*
19. "Egyptians Riot over Bread Crisis." 2008. *The Telegraph* (U.K.), 8 April. *(www.telegraph.co.uk).*
20. David D. Kirkpatrick. 2011. "Surge in Crime Imperils Effort to Remake Egypt." *New York Times*, 12 May.
21. Louise Sheldon. 2004. "Reflections on the Status of Women in Islam." *Baltimore Chronicle and Sentinel*, 2 June. *(www.baltimorechronicle.com).*
22. "African Women in Engineering and Science: Egypt." 2011. Global Alliances. *(www.globalalliancesnet.org).*
23. Charles Levinson. 2005. "Egyptian Women See Divorce as Religious Right." Women's e-News, 9 January. *(www.womensnews.org).*
24. Ernesto Londono. 2011. "Clashes kill 23 in heart of Cairo." *Washington Post*, 10 October.

## Sudan

1. "Sudan: Population." 2005. *Encyclopedia Britannica Online*, 13 February. *(www.britannica.com).*
2. Tessa Merrod. 2003. "Too Little: The Vicious Circle of Drought in North Darfur." Intermediate Technology Development Group (U.K.), October. *(www.itdg.org).*
3. Josh Kron. 2011. "Sudan Leader to Accept Secession of South." *New York Times*, 7 February.
4. *Ibid.*
5. John Daniszewski. 1997. "A Ray of Hope in a War-Torn Sudan." *New York Times*, 18 October.
6. "Sudan at War With Itself." 2007. *Washington Post*, 7 April.
7. "Sudan 2010." 2010. Freedom House. *(www.freedomhouse.org).*
8. *Ibid.*
9. Stephanie McCrummen. 2007. "Sudan, in Mud Brick and Marble," *Washington Post*, 26 February.
10. "Population and Failing States: Sudan." 2009. Population Institute. *(www.populationinstitute.org).*
11. *Ibid.*
12. "Sudan." 2011. *World Factbook.* Central Intelligence Agency.
13. William Finnegan. 1999. "The Invisible War." *The New Yorker*, 25 January, 71.
14. "Sudan at War With Itself," *op. cit.*
15. Randa Takieddine. 2011. "The Southern Sudan Referendum and Sanctions on Sudan." *Al-Hayat* (Beirut), 9 February. *(www.daralhayat.com).*
16. "Sudan 2010," *op. cit.*
17. *Ibid.*
18. "Sudan Migration Country Profile." 2011. Secretariat for Sudanese Working Abroad. Zunia, 27 February. *(http://zunia.org).*
19. "Fertility Rate, Total Births per Woman, Sudan." 2009. World Bank. *(www.worldbank.org).*
20. "Gender Equality and Social Institutions in Sudan." 2004. Social Institutions and Gender Index. *(genderindex.org).*
21. Rosebell. 2011. "South Sudan women Seek 30 Percent Representation in a New State." *Rosebell's Blog*, 20 April. *(http://rosebellkagumire.com).*
22. Jason Straziuso and Michael Onyiego. 2012. "South Sudan's Surging Violence Draws Emergency Aid Response." *Washington Post.* 8 January.

# Chapter 15

## Lebanon

1. Alia Ibrahim, Robin Wright, and Ellen Knickmeyer. 2008. "As Tensions Rise in Lebanon, Residents Again Fear the Worst." 2008. *Washington Post*, 21 March.
2. "Lebanese Unemployment Rate." 2011. Index Mundi. *(www.indexmundi.com).*
3. Schumpeter. 2011. "Young, Jobless and Looking for Trouble." *The Economist*, 3 February.
4. "Demographics of Lebanon." 2011. Wikipedia.
5. *Ibid.*
6. *Ibid.*

7. Bassem Mroue. 2011. "Hezbollah's Candidate to Form Lebanese Government." *Washington Times*, 25 January.
8. *Ibid.*
9. "2008 Conflict in Lebanon." 2011. Wikipedia.
10. Jean Aziz, 2014, "Lebanon's new government based on mutual oversight." *Al-Monitor*, 18 February.
11. "Women, Media and Politics in Lebanon." 2008. *Menassat*, 16 July. *(www.menassat .com).*
12. "Gender: Lebanon." 2004. POGAR, Programme on Governance in the Arab Region. U.N. Development Programme. *(www.pogar.org).*
13. "Women, Media", *op. cit.*

## Syria

1. "Help Syrian Refugees Survive." 2012. U.N. High Commission for Refugees. *(https:// donate.unrefugees.org)*
2. "Syrian refugee camps slammed by rain, cold, making miserable conditions unbearable." 2013. CBS/AP. 9 January. *(www.cbsnews.com)*
3. Matthew Lee and Martin Crutsinger. 2011."U.S. Slaps Sanctions on Syria's Assad for Abuses." Associated Press, 18 May.
4. "Education in Syria." 2006. Wikipedia.
5. David Hirst. 2005. "Syria's Unpredictable Storm." *Los Angeles Times*, 7 June.
6. "Syria Unemployment Rate." 2011. Index Mundi. *(www.indexmundi.com).*
7. Catherine Bellafronto. 2004. "Syria." Freedom House. *(www.freedomhouse.org).*
8. Sharifa Shafie. 2003. "Palestinian Refugees in Syria." FMO Research Guide. *(www .forcedmigration.org).*
9. "Iraqi Refugees in Syria Reluctant to Return Home Permanently." 2010. U.N. High Commission for Refugees, 8 October. *(www.unhcr.org).*
10. Sarah Birke. 2010. "In Syria, the Fight for Women's Rights Means Helping Both Genders." *Christian Science Monitor*, 7 June. *(www.csmonitor.com).*
11. Sarah Birke. 2010. "In Syria, the Fight for Women's Rights Means Helping Both Genders." *Christian Science Monitor*, 7 June.

## Palestinian Territories

1. Kim Murphy. 2006. "Hamas Victory Is Built on Social Work." *Los Angeles Times*, 2 March.
2. "Line of Separation." 2006. *Washington Post*, 30 May.
3. Ed Pilkington. 2011. "US Vetoes U.N. Condemnation of Israeli Settlements." *The Guardian* (U.K.), 19 February.
4. Mousa Abu Marzook. 2006. "What Hamas Is Seeking." *Washington Post*, 31 January.
5. "Israelis and Palestinians Killed in the Current Violence." 2011. If Americans Knew, 2 February. *(www.ifamericansknew.org).*
6. "Palestinians Try for Their Own Arab Spring." 2011. *Time*, 30 May, 12.
7. Sheera Frenkel. 2011. "Israel's '67 Borders Have Long Been at Root of Peace Debate." *Kansas City Star*, 20 May.

8. Isabel Kershner. 2009. "U.N. Seeks End to Razing of Homes in East Jerusalem." *New York Times*, 1 May.

9. The View from Here. 2009. 9 January. *(http://israeltheviewfromhere.blogspot.com)*

10. "Palestinians Try for Their Own Arab Spring," *op. cit.*

11. Jeremy M. Sharp. 2010. "U.S. Foreign Aid to Israel." Congressional Research Service. 16 September. *(www.fas.org)*.

12. "U.S. Military Aid and the Israel/Palestine Conflict." 2011. If Americans Knew. *(www.ifamericansknew.org)*.

13. *Ibid.*

14. Yusef Daher. 2004. "Palestinian Christians: Down from 2% to 1%. What Is Next?" Laity Committee on the Holy Land. 17 February. *(www.holylandchristians.com)*.

15. Silvia Nicolaou-Garcia. 2010. "Christian-Muslim Relations in Palestine." *Middle East Monitor*, 24 June. *(www.middleeastmonitor.org.uk)*.

16. "West Bank." 2011. *The World Factbook*. Central Intelligence Agency, 3 May.

17. *Ibid.*

18. Ethan Bronner. 2011. "Before a Diplomatic Showdown, a Budget Crisis Saps Palestinians' Confidence." *New York Times*, 27 July.

19. "Gaza." 2011. *The World Factbook*. Central Intelligence Agency, 25 April.

20. Yair Amikam. 2007. "The Palestinian Medical Crisis: An Exchange." *New York Review*, 14 June.

21. "Palestinian Central Bureau of Statistics, 2011." 2011. *Annual Report, Palestine Children, Child Statistics Series No. 14*. Ramallah.

22. "Women's Rights in the Middle East and North Africa: Citizenship and Justice, Palestine (Palestinian Authority and Israeli-Occupied Territories)." 2011. Freedom House. *(www.freedomhouse.org)*.

## Jordan

1. "Jordan." 2011. *The World Factbook*. Central Intelligence Agency, 17 May.

2. Syria Regional Refugee Response. 2013. UNHCR. *(http://dataunhcr.org)*

3. Fawwaz Al-Abed Al-Haq. 2009 "Islam and Language Planning in the Arab World: A Case Study in Jordan." *Iranian Journal of Language Studies*, 3 (3), 267–302.

4. Sylvia Smith. 2009. "New Ideas for Jordan's Traditional Bedouin." BBC News, 22 May.

5. Joby Warrick. 2010. "In Jordan, U.S. Finds Quiet Ally in Arab World." *Washington Post*, 4 October.

6. Alan Cooperman. 2005. "Jordan's King Abdullah Pushes for Moderation." *Washington Post*, 14 September.

7. Ellen Knickmeyer and Yasmin Mousa. 2007. "Jordan's Limited Democracy Leaves Voters Discontented." *Washington Post*, 20 November.

8. *Ibid.*

9. "Jordanian Parliamentary Election, 2010." 2011. Wikipedia.

10. Imtiaz Muqbil. 2011. "Ten Years After 9/11, Pew Poll Shows U.S.-Muslim Schism as Wide as Ever." *Travel Impact Newswire*, 18 May. *(www.travel-impact-newswire.com)*.

11. "Jordan Creates Commission to Examine Reform." 2011. Agence France-Presse. France 24, International News, 14 March. *(www.france24.com)*.

12. Joel Greenberg. 2011. "Motorcade of Jordan's King Said to Be Attacked." *Washington Post*, 14 June.

13. Jamal Halaby. 2011. "Jordan's King Will Share Power in Forming Cabinet." *Washington Post*, 27 October.

14. "Jordan. " *The World Factbook, op. cit.*

15. "Economy of Jordan." 2011. Wikipedia.

16. Neil MacFarquhar. 2001. "Syria Reaches Turning Point, but Which Way Will it Turn?" *New York Times*, 12 March.

17. "Education in Jordan." 2011. Wikipedia.

## Iraq

1. Andrew Hammond. 2007. *Popular Culture in the Arab World.* Cairo: American University in Cairo Press, 8.

2. "Half Million Child Deaths 1991–1998." 2000. Global Policy Forum. United Nations. *(www.globalpolicy.org).*

3. Ellen Knickmeyer. 2006. "Ghosts of Iraq's Birth." *Washington Post National Weekly Edition,* 13–19 March.

4. "Health Situation in Iraq." 2003. World Health Organization, United Nations. *(www.who.int).*

5. "Iraq: Briefing on Health." 2002. Office for Coordination of Humanitarian Affairs. United Nations, 18 May. *(www.ochaonline.un.org).*

6. John Pilger. 2005. "Squeezed to Death." *The Guardian* (U.K.), 4 March.

7. "An Iraq Fit for Children: Building Iraq's Future." 2010. *Quarterly Newsletter,* United Nations Children's Fund, Issue 02.

8. "Prevalence of Child Malnutrition (Percentage Underweight under Age Five), 2000–2009." 2009. Global Health Facts. Kaiser Foundation. *(www.globalhealthfacts. org).*

9. Alissa J. Rubin. 2009. "Iraqi Surveys Start to Unveil the Mental Scars of War, Especially Among Women." *New York Times*, 7 March.

10. Joost Hillermann. 2011. "Waiting for Baghdad." *The New York Review*, 14 April, 55.

11. "Education and Development in Iraq." 2011. U.N. Inter-Agency Info and Analysis Unit. *(www.iauiraq.org).*

12. "Iraq." 2011. *The World Factbook*. Central Intelligence Agency, 12 January.

13. "Iraqi Women and Children's Liberation Act of 2004, S 2519." 2004. *The Orator.* U.S. Congress, 15 June. *(www.theorator.com).*

14. "Background on Women's Status in Iraq Prior to the Fall of the Saddam Hussein Government." 2003. *Human Rights Watch Briefing Paper.* Human Rights Watch, November. *(http://hrw.org).*

15. Sanjay Suri. 2006. "Saddam Better for Women." Inter Press Service, 30 March. *(http://ipsnews.net).*

16. Tina Susman. 2007. "Iraqis Divided by Treatment of Women in Constitution." *Los Angeles Times*, 9 October.

17. John Leland and Riyadh Mohammed. 2010. "Iraqi Women Are Seeking Greater Political Influence." *New York Times*, 17 February.

18. Ellen Knickmeyer. 2005. "Iraqi Women See Little but Darkness." *Washington Post*, 15 October.

19. Nancy Trejos. 2006. "Women Lose Ground in the New Iraq." *Washington Post*, 16 December.

20. "Gender Cleansing in Iraq: Women in Politics." 2008. Layalina Productions, Inc., 5 June. *(www. layalina.tv)*.

21. *Ibid.*

22. Rubin, *op. cit.*

23. Leland and Mohammed, *op. cit.*

24. *Ibid.*

25. "4.5 Million Orphans in Iraq: Protests over Food and Shelter." 2011. Global Research, 22 February. *(http://globalresearch.ca)*.

26. "First Annual SICF Orphan's Conference in Baghdad." 2009. Rescue Iraq, World Orphans, 25 April. *(http://rescue.typepad.com)*.

27. *Ibid.*

28. "Current Projects." 2011. Iraqi Orphan Foundation, 15 October. *(www.iraqiorphan-foundation.com)*.

29. Iraq Body Count Project. 2011. February. *(www.iraqbodycount.org)*.

30. "Why Does Iraq Body Count Report a Much Lower Number?" 2011. Unknown News, April 25. *(www.unknownnews.org)*.

31. "Iraq Deaths." 2009. Just Foreign Policy. *(www.justforeignpolicy.org)*.

## Chapter 16

**Saudi Arabia**

1. "Saudi Arabia." 2011. *The World Factbook*. Central Intelligence Agency, 17 May.

2. Andrew Martin. 2008. "Mideast Facing Choice Between Crops and Water." *New York Times*, 21 July.

3. *Ibid.*

4. Florence Foster. 2010. "New Rules for Foreign Workers in Saudi Arabia." Move One, Inc., 22 April. *(www.moveoneinc.com)*.

5. "Saudi Arabia," *op. cit.*

6. Foster, *op. cit.*

7. "Saudi Arabia's Foreign Workforce." 2003. *BBC News World Edition*. BBC News, 13 May. *(http://news.bbc.co.uk)*.

8. "Egypt's Youth Unemployment Problem Has Erupted—But What About Britain's?" 2011. *Money Week*, 31 January. *(www.moneyweek.com)*.

9. "Saudi Arabia Opens First Mixed-Gender University." 2009. *Los Angeles Times*, 23 September.

10. Caryle Murphy and Susan Kinzie. 2006. "Saudis Again Head to U.S. Campuses." *Washington Post*, 11 November.

11. "Saudi Arabia Opens," *op. cit.*

12. Afshin Molavi. 2006 "Challenge for reform-Minded King: To Weaken Religious Radicals." *St. Paul Pioneer Press*, 3 September.

13. "Saudi Arabia," *op. cit.*

14. David Ignatius. 2010. "A Saudi Fatwa for Moderation." *Washington Post*, 13 June.

15. "Saudi Arabia, International Religious Freedom Report 2004." 2004. Bureau of Democracy, Human Rights, and Labor. U.S. Department of State, 15 November. *(www.state.gov).*

16. *Advancement of Saudi Women.* 2012. Saudi Arabian Ministry of Higher Education. (*www.pnu.edu.sa*)

17. "Shi's [Shia] in Saudi Arabia." 2004. *Minorities at Risk Project.* Center for International Development and Conflict Management. University of Maryland, 15 July. *(www.cidem.umd.edu).*

18. Scott Wilson. 2005. "Shiites See an Opening in Saudi Arabia." *Washington Post,* 28 February.

19. *Ibid.*

20. Robert Lacey. 2009. *Inside the Kingdom.* London: Penguin Books Ltd., 169.

20. "Saudis to Allow Female Drivers and Award Female Journalists, Qatar's First Female Jockey." 2008. Layalina Productions, Inc., 18–31 January. *(www.layalina.tv).*

21. "Saudi Arabia," *op. cit.*

22. Faiza Saleh Ambah. 2008. "Saudi Women See a Brighter Road on Rights." *Washington Post,* 31 January.

23. Kelly McEvers. 2008. "Saudis Slow to Accept Working Women." *Marketplace,* 23 April. *(http://marketplace.publicradio.org).*

24. *Advancement of Saudi Women, op. cit.*

25. Andrew Lee Butters. 2009. "Saudi's Small Steps," *Time,* 19 October.

26. *Ibid.*

27. Neil MacFarquhar. 2011. "In Saudi Arabia, Royal Funds Buy Peace for Now." *New York Times,* 9 June.

28. Mike Giglio. 2011. "Saudi's Surprise Renegades." *Newsweek,* 9 May.

**Yemen**

1. Max Rodenbeck. 2010."Yemen, Al-Qaeda, and the U.S." *The New York Review,* 30 September, 39.

2. Karl Vick. 2001. "Yemen Walks Tightrope in Terrorism Stance." *Washington Post,* 29 September.

3. Ian Fisher. 2003. "Hate of the West Finds Fertile Soil in Yemen. But Does Al-Qaeda?" *New York Times,* 9 January.

4. "Pilgrimage to Karbala, Sunni and Shia, the Worlds of Islam." 2007. PBS, 26 March. *(www.pbs.org).*

5. "Yemen." 2011. *The World Factbook.* Central Intelligence Agency, 17 May.

6. Sudarsan Raghavan. 2011. "Oil-Site Attacks Hit Yemen Hard." *Washington Post,* 2 July.

7. Christopher Boucek and David Donadio. 2010. "A Nation on the Brink," *The Atlantic,* April, 53.

8. "Yemen," *op. cit.*

9. "Yemen Remittances Total $1.5 Billion." 2011. Al-Shorfa, 8 January. *(alshorfa.com).*

10. Boucek and Donadio, *op. cit.,* 53.

11. Christopher Ward. 2001. "Yemen's Water Crisis." The British-Yemeni Society, July. *(www.al-bab.com).*

12. Rodenbeck, *op. cit.,* 42.

13. Robert F. Worth. 2009. "Thirsty Plant Dries Out Yemen." *New York Times*, 1 November.
14. Rodenbeck, *op. cit.*, 39.
15. "Yemen," *op. cit.*
16. Boucek, op. cit., 53.
17. "Yemen Education." NationMaster. *(www.nationmaster.com).*
18. "Young and Unmarried Yemeni Women More Likely to Pursue Career and Financial Independence." 2010. Newsdesk. Wowelle, 12 March. *(http://wowelle.com).*
19. Sudarsan Raghavan. 2011. "For Yemeni Women, Fruits of Revolution Still Out of Reach." *Washington Post.* 26 December.

## The Arabian Gulf States (Persian Gulf)

1. "The Situation of Female Membership of Governments by 2011." Worldwide Guide to Women in Leadership. *(www.guide2womenleaders.com).*

## Kuwait

1. "Islamists Dominate Kuwait Polls." 2008. BBC News, 18 May. *(http://news.bbc.co.uk).*
2. "Kuwait." 2011. *The World Factbook.* Central Intelligence Agency, 17 May.
3. "Kuwait's Ruler Orders 'Stricter' Security." 2011. *Newsday.* 17 November. *(www.newsday.com)*
4. *Ibid.*
5. *Ibid.*
6. Peter Mansfield. 1981. *The New Arabians.* New York: Doubleday, 112.
7. "Kuwait's Ruler," *op. cit.*
8. "Women's Rights in Kuwait." 2011. Wikipedia.
9. "Kuwait: New Labor Law Grants Grants Women the Right—and Flexibility—to Work Late." 2010. *Los Angeles Times,* 5 June.

## Bahrain

1. Joby Warrick. 2011. "Bahrain Ends State of Emergency, Vows Talks on Political Reform." *Washington Post,* 1 June.
2. "Bahrain's Brewing Crisis." 2011. *Washington Post,* 10 September.
3. Barbara Surk. 2011. "Bahrain court gives harsh sentences to protesters, those who treated them." *Washington Post,* 30 September.
4. "Tipping Point in Bahrain?" 2011. *Washington Post,* 24 November.
5. Alexandria Sandels. 2010. "Bahrain's Shiite Majority Makes Electoral Gains." *Los Angeles Times,* 24 October.
6. "Bahrain." 2011. *The World Factbook.* Central Intelligence Agency, 17 May.
7. "Foreigners Now Majority of Bahrain's Population." 2011. Agence France-Presse. Global Nation, 2 August. *(http://globalnation.inquirer.net).*
8. "Efforts Are Exerted to Fight Unemployment, Says Humaidan." 2011. Bahrain New Agency, 6 March. *(www.bna.bh).*
9. Peter Kennicott. 2011. "Splitting image." *Washington Post,* 11 May.
10. "Bahrain, People and Heritage." 2011. Wikipedia.

### Qatar

1. Dina Al-Shibeeb. 2011. "Qatar Holds Fourth Municipal Elections, and Nationals Welcome Opportunity to Vote." *Al-Arabiyya News*, 11 May.
2. "Qatar." 2011. Wikipedia.
3. "Kuwait's Ruler Orders Stricter Security." 2011, *Newsday*, 17 November. (*www.newsday.com*)
4. "Qatar." 2011. *The World Factbook*. Central Intelligence Agency, 17 May.

### The United Arab Emirates (UAE)

1. "Financial Management: United Arab Emirates." 2004. POGAR, Programme on Governance in the Arab Region. U.N. Development Programme. *(www.pogar.org)*.
2. *Ibid.*
3. "United Arab Emirates." 2011. *The World Factbook*, Central Intelligence Agency, 17 May.
4. "United Arab Emirates." 2011. Wikipedia.
5. *The World Factbook, op. cit.*
6. Eman Mohammed. 2008. "Arab First Ladies Speak Up for Women." *Gulf News* (UAE), 12 November. *(http://gulfnews.com).*
7. "Arabic or English?" 2009. *Khaleej Times*, 7 December. *(www.khaleejtimes.com).*
8. Wikipedia, *op. cit.*
9. *World Factbook, op. cit.*
10. Jason DeParle. 2007. "Fearful of Restive Foreign Labor, Dubai Eyes Reforms." *New York Times*, 6 August.
11. *Ibid.*
12. Wikipedia, *op. cit.*

### Oman

1. "Oman." 2011. *The World Factbook*. Central Intelligence Agency, 17 May.
2. "Oman." 2011. Wikipedia.
3. Meir Javedanfar. 2005. "Economic Analysis—Forecast of the Omani Economy for the Year 2007." *Middle East Analysis Review*, 20 July. *(www.meepas.com).*
4. Saleh Al-Shaibany. 2009. "Oman Oil Revenues Tumble 51 Pct Jan-April, Spending Up." Reuters, 13 June.
5. Javedanfar, *op. cit.*
6. *The World Factbook, op. cit.*
7. *Ibid.*
8. Wikipedia, *op. cit.*
9. "Oman's Women in Business and Government." 2005. International Business Wiki. *(http://internatonalbusiness.wikia.com).*
10. *The World Factbook, op. cit.*
11. Michael Slackman. 2009. "With Murmurs of Change, Sultan Tightens His Grip." *New York Times*, 15 May.

# BIBLIOGRAPHY

"4.5 Million Orphans in Iraq: Protests over Food and Shelter." 2011. Global Research. 22 February. <http://globalresearch.ca>.

"2008 Conflict in Lebanon." 2011. Wikipedia.

Abdallah, Abdel Mahdi. 2003. "Causes of Anti-Americanism in the Arab World: A Socio-Political Perspective." *Middle East Review of International Affairs* 7, 4 (December). 68.

"About Free Muslims Coalition." 2011. Free Muslims Coalition. 30 May. <www.free-muslims.org>.

Abrahamyan, Hovik. 2010. "Hovik Abrahamyan: Terrorism Is an Evil that Threatens All Humanity." 29 March. PanArmenian Network. <www.panarmenian.net>.

Abouzeid, Rania. 2011. "After the Revolution: Young Tunisians Are Still Looking for Work." *Time.* 7 February.

Abu Marzook, Mousa. 2006. "What Hamas Is Seeking." *Washington Post.* 31 January.

Adler, Margot. 2011. "Developer: Plans for N.Y. Mosque Moving Forward." *All Things Considered.* National Public Radio. 5 May.

"African Women in Engineering and Science: Egypt." 2011. Global Alliances. <www.globalallianmcesnet.org>.

Ajami, Fouad. 2005. "Bush Country." *The Daily Star* (Beirut). 23 May. <www.dailystar.com.lb>.

Ajami, Fouad. 2005. "The Meaning of Lebanon." The Foundation for the Defense of Democracy. 1 May. <www.defenddemocracy.org>.

Akl, Aida F. 2011. "Will Women Benefit from Middle East Revolution?" *Arab News.* 9 March. <www.voanews.com>.

Akyol, Mustafa. 2006. "Sexism Deleted in Turkey." *Washington Post.* 16 July.

Al-Ajmi, Nassir M. 2003. "Heart-to-Heart Talk—A Friend to Friend Discussion." The Ladah Foundation. 23 October. <www.ladah.org>.

Alam, M. Shahid. 2004. "The Clash Thesis: A Failing Ideology." Common Dreams News Center. <www.commondreams.org>.

Al-Marayati, Laila and Basil Abdelkarim. 2006. "The Crime of Being a Muslim Charity." *Washington Post.* 11 March.

Al Aswany, Alaa. 2011. *On the State of Egypt.* New York: Vintage Books. 87.

Al-Ba'albaki, Mounir. 2004. *Al-Mawrid: A Modern English-Arabic Dictionary.* Beirut: Dar El-Ilm lil-Malayen. 101–12.

"Algeria." 2011. *The World Factbook.* Central Intelligence Agency.

"Algeria Election: Reluctant Youth." 2005. *Arab-American Journal.* 23 December. <www.arabamerican.com>.

Al-Haq, Fawwaz Al-Abed. 2009. "Islam and Language Planning in the Arab world: A Case Study in Jordan." *Iranian Journal of Language Studies*, 3 (3). 267–302.

Al-Krenawi, Alean and John R. Graham. 2003. "Principles of Social Work Practice in the Muslim Arab World." *Arab Studies Quarterly* 25, 4 (Fall). 85.

Al-Shaibany, Saleh. 2009. "Oman Oil Revenues Tumble 51 Pct Jan-April, Spending Up." Reuters. 13 June.

Al-Shibeeb, Dina. 2011. "Qatar Holds Fourth Municipal Elections, and Nationals Welcome Opportunity to Vote." *Al-Arabiyya News.* 11 May.

Allen, J. A. 1981. *Libya, The Experience of Oil.* Boulder, CO: Westview Press. 22.

"The Amazigh (Berber)." 2011. Phoenician International Research Center. <www.phoenicia.org>.

Ambah, Faiza Saleh. 2008. "Saudi Women See a Brighter Road on Rights." *Washington Post.* 31 January.

Amikam, Yair. 2007. "The Palestinian Medical Crisis: An Exchange." *New York Review of Books.* 14 June.

"Amr Khaled." 2011. Wikipedia.

*Annual Report, Palestine Children, Child Statistics Series No. 14.* 2011. Palestinian Central Bureau of Statistics. Ramallah.

Applebaum, Anne. 2009. "In Morocco, an Alternative to Iran." *Washington Post.* 30 June.

*Arab Human Development Report 2009.* 2009. U.N. Development Programme. <www.arab-hdr.org>.

"Arab Spring Fails to Improve U.S. Image." 2011. Pew Research Center Publications. 17 May . <http://pewresearch.org>.

"Arab World." 2011. Wikipedia. February.

"Arabic or English?" 2009. *Khaleej Times* (UAE). 7 December. <www.khaleejtimes.com>.

"Are Women on Their Way at Last?" 2010. *The Economist.* 1 May.

Armas, Gennaro. 2005. "Census Bureau Says People of Arab Descent Doing Well in the United States." *Detroit Free Press.* 9 March.

Armstrong, Karen. 1992. *Muhammad, A Biography of the Prophet.* San Francisco: HarperSanFrancisco. 198.

Atiyeh, George N. 1977. *Arab and American Cultures.* Washington, D.C.: American Enterprise Institute for Public Policy Research. 179.

Audi, Nadim. 2011. "Offering Slow, Small Changes, Morocco's King Stays in Power." *New York Times.* 10 July.

"Background Note: Algeria." 2011. U.S. Department of State. 17 February.

"Background Note: Egypt." 2010. U.S. Department of State. 10 November.

"Background Note: Libya." 2010. U.S. Department of State. 17 November.

"Background on Women's Status in Iraq Prior to the Fall of the Saddam Hussein Government." 2003. *Human Rights Watch Briefing Paper.* Human Rights Watch. November. <http://hrw.org>.

"Bahrain." 2011. *The World Factbook.* Central Intelligence Agency. 17 May.

"Bahrain, People and Heritage." 2011. Wikipedia.

"Bahrain's Brewing Crisis." 2011. *Washington Post.* 10 September.

Bakar, Osman. 1999. *The History and Philosophy of Islamic Science.* Cambridge, U.K.: Islamic Texts Society. 214.

Bandew, Doug. 2009. "Maybe Europe Isn't Lost to Islamic Terrorism." Cato @ Liberty. 26 July. <www.cato-at-liberty.org>.

Barakat, Halim. 1993. *The Arab World: Society, Culture, and the State.* Berkeley: University of California Press. 21.

Baram, Marcus. 2011. "Threat of Right-Wing Extremism in U.S. Debated by Feds, Analysts." *Huffington Post.* 28 July. <www.huffingtonpost.com>.

Barber, Mike. 2001. "Muslims in the U.S. Military Are as Loyal as Any, Chaplain Says." *Seattle Post-Intelligencer.* 19 October.

Bashir, Abdul Wahab. 2002. "Scholars Define Terrorism, Call for Joint Action to Defend Islam." *Arab News*, 12 January.

Beck, Glenn. 2009. "Remember Why We Were Attacked on Sept. 11." Fox News, 11 September. <www.foxnews.com>.

Bellafronto, Catherine. 2004. "Syria." Freedom House. <www.freedomhouse.org>.

Bennett, William J. and Alan M. Dershowitz. 2006. "A Failure of the Press." *Washington Post.* 23 February.

"Berber Languages." 2005. *Columbia Encyclopedia*, 6th ed. <www.bartleby.com>.

"Berber Languages." 2004. Wikipedia.

Bhutto, Benazir. 1998. "Politics and the Modern Woman." In *Liberal Islam, A Sourcebook*, edited by Charles Kurzman. New York: Oxford University Press. 107.

Birke, Sarah. 2010. "In Syria, the Fight for Women's Rights Means Helping Both Genders." *Christian Science Monitor.* 7 June.

Blank, Jonah. 1998. "The Muslim Mainstream." *U.S. News and World Report.* 10 July. 22.

Blythe, Gilbert P. 2003. "We Are All Jews Now." *The Last Ditch*. WTM Enterprises. 19 October. <www.thornwalker.com>.

Bochlert, Eric. 2002. "Terrorists Under the Bed." *Salon.* 5 March. <www.salon.com>.

Boorstein, Michelle. 2010. "For Critics of Islam, 'Sharia' Is a Loaded Word." *Washington Post.* 27 August.

Boorstein, Michelle and Felicia Sonmez. 2011. "Familiar Sparring in Hearing on Civil Rights of Muslims." *Washington Post.* 30 March.

Booth, William. 2007. "Cast of Villains." *Washington Post.* 23 June.

Bordat, Stephanie Willman and Saida Kouzzi. 2004. "The Challenge of Implementing Morocco's New Personal Status Law." Global Rights. <www.globalrights.org>.

Boustany, Nora. 2006. "U.N. Cites Arab World's 'Empty Gestures' on Women." *Washington Post.* 8 December.

Bowen, Donna Lee and Evelyn A. Early, eds. 1993. *Everyday Life in the Muslim Middle East.* Bloomington: Indiana University Press. 77.

Bronner, Ethan. 2011. "Before a Diplomatic Showdown, a Budget Crisis Saps Palestinians' Confidence." *New York Times.* 27 July.

Brown, David. 2006. "Global Study Examines Toll of Genetic Defects." *Washington Post.* 30 January.

Butters, Andrew Lee. 2009. "Saudi's Small Steps." *Time.* 19 October.

Caldwell, Christopher. 2011. "Europe's Arizona Problem." *New York Times.* 11 June.

Charai, Ahmed and Joseph Braude. 2011. "All Hail the (Democratic) King." *New York Times.* 11 July.

Chivers, C. J. 2011. "Amid a Berber Reawakening in Libya, Fears of Revenge." *New York Times.* 9 August.

Choucair, Julia. 2004. "Dates of Women's Suffrage and Current Ministerial Positions Held by Women in Arab Countries." Carnegie Endowment for International Peace. <http://ceip.org>.

"CIA Insider: The Threat We Refuse to Get." 2004. *Washington Post.* 11 July.

Clayton, Mark. 2004. "How Are Mosques Fighting Terror?" *Christian Science Monitor.* 12 August.

Cody, Edward. 2010. "Belgium Approves Ban on Full-Face Veils in Public." *Washington Post.* 30 April.

Cody, Edward. 2009. "Tensions Grow for Muslims as French Debate National Identity." · *Washington Post.* 19 December.

Cohn, D'Vera. 2001. "Statistics Portray Settled, Affluent Mideast Community." *Washington Post.* 20 November.

Collins, Lauren. 2011. "England, Their England." *The New Yorker.* 4 July.

"Complete Text of President Bush's National Address." 2001. *Globe and Mail* (Canada). 12 September.

Conason, Joe. 2010. "Why Nobody Watches Our Arab TV Channel." *Salon.* 12 May.

Conlin, Jennifer. 2010. "Life Lessons in the Mideast." *New York Times.* 8 August.

"A Conservative Christian Group Sues the U.M.C. for Assigning a Book on Islam." 2002. Democracy Now. 8 August. <www.democracynow.org>.

Cooperman, Alan. 2005. "Jordan's King Abdullah Pushes for Moderation." *Washington Post.* 4 October.

Cooperman, Alan. 2002. "September 11 Backlash Murders and the State of Hate." *Washington Post*, 20 January.

Cooperman, Alan and Mary Beth Sheridan. 2005. "Muslims to Provide Food on Sept. 11." *Washington Post.* 9 September.

"Court Upholds Spanish City's Ban on Face-Covering Islamic Veils in Municipal Buildings." 2011. Associated Press. *Washington Post World.* 9 June. <www.washingtonpost.com/world>.

Culver, Virginia. 2002. "Many American Muslims Well-Off, College Educated, Poll Shows." *Denver Post.* 18 January.

"Current Projects. 2011. Iraqi Orphan Foundation. 15 October. <www.iraqiorphanfoundation.com>.

Curtis, Edward E., IV. 2010. "5 Myths About Mosques in America." *Washington Post.* 29 August.

Daher, Yusuf. 2004. "Palestinian Christians: Down from 2% to 1%. What Is Next?" Laity Committee on the Holy Land. 17 February. <www.holylandchristians.com>.

Daniszewski, John. 1997. "A Ray of Hope in a War-Torn Sudan." *New York Times.* 18 October.

Daragahi, Borzou. 2011. "Libya's Fed-Up Berbers Aiming for Equality." *Los Angeles Times.* 17 July.

Dawood, Khaled. 2004. "Arab Opinions." *Al-Ahram Weekly.* 30 July. <www.ahram.org.eg>.

Deane, Claudia and Darryl Fears. 2006. "Negative Perception of Islam Increasing." *Washington Post*. 9 March.

"Demographics." 2003. Arab American Institute. <www.aaiusa.org>.

"Demographics of Lebanon." 2011. Wikipedia.

"Denmark Imposes Restrictions on Imams." 2004. Islam Online. 18 February. <islamon-line.net>.

DeParle, Jason. 2007. "Fearful of Restive Foreign Labor, Dubai Eyes Reforms." *New York Times*. 6 August.

DeYoung, Karen. 2011. "Saleh Surrenders to Opposition, Yields Power." *Washington Post*. 24 November.

Diehl, Jackson. 2011. "Iraq, Mideast Model." *Washington Post*. 10 October.

"Economy of Algeria." 2011. Wikipedia.

"Economy of Jordan. 2011. Wikipedia.

"Education and Development in Iraq." 2010. U.N. Inter-Agency Info and Analysis Unit. <www.iauiraq.org>.

"Education in Jordan." 2011. Wikipedia.

"Education in Syria." 2006. Wikipedia.

"Efforts Are Exerted to Fight Unemployment, Says Humaidan." 2011. Bahrain New Agency. 6 March. <http://globalnation.inquirer.net>.

"Egypt." 2005. *Encarta Online Encyclopedia*. Microsoft Corp. <www.encarta.msn.com>.

"Egypt." 2011. Index Mundi. <www.indexmundi.com>.

"Egypt: Population Under Age 15." 2011. Human Development Report. UNDP. Globalis-Egypt.

"The Egyptian Revolution." 2011. Wikipedia.

"Egyptians Riot over Bread Crisis." 2008. *The Telegraph* (U.K.). 8 April.

"Egypt's Youth Unemployment Problem Has Erupted—But What About Britain's?" 2011. *Money Week*. 31 January. <www.moneyweek.com>.

Elliott, Andrea. 2007. "Where Boys Grow Up to Be Jihadis." *New York Times Magazine*. 27 November.

Elliott, Andrea. 2011. "The Man Behind the Anti-Shariah Movement." *New York Times*. 30 July.

El-Tablawy, Tarik. 2011. "Egyptian Food Prices Have Risen 20 Percent in the Last Year." Huffpost Business. *The Huffington Post*. 10 May.

Eltahawy, Mona. 2010. "Rending the Veil—With Little Help." *Washington Post*. 18 July.

Emerson, Steve. 2002. *American Jihad: The Terrorists Living Among Us*. New York: Free Press. 41.

Esposito, John L. 2004. "Preface," *The Islamic World: Past and Present*. Cary, N.C.: Oxford University Press USA.

Esposito, John and Dalia Mogahed. 2008. "Muslim True/False." *Los Angeles Times*. 2 April.

"E.U. Opens Debate on Economic Migration." 2005. EurActiv. 14 January. <www.euractiv.com>.

Fahim, Kareem. 2011. "Libya Revolt Leaves Women, Who Led It, on Sidelines." *New York Times*. 20 May.

Faiola, Anthony. 2010. "Anti-Muslim Feelings Propel Right Wing." *Washington Post*. 26 October.

Farhi, Paul. 2005. "Talk Show Host Graham Fired by WMAL Over Islam Remarks." *Washington Post.* 23 August.

Farrell, Michael B. 2010. "Tariq Ramadan Visits U.S. Part of a Fresh Start for West and Islam?" *Christian Science Monitor.* 9 April.

"Fatima Urges Protection of Arab Family." 1999. *UAE Interact.* Ministry of Information and Culture. <www.uaeinteract.com>.

Feiler, Bruce. 2011. *Generation Freedom.* New York: HarperCollins Publishers.

Fernea, Elizabeth. 2000. "Islamic Feminism Finds a Different Voice." *Foreign Service Journal* (May), 30.

"Fertility Rate, Total Births per Woman, Sudan." 2009. World Bank. <www.worldbank.org>.

"Fertilizer Use by Crop in Egypt." 1998. National Resources Management and Environmental Development. FAO Corporate Document Repository. <www.fao.org>.

Filiu, Jean-Pierre. 2011. *The Arab Revolution.* London: Hurst.

"Financial Management: United Arab Emirates." 2004. POGAR, Programme on Governance in the Arab Region. U.N. Development Programme. <www.pogar.org>.

Finnegan, William. 1999. "The Invisible War." *The New Yorker.* 25 January. 71.

"First Annual SICF Orphan's Conference in Baghdad." 2009. Rescue Iraq, World Orphans. April 25. <http://rescue.typepad.com>.

Fisher, Ian. 2003. "Hate of the West Finds Fertile Soil in Yemen, But Does Al-Qaeda?" *New York Times.* 9 January.

Fisher, Milia and Sara Birkenthal. 2011. "Jordan Becoming Choice Destination for Arabic- Language Study." *The Jordan Times.* 5 August.

Fleishman, Jeffrey. 2010. "Egypt's Provocative Voice of Moderate Islam." *Los Angeles Times.* 6 August.

Fleishman, Jeffrey and Kath Linthicum. 2010. "Demands on the Nile Imperil Egypt's Lifeline." *Los Angeles Times.* 12 September.

"Foreigners Now Majority of Bahrain's Population." 2011. Agence France-Presse. Global Nation. 2 August. <http://globalnation.inquirer.net>.

Foster, Florence. 2010. "New Rules for Foreign Workers in Saudi Arabia." Move One, Inc. 22 April. < www.moveoneinc.com>.

Foxman, Abraham H. 2011. "The New Shape of Anti-Muslim Hatred." *Washington Post.* 30 July.

Frenkel, Sheera. 2011. "Israel's '67 Borders Have Long Been at Root of Peace Debate." *Kansas City Star.* 20 May.

Fromkin, David. 1989. *A Peace to End All Peace.* New York: Henry Holt: 306.

"Gaza." 2011. *The World Factbook.* Central Intelligence Agency. 25 April.

"Gender Cleansing in Iraq: Women in Politics." 2008. Layalina Productions, Inc. 5 June. <www.layalina.tv>.

"Gender Equality and Social Institutions in Libya. 2006. Social Institutions and Gender Index. <http://genderindex.org>.

"Gender Equality and Social Institutions in Sudan." 2004. Social Institutions and Gender Index. <http://genderindex.org>.

"Gender: Lebanon." 2004. POGAR, Programme on Governance in the Arab Region. U.N. Development Programme. <www.pogar.org>.

Geranios, Nicholas K. 2011. "Libya Ends College Funding for 2,000 U.S. Students." Associated Press. 13 May.

Ghannoushi, Soumaya. 2011. "Obama, Hands Off Our Spring." *The Guardian* (U.K.). 26 May.

Ghosh, Bobby. 2011. "The Rebels' Road to Democracy," in "The Liberation of Libya." *Time*, 5 September. 34–37.

Giglio, Mike. 2011. "Saudi's Surprise Renegades." *Newsweek.* 9 May.

Goldberg, Jeffrey. 2011. "Danger, Falling Tyrants." *The Atlantic.* June. 50.

Goldfarb, Zachary A. 2006. "Va. Lawmaker's Remarks on Muslims Criticized." *Washington Post.* 21 December.

Goodman, David. 2011. "United States and Other Nations Step Up Libyan Evacuations." *New York Times.* 23 February

Goodstein, Laurie. 2011. "Forecast Sees Muslim Population Leveling Off." *New York Times.* 27 January.

Goodstein, Laurie. 2009. "Poll Finds U.S. Muslims Thriving, but Not Content." *New York Times.* 2 March.

Gowen, Annie. 2010. "Nowhere Near Ground Zero, but No More Welcome." *Washington Post.* 23 August.

Graham, Franklin. 2001. "My View of Islam." *Covenant News.* 9 December. <www.covenantnews.com>.

Green, William. 2011. "Libyan Students Worth More Than 160 Million Pounds To UK Universities." Journal Live. 4 March. <http://blogs.journallive.co.uk>.

Greenberg, Joel. 2011. "Motorcade of Jordan's King Said to Be Attacked." *Washington Post.* 14 June.

Greenwald, Glenn. 2007. "Large Number of Americans Favor Violent Attacks Against Civilians." *Salon.* 23 May. <www.salon.com>.

Grimsley, Kerstin. 2001. "More Arabs, Muslims Allege Bias on the Job." *Washington Post.* 12 February.

"Growing Urbanization." *Human Development Report, 1999.* 1999. U.N. Development Programme. <www.hdr.undp.org>.

Habeck, Mary. 2006. "Knowing the Enemy." Essay for *Book Talk.* 17 November. 4.

Haddad, Yvonne and Jane Smith. 2002. *Muslim Minorities in the West: Visible and Invisible.* New York. Altamira Press. xii.

Haddad, Yvonne Yazbek and Michael J. Balz. 2008. "Taming the Imams: European Governments and Islamic Preachers since 9/11." *Islam and Christian-Muslim Relations, 19,* 2 (April). *215.*

Halaby, Jamal. 2011. "Jordan's King Will Share Power in Forming Cabinet." *Washington Post.* 27 October

"Half Million Child Deaths 1991–1998." 2000. Global Policy Forum. United Nations. <www.globalpolicy.org>.

Hall, Edward T. 1966. *The Hidden Dimension.* New York: Doubleday. 15.

Hamamy, Hanan. 2003. "Consanguineous Marriages in the Arab World." National Centre for Diabetes, Endocrinology and Genetics: Amman, Jordan. July. <www.ambassadors.net>.

Hammond, Andrew. 2007. *Popular Culture in the Arab World.* Cairo: American University in Cairo Press.

Hanania, Ray. 2005. "Failure to Understand Arab Muslim Issues Exposes Nation to Attacks." 11 March. <www. hananiacreators/blogspot.com>.

Hasan, Aida. 1999. "Arab Culture and Identity: Arab Food and Hospitality." Suite University Online. <www.suite101.com>.

Hazleton, Leslie. 2009. *After the Prophet.* New York: Anchor Books. 108.

"Healing the Nation: Arab American Responses to September 11 Attacks." 2001. Arab American Institute. <www.aaiusa.org>.

"Health Situation in Iraq." 2003. World Health Organization, United Nations. <www.who.int>.

"Hijab by Country." 2011. Wikipedia.

Hillerman, Joost. 2011. "Waiting for Baghdad." *The New York Review.* 14 April. 55.

Hirst, David. 2005. "Syria's Unpredictable Storm." *Los Angeles Times.* 7 June.

"Historical Ties Leave Trying Legacy." 1993. *Christian Science Monitor.* 27 January.

"History of the Jews in Morocco." 2011. Wikipedia. 29 April.

Holzman, Michael. 2003. "Washington's Sour Sales Pitch." *New York Times.* 4 October.

House, Karen Elliott. 2012. *On Saudi Arabia: Its People, Past, Religion, Fault Lines—and Future.* New York: Alfred A. Knopf.

Hudson, Saul. 2005. "U.S. Halts Arabic Magazine Meant to Boost U.S. image." Reuters. 22 December. <www.alertnet.org>.

Humphreys, R. Stephen. 1999. *Between Memory and Desire: The Middle East in a Troubled Age.* Berkeley: University of California Press. 174.

Huntington, Samuel P. 1993. "The Clash of Civilizations." *Foreign Affairs* 72, 3 (Summer). 31– 32.

Huntington, Samuel P. 1996. *The Clash of Civilizations and the Remaking of World Order.* New York: Simon and Schuster. 211.

Hurdle, Jon. 2010. "Arabic Flashcards Land Student in U.S. Detention." Reuters. 10 February.

Hymas, Lisa. 2011. "Egypt Has a Population Crisis as Well as a Democracy Crisis." *Grist,* 5. February. <www.grist.org>.

Ibrahim, Alia, Robin Wright, and Ellen Knickmeyer. 2008. "As Tensions Rise in Lebanon, Residents Again Fear the Worst." 2008. *Washington Post.* 21 March.

Ignatius, David. 2010. "A Saudi Fatwa for Moderation." *Washington Post.* 13 June.

Ignatius, David. 2010. "Saudis Act Aggressively to Denounce Terrorism." *Washington Post.* 13 June.

Ignatius, David. 2005. "Taking Back Islam." *Washington Post.* 18 September.

Ignatius, David. 2010. "The Mideast's Generational Shift." *Washington Post.* 28 November.

"Internet Users per 1,000 People." 2004. *Human Development Report 2004.* 2004. U.N. Development Programme. <www.hdr.undp.org>.

"Intolerance." 2010. *The New Yorker.* 20 September. 47.

"Iraq." 2011. *The World Factbook.* Central Intelligence Agency. 12 January.

"Iraq: Briefing on Health." 2002. Office for Coordination of Humanitarian Affairs. United Nations. 18 May. <www.ochaonline.un.org>.

Iraq Body Count Project. 2011. February. <www.iraqbodycount.org.>.

"Iraq Deaths." 2009. Just Foreign Policy. <www.justforeignpolicy.org>.

"An Iraq Fit for Children: Building Iraq's Future." 2010. *Quarterly Newsletter.* United Nations Children's Fund, Issue 02.

"Iraqi Refugees in Syria Reluctant to Return to Home Permanently." 2010. U.N. High Commission for Refugees. 8 October. <www.unhcr.org>.

"Iraqi Women and Childdren's Liberaton Act of 2004, S2519." 2004. *The Orator.* U.S. Congress. 15 June. <www.theorator.com>.

"Islam in Australia." 2011. Wikipedia.

"Islam in Europe." 2011. Wikipedia.

"Islam Is Violent." 2008. Jesus-is-Lord. 29 November. <www.jesus-is-lord.com>.

"Islam, Jihad, and Terrorism." 2004. Institute of Islamic Information and Education. 14 October. <www.iiie.net>.

"Islamic Dress in Europe." 2011. Wikipedia.

"Islamists Dominate Kuwait Polls." 2008. BBC News. 18 May. <http://news.bbc.co.uk>.

"Israelis and Palestinians Killed in the Current Violence." 2011. If Americans Knew. 2 February. <www.ifamericansknew.org>.

Javendar, Meir. 2005. "Economic Analysis—Forecast of the Omani Economy for the Year 2007." *Middle East Analysis Review.* 20 July. <www.meepas.com>.

Jawad, Rana. 2008. "Women's Lib Takes Off in Libya." BBC News. 29 April. <http://newsvote.bbc.co.uk>.

"Jordan." 2011. *The World Factbook.* Central Intelligence Agency. 17 May.

"Jordan Creates Commission to Examine Reform." 2011. Agence France-Presse. France 24, International News. 14 March. <www.france24.com>.

"Jordanian Parliamentary Election, 2010." 2011. Wikipedia.

Karam, Ghassan. 2010. "Human Development in the Arab World." *Ya Libnan.* 7 November. (based on UNDP figures). <www.yalibnan.com>.

Karmi, Ghada. 2002. *In Search of Fatima, A Palestinian Story.* London: Verso. 181.

Kawatch, Nadim. 2010. "Arab World Needs to Rise to the Literacy Challenge." Emirates 24/7 News. 28 July. <www.emirates247.com>.

Kennicott, Peter. 2011. "Splitting Image." *Washington Post.* 11 May.

Kennicott, Philip. 2004. "An About-Face on America." *Washington Post.* 24 August.

Kern, Soeren. 2010. "Europe's Mosque Wars." Pundicity. 18 August. <http://kern.pundicity.com>.

Kershaw, Sarah. 2010. "The Terrorist Mind: An Update." *New York Times.* 10 January.

Kershner, Isabel. 2009. "U.N. Seeks End to Razing of Homes in East Jerusalem." *New York Times.* 1 May.

Kessler, Glenn and Robin Wright. 2005. "Report: U.S. Image in Bad Shape." *Washington Post*, 24 September.

Kettani, Housain. 2009. *Muslim Population in Europe.* Proceedings of the 2009 International Conference on Social Sciences and the Humanities, 9-11 October. Table 4, "Muslim Population in Northeastern Europe in 2010." Table 4.1, "Muslim Population in Souhwestern Europe in 2010."

Khalidi, Rashid. 2004. *Resurrecting Empire: Western Footprints and America's Perilous Path in the Middle East.* Boston: Beacon Press. xii.

Kharoufi, Mostafa. 1996. "Urbanization and Urban Research in the Arab World." UNESCO. <www.unesco.org>.

Khouri, Rami. 2003. "For Arabs, a Cruel Echo of History." *The Daily Star* (Beirut). 21 March. <www.dailystar.com.lb>.

Kirkpatrick, David D. 2011. "Egypt's Military Expands Power, Raising Alarms." *New York Times*. 14 October.

Kirkpatrick, David D. 2011. "Egypt Military Moves to Cement a Muscular Role in Government." *New York Times*. 16 July.

Kirkpatrick, David D. 2011. "Egypt Purges Mubarak-Era Police Officers." *New York Times*. 13 July.

Kirkpatrick, David D. 2011. "Surge in Crime Imperils Effort to Remake Egypt." *New York Times*. 12 May.

Kirkpatrick, David D. and Mona El-Naggar. 2011. "Poll Finds Egyptians Full of Hope About Future." *New York Times*. 26 April.

Klein, Helen Altman and Gilbert Kuperman. 2008. "Through an Arab Cultural Lens." *The Military Review*, (May-June). 103.

Knickmeyer, Ellen. 2006. "Ghosts of Iraq's Birth." *Washington Post National Weekly Edition*. 13–19 March.

Knickmeyer, Ellen. 2005. "Iraqi Women See Little but Darkness." *Washington Post*. 15 October.

Knickmeyer, Ellen and Yasmin Mousa. 2007. "Jordan's Limited Democracy Leaves Voters Discontented." *Washington Post* 20 november.

Kramer, Jane. 2006. "The Crusader." *The New Yorker*. 16 October.

Krauthammer, Charles. 2006. "'Munich,' the Travesty." *Washington Post*. 13 January

Krauthammer, Charles. 2005. "Syria and the New Axis of Evil." *Washington Post*. 1 April.

Krauthammer, Charles. 2005. "Why It Deserves the Hype." *Time*. 14 February. 80.

Kristof, Nicholas D. 2002. "Bigotry in Islam and Here." *New York Times*. 9 July.

Kristof, Nicholas D. 2009. "Islam, Virgins, and Grapes." *New York Times*. 23 April.

Kron, Josh. 2011. "Sudan Leader to Accept Secession of South." *New York Times*. 7 February.

Kronemer, Alexander. 2002. "Understanding Muhammad." *Christian Science Monitor*. 9 December.

Kunkle, Frederick. 2011. "Are Good Works Good Politics?" *Washington Post*. 9 April.

"Kuwait." 2011. Index Mundi. <www.indexmundi.com>.

"Kuwait." 2011. *The World Factbook*. Central Intelligence Agency. 17 May.

"Kuwait: New Labor Law Grants Women the Right—and Flexibility—to Work Late." 2010. *Los Angeles Times*. 5 June.

Lacey, Robert. 2009. *Inside the Kingdom*. London: Penguin Books Ltd. 169.

Lacey, Terry. 2009. "Muslim Population Current Estimate: 1.8 Billion, Christians 2.2 Billion—Only 20% of Muslims Live in the Middle East/North Africa Combined." Pew Forum on Religion and Public life. 10 September. <www.waryatv.com>.

Lally, Kathy. 2011. "Egypt Calls." *Washington Post*. 1 May.

Lampman, Jane. 2002. "Muslim in America." *Christian Science Monitor*. 10 January.

Laurence, Jonathan. 2007. "The Prophet of Moderation: Tariq Ramadan's Quest to Reclaim Islam." *New York Times*. 18 June.

Lawrence, T. E. 1926. *The Seven Pillars of Wisdom*. New York: Doubleday. 24.

"Leading Indicators of Revolt in the Middle East and North Africa: Corruption, Unemployment and Percentage of Household Money Spent on Food." 2011. "Arab League Index of Unrest." *The Big Picture*. Ritholtz. February. <www.ritholtz.com>.

"Lebanese Unemployment Rate." 2011. Index Mundi. <www.indexmundi.com>.

Lee, Martin A. 2004. "Not a Prayer." *Harper's Magazine* (June). 79.

Lee, Matthew and Martin Crutsinger. 2011. "U.S. Slaps Sanctions on Syria's Assad for Abuses." Associated Press. 18 May.

Leland, John and Riyadh Mohammed. 2010. "Iraqi Women Are Seeking Greater Political Influence." *New York Times.* 17 February.

Levinson, Charles. 2005. "Egyptian Women See Divorce as Religious Right." Women's e-News. 9 January. <www.womensnews.org>.

Lewis, Bernard. 2002. "Targeted by a History of Hatred." *Washington Post.* 10 September.

Lewis, Bernard. 1990. "The Roots of Muslim Rage." *The Atlantic Monthly.* (September). 56.

"Libya." 2011. *The World Factbook.* Central Intelligence Agency.

"Libyan Students in U.S. Blackmailed into Attending Pro-Qaddhafi Rallies." 2011. *The Arab- American News.* 18 February. <www.arabamericannews.com>.

"Libya's Well-Oiled Revolution." 2011. *Time.* 7 November.

"Line of Separation." 2006. *Washington Post.* 30 May.

Londono, Ernesto. 2011. "Clashes kill 23 in heart of Cairo." *Washington Post.* 10 October.

Londono, Ernesto. 2006. "Teacher Charged After Uproar Over Arabic." *Washington Post.* 13 September.

Lynch, Colum. 2005. "Report Urges Arab Governments to Share Power." *Washington Post.* 5 April.

MacFarquhar, Neil. 2011. "In Saudi Arabia, Royal Funds Buy Peace, For Now." *New York Times,* 9 June.

MacFarquhar, Neil. 2007. "New Translation Prompts Debate on Islamic Verse." *New York Times.* 23 March.

MacFarquhar, Neil. 2001. "Syria Reaches Turning Point, but Which Way Will It Turn?" *New York Times.* 12 March.

Maghraoui, Abdeslam. 2006. *American Foreign Policy and Islamic Renewal.* United States Institute of Peace, Special Report. July. <www.usip.org>.

"Making Egypt More Food Secure: Short-Term and Long-Term U.S. Actions." 2011. Center for American Progress. <www.americanprogress.org>.

Mansfield, Peter. 1981. *The New Arabians.* New York: Doubleday. 112.

Martin, Andrew. 2008. "Mideast Facing Choice Between Crops and Water." *New York Times.* 21 July.

Martinson, Jane. 2011. "The Fight for Women's Rights in the Middle East." *The Guardian* (U.K.). 11 March.

McConnell, Scott. 2001. "Why Many Arabs Hate America." Media Monitors Network. 12 September. <www.mediamonitors.net>.

McCrummen, Stephanie. 2007. "Sudan, in Mud Brick and Marble." *Washington Post.* 26 February.

McDermott, Terry. 2011. "Counting Muslim Terrorists and Coming Up Short." (A review of *The Missing Martyrs* by Charles Kurzman, published by Oxford University.) *Washington Post,* 21 August.

McEvers, Kelly. 2008. "Saudis Slow to Accept Working Women." *Marketplace.* 23 April. <http://marketplace.publicradio.org>.

McGirk, Tim. 2008. "Morocco's Gentle War on Terror." *Time.* 6 August.

McLoughlin, Leslie J. 1982. *Colloquial Arabic (Levantine).* London: Routledge and Kegan Paul. 2–3.

Merrod, Tessa. 2003. "Too Little: The Vicious Circle of Drought in North Darfur." Intermediate Technology Development Group (U.K.). October. <www.itdg.org>.

Michaels, Adrian. 2009. "The E.U. Is Facing an Era of Vast Social Change, Reports Adrian Michaels, and Few Politicians Are Taking Notice." *The Telegraph* (U.K.). 8 August.

"Middle East Population Set to Double." 2002. *Popline.* Population Institute. 25 April. <www.populationinstitute.org>.

Milne, Seamus. 2010. "This Tide of Anti-Muslim Hatred Is a Threat to Us All." *The Guardian* (U.K.). 25 February.

Mohammed, Eman. 2008. "Arab First Ladies Speak Up for Women." *Gulf News* (UAE). 12 November. <http://gulfnews.com>.

Molavi, Afshin. 2006. "Challenge for Reform-Minded King: To Weaken Religious Radicals." *St. Paul Pioneer Press.* 3 September.

Moore, Molly. 2007. "In a Europe Torn Over Mosques, A City Offers Accommodation." *Washington Post.* 9 December.

Moore, Tristana. 2011. "After Norway, Will Germany Ban a Far-Right Political Party?" *Time World.* 10 August. <www.time.com>.

"More than 99% of Terrorism Is Not Islamic." 2010. Disclose TV. 7 October. <www. disclosetv>.

Morello, Carol. 2011. "In Poll, Muslims Largely Upbeat About Life in U.S." *Washington Post*,30 August.

"Moroccan Women and Gender Inequality in the Workplace." 2010. European Professional Women's Network. 27 April. <www.EuropeanPWN.net>.

"Morocco." 2011. Index Mundi. <www.indexmundi.com>.

"Morocco Age Structure." 2010. Index Mundi. <www.indexmundi.com>.

"Mosques and Islamic Centers in Canada." 2010. Islamic Supreme Council. 20 January. <www.islamicsupremecouncil.com/canada.htm>.

Mouallem, Mona Lisa. 2011. "Will the Revolutions Help or Hurt Women? A Country-by-Country Look." Global Public Square. CNN World. 16 March. <http://global-publicsquare.blogs.cnn.com>.

Mousalli, Ahmad S. 1999. *Moderate and Radical Islamic Fundamentalism.* Gainesville: University of Florida Press. 181–86.

Mroue, Bassem. 2011. "Hezbollah's Candidate to Form Lebanese Government." *Washington Times.* 25 January.

Mujahid, Abdel Malik. 2001. "Muslims in America: Profile 2001." SoundVision. <www. soundvision.com>.

Muqbil, Imtiaz. 2011. "Ten Years after 9/11, Pew Poll Shows U.S.-Muslim Schism as Wide as Ever." *Travel Impact Newswire.* 18 May. <www.travel-impact-newswire.com>.

Murphy, Caryle and Susan Kinzie. 2006. "Saudis Again Head to U.S. Campuses." *Washington Post.* 11 November.

Murphy, Kim. 2006. "Hamas Victory Is Built on Social Work." *Los Angeles Times.* 2 March.

"Muslim Americans: Middle Class and Mostly Mainstream." 2007. Pew Research Center. 22 May. <http://people-press.org>.

"Muslim Population in Canada to Double by 2017." 2009. Madinat Al Muslimeen. 10 March. <http://jannah.org>.

"Muslim Women Wearing Veil 'Refused Bus Ride' in London." 2010. BBC News. 23 July.

Myers, Steven Lee. 2005. "Growth of Islam in Russia Brings Soviet Response." *New York Times*. 22 November.

"New MLA Survey Report Finds that the Study of Languages Other Than English Is Growing and Diversifying at U.S. Colleges and Universities." 2010. Modern Language Association. 8 December. <www.mla.org>.

Ngawi, Rodrique. 2002. "Rwanda Turns to Islam after Genocide." *Times Daily*. 7 November. <www.timesdaily.com>.

Nicolaou-Garcia, Silvia. 2010. "Christian-Muslim relations in Palestine." *Middle East Monitor*. 24 June. <www.middleeastmonitor.org.uk>.

"Obama Renews Syria Sanctions." 2010. Agence France-Presse. *New York Times*. 3 May.

"Oman." 2011. Wikipedia.

"Oman." 2011. *The World Factbook*. Central Intelligence Agency. 17 May.

"Oman's Women in Business and Government." 2005. International Business Wiki. <http://internationalbusiness.wikia.com>.

Omstad, Thomas. 2005. "The Casbah Connection." *U.S. News and World Report*. 9 May. 28.

Onyiego, Michael and Staziuso, Jason. 2012. "South Sudan's Surging Violence Draws Emergency Aid Response." *Washington Post*. 8 January.

"Palestinians Try for Their Own Arab Spring." 2011. *Time*. 30 May. 12.

Pape, Robert A. 2005. *Dying to Win: The Strategic Logic of Suicide Terrorism*. New York: Random House. 23.

"Paper or Plastic?—A More Perfect Union Project." 2010. Flikr. 6 April. <www.flikr.com>.

Parker, Kathleen. 2010. "What Americans Can Do to Discourage Future McVeighs." *Washington Post*. 18 April.

Patai, Raphael. 2002. *The Arab Mind* (1973; reprint). Long Island: The Hatherleigh Press.

Peters, Ralph. 2002. *Beyond Terror*. Mechanicsburg, P.A.: Stackpole Books. 35.

Peters, Ralph. 2003. *The Tragedy of the Arabs*. Word Gems. March 30. <www.wordgems.com>.

Pilger, John. 2005. "Squeezed to Death." *The Guardian* (U.K.). 4 March.

"Pilgrimage to Karbala, Sunni and Shia, the Worlds of Islam." 2007. PBS, 26 March. <www.pbs.org>.

Pilkington, Ed. 2011. "U.S. Vetoes U.N. Condemnation of Israeli Settlements." *The Guardian* (U.K.). 19 February.

Pipes, Daniel. 2003. *Militant Islam Reaches America*. New York: W.W. Norton & Co. 247–48.

"Poll Data: Arabs Doubt U.S." 2007. Layalina Productions, Inc. April 13–26. <www.layalina.tv>.

"Poll: Islamic Women Liked as Leaders." 2006. United Press International. 30 March. <www.upi.com>.

"Polls Point to American-Muslim Rift." 2007. Layalina Productions, Inc. July 20–August 2. <www.layalina.tv>.

"Population and Failing States: Sudan." 2009. Population Institute. <www.populationinstitute.org>.

"Population Density." 2011. Palestinian Central Bureau of Statistics. Palestine National Authority. 12 May.

"Population Density per Square Mile of Countries." 2009. <www.infoplease.com>.

"Population Trends in Europe and Their Sensitivity to Policy Measures." 2004. Committee on Migration, Refugees and Population. <http://assembly.coe.int>.

Potok, Mark. 2008. "Hate Rises." *Washington Post.* 9 March.

Potok, Mark. 2010. "Rage on the Right." *Intelligence Report*, 137 (Spring).

"Post-Revolutionary Tunisia: Moving Ahead." 2011. *The Economist.* 16 July.

"Prevalence of Child Malnutrition (Percentage Underweight Under Age Five) 2000–2009." 2009. Global Health Facts. Kaiser Foundation. <www.globalhealthfacts.org>.

"Qatar." 2011. Wikipedia.

"Qatar." 2011. *The World Factbook.* Central Intelligence Agency. 17 May.

Qutb, Muhammad Sayyid. 1979. "The Role of Religion in Education." In *Aims and Objectives of Islamic Education*, edited by S. N. Al-Attas. Jeddah: King Abdulaziz University. 60.

Raghavan, Sudarsan. 2011. "For Yemeni Women, Fruits of Revolution Still Out of Reach." *Washington Post.* 26 December.

Raghavan, Sudarsan. 2011. "Oil-Site Attacks Hit Yemen Hard." *Washington Post.* 2 July.

Ramadan, Tariq. 2008. "Anti-Muslim Bias Taints 'Tolerant' Europe." Topix. 10 December. <www.topix.com>.

Ramadan, Tariq. 2004. *Western Muslims and the Future of Islam.* Oxford: Oxford University Press. 6.

Raz, Guy. 2006. "The War on the Word 'Jihad.'" *All Things Considered.* National Public Radio. 31 October.

"Report Instances of Extremism or Support of Terrorism." 2005. Free Muslims Coalition. <www.freemuslims.org>.

Richman, Sheldon. 2002. "Another Frankenstein's Monster." *Commentaries.* The Future of Freedom Foundation. 27 December. <www.fff.org>.

Ripley, Amanda. 2008. "Reverse Radicalism." *Time.* 24 March. *The New York Review.* 30 September. 39.

Rosebell. 2011. "South Sudan Women Seek 30 Percent Representation in a New State." *Rosebell's Blog.* 20 April. <http://rosebellkagumire.com>.

Rubin, Alissa J. 2009. "Iraqi Surveys Start to Unveil the Mental Scars of War, Especially Among Women." *New York Times.* 7 March.

Rubin, Barry. 2002. "The Real Roots of Arab Anti-Americanism." *Foreign Affairs* (November/December). 80.

Ruiz, Maricelle, ed. 2006. "The United Arab Emirates Tops the List of Internet Use in the Middle East." Internet Business Law Services. 31 May. <https://ibis.com>.

Ruthven, Malise. 2009. "The Big Muslim Problem!" *The New York Review.* 17 December.

Sacirbey, Omar. 2006. "Did Muhammad Really Say That? Muslims Re-Examine the Words of the Prophet in Today's Light." *Washington Post.* 5 August.

Sacirbey, Omar. 2011. "Islamic Law Ban in State Courts Petitioned by Muslims." *Huffington Post*, 13 September.

Saloojie, Riad. 2000. "The Nature of Islam." *The Globe and Mail* (Canada). 16 January.

Samhan, Helen. 2001. "Arab Americans." Arab American Institute. <www.aaiusa.org>.

Sandels, Alexandra. 2010. "Bahain's Shiite Majority Makes Electoral Gains." *Los Angeles Times.* 24 October.

"Saudi Arabia." 2011. Index Mundi. <www.indexmundi.com>.

"Saudi Arabia." 2011.*The World Factbook*. Central Intelligence Agency. 17 May.

"Saudi Arabia, International Religious Freedom Report 2004." 2004. Bureau of Democracy, Human Rights, and Labor. U.S. Department of State. 15 November. <www. state.gov>.

"Saudi Arabia's Foreign Workforce." 2003. *BBC News World Edition*. BBC News. 13 May.

"Saudis to Allow Female Drivers and Award Female Journalists, Qatar's First Female Jockey." 2008. Layalina Productions, Inc. 18–31 January. <www.layalina.tv>.

Sayare, Scott. 2011. "Tunisia Is Uneasy Over Party of Islamists." *New York Times*. 15 May.

Scheuer, Michael. 2004. *Imperial Hubris: Why the West Is Losing the War on Terror.* Washington D.C.: Brassey's Inc. 17.

"School Enrollment, Tertiary." 2008. Index Mundi (from UNESCO data). <www.index-mundi.com>.

Schrank, Delphine. 2006. "Survey Details 'Deep' Divide Between Muslims, Westerners." *Washington Post*. 23 June.

Schuman, Michael. 2011. "Seeking Growth After the Arab Spring." *Time*. 22 August.

Schumpeter. 2011. "Young, Jobless and Looking for Trouble." *The Economist*. 3 February.

Schwartz, Emma. 2008. "Giving Voice to a Long-Repressed People." *U.S. News & World Report*. 24–31 March. 29.

Seib, Philip. 2011. "Obama Tries Again in the Arab World." Scrollpost. 13 May. <http://scrollpost.com>.

Shafie, Sharifa. 2003. "Palestinian Refugees in Syria." FMO Research Guide. <www. forcedmigration.org>.

Shapiro, Samantha M. 2006. "Ministering to the Upwardly Mobile Muslim." *New York Times Magazine*. 30 April.

Sharp, Jeremy M. 2010. "U.S. Foreign Aid to Israel." Congressional Research Service. 16 September. <www.fas.org>.

Sheldon, Louise. 2004. "Reflections on the Status of Women in Islam." *Baltimore Chronicle and Sentinel*. 2 June. <www.baltimorechronicle.com>.

Shenker, Jack. 2011. "Egypt Election Results Put Muslim Brotherhood Ahead." *The Guardian* (UK). 30 November.

Sheridan, Mary Beth. 2005. "U.S. Muslim Groups Cleared." *Washington Post*. 18 November.

Shi's [Shia] in Saudi Arabia." 2004. *Minorities at Risk Project*. Center for International Development and Conflict Management. University of Maryland. 15 July. <www. cidem.umd.edu>.

Shipler, David. 1986. *Arab and Jew, Wounded Spirits in a Promised Land*. New York: Penguin Books. 387.

Shulman, Robin. 2007. "In New York, a Word Starts a Fire." *Washington Post*. 24 August.

Simmons, Erica. 1990. "A Passion for Justice." *New Internationalist*, 210 (August). 9.

Simmons, Jonathan. 2011. "Lebanon's First Lady to Arab world: Make Women's Rights a Priority." *Daily Star* (Beirut). <www.dailystar.com.lb>.

Slackman, Michael. 2007. "A Quiet Revolution in Algeria: Gains by Women." *New York Times*. 26 May.

Slackman, Michael. 2008. "In Algeria, a Tug of War for Young Minds." *New York Times*. 23 June.

Slackman, Michael. 2009. "With Murmurs of Change, Sultan Tightens His Grip." *New York Times*. 15 May.

Slade, Shelley. 1981. "The Image of the Arab in America: Analysis of a Poll of American Attitudes." *Middle East Journal* 35, 2 (Spring). 143.

Sly, Liz. 2011. "Six Italian U.N. Peacekeepers Injured in Bomb Attack in Southern Lebanon." *Washington Post.* 28 May.

Smith, Craig. 2004. "Voices of the Dead Echo Across Algeria." *New York Times.* 18 April.

Smith, Helena. 2009. "The First Ladies of the Arab World Blaze a Trail for Women's Rights." *The Observer* (U.K.). 8 March.

Smith, Lee. 2004. "Democracy Inaction: Understanding Arab Anti-Americanism." *Slate* 23. (April). <www.slate.msn.com>.

Smith, Sylvia. 2009. "New Ideas for Jordan's Traditional Bedouin." BBC News. 22 May.

Spinner, Jackie. 2005. "An Attack Burns Anguish into Kurdish Region." *Washington Post.* 6 February.

Stack, Megan. 2005. "The Many Layers of the Veil." *Los Angeles Times.* 12 January.

Steele, Jonathan. 2003. "Terrorism Is Not an Enemy State that Can Be Defeated." *The Guardian* (U.K.). 23 November.

Stengel, Richard. 2006. "One Thing We Need to Do." *Time.* 11 September.

Stern, Jessica. 2010. "5 Myths About Who Becomes a Terrorist." *Washington Post.* 10 January.

"Sudan." 2011. *World Factbook.* Central Intelligence Agency.

"Sudan 2010." 2010. Freedom House. <www.freedomhouse.org>.

"Sudan at War With Itself." 2007. *Washington Post.* 7 April.

"Sudan Migration Country Profile." 2011. Secretariat for Sudanese Working Abroad. Zunia. 17 February. <http://zunia.org>.

"Sudan: Population." 2005. *Encyclopedia Britannica Online.* 13 February. <www.britannica.com>.

Sullivan, Amy. 2011. "Articles of Faith: The Conservative Double Standard on Christian Terrorism." *Time Swampland.* 29 July. <http://swampland.time.com>.

Sullivan, Andrew. 2011. "Breivik: A Living Definition of Christianism." *The Daily Beast,* 25 July. <www.thedailybeast.com>.

Sullivan, Kevin. 2007. "Younger Muslims Tune In to Upbeat Religious Message." *Washington Post,* 2 December.

Suri, Sanjay. 2006. "Saddam Better for Women." Inter Press Service. 30 March. <http://ipsnews.net>.

Susman, Tina. 2007. "Iraqis Divided by Treatment of Women in Constitution." *Los Angeles Times.* 9 October.

*Syria, A Country Study.* Thomas Collelo, ed. 1988. Washington, D.C.: Department of the Army. 81–82

*Syria, Country Study Guide.* 2007. Washington D.C.: International Business Publications, USA.

"Syria Unemployment Rate." 2011. Index Mundi. <www.indexmundi.com>.

Takieddine, Randa. 2011. "The Southern Sudan Referendum and Sanctions on Sudan." *Al- Hayat* (Beirut). 9 February. <www.daralhayat.com>.

"Tariq Ramadan." 2011. Wikipedia.

Taspinar, Omer. 2003. "Europe's Muslim Street." *Foreign Policy* 135, (March-April). 77.

"Terrorism: Is Anders Breivik a Christian?" 2011. *The Week.* 12 August.

Timberg, Scott. 2007. "Middle East through Western Eyes." *Los Angeles Times*. 7 September.

"Top U.S. evangelist targets Islam." 2006. BBC News. 14 March. <http://news.bbc.co.uk>.

"Tourism in Tunisia." 2011. Focus Multimedia. <www.focusmm.com>.

"Transcript of Bin Ladin's speech." 2004. Al-Jazeera. 30 October. <www.aljazeera.net>.

Trejos, Nancy. 2006. "Women Lose Ground in the New Iraq." *Washington Post*. 16 December.

Trescott, Jacqueline. 2006. "Kennedy Center Plans Festival as Olive Branch to Arab Culture." *Washington Post*. 28 April.

"The Truth About American Muslims." 2011. *New York Times*. 1 April.

"Tunisia." 2011. *The World Factbook*. Central Intelligence Agency.

"Tunisia: International Religious Freedom Report 2003." 2003. Bureau of Democracy, Human Rights and Labor. U.S. Department of State. 18 December.

"Tunisia: Minister, Jobs Abroad for 35,000 Tunisians by 2013." 2011. Ansamed. 23 May. <www.ansamed.info>.

"Tunisian Economy to Grow 1–2 Pct in 2011: Cenbank." 2011. Reuters. 30 April. <http://afreuters.com>.

"Unemployment in the Arab World." 2008. Layalina Productions, Inc. July 18–31. <www.layalina.tv>.

"United Arab Emirates." 2011. Wikipedia.

"United Arab Emirates." 2011. *The World Factbook*. Central Intelligence Agency. 17 May.

"Unmarried Childbearing." 2008. Centers for Disease Control and Prevention. <www.cdc.gov>.

"Unprecedented Opportunity." 2005. The Center for Public Integrity, interview with Rami Khoury. 2 March. <www.publicintegrity.org>.

"U.S. Military Aid and the Israel/Palestine Conflict." 2011. If Americans Knew. <www.ifamericansknew.org>.

"U.S. Needs to Go Goodwill Hunting." 2005. *Washington Post*. 30 September.

"U.S. Public Diplomacy in the Middle East on a New Course." 2009. Layalina Productions, Inc. December 18–31. <www.layalina.tv>.

Vick, Karl. 2011. "Yemen Walks Tightrope in Terrorism Stance." *Washington Post*. 29 September.

"Views of a Changing World." 2003. Pew Global Attitudes Project. June. <www.people-press.org>.

Vu, Michelle. 2011. "Muslim Population to Double in U.S. by 2030, Report Projects." *Free Republic*. 29 January.

Walker, Martin. 2009. "The World's New Numbers." *The Wilson Quarter*, (Spring), 26.

"War in Libya: Closing in on Tripoli." 2011. *The Economist*. 16 July.

Ward, Christopher. 2001. "Yemen's Water Crisis." The British Yemeni Society. July. <www.al- bab.com>.

Warrick, Joby. 2011. "Bahrain Ends State of Emergency, Vows Talks on Political Reform." *Washington Post*. 1 June.

Warrick, Joby. 2010. "In Jordan, U.S. Finds Quiet Ally in Arab World." *Washington Post*. 4 October.

Warrick, Joby. 2011. "U.S. envoy accosted by mob in Syria." *Washington Post*. 30 September.

Wax, Emily. 2002. "Jihad Is Taught as Struggle to Heal." *Washington Post.* 23 September.

"West Bank." 2011. *The World Factbook.* Central Intelligence Agency. 3 May.

"What Lies behind Egypt's Problems?" 2011. Bill Totten's Weblog. 4 February. <http://billtotten.blogspot.com>.

Whitaker, Brian. 2000. "Why the Rules of Racism Are Different for Arabs." *The Guardian* (U.K.). 18 August.

Whitlock, Craig and Greg Miller. 2011. "U.S. Creating a Ring of Secret Drone Bases." *Washington Post,* 21 September.

"Why Does Iraq Body Count Report a Much Lower Number?" 2011. Unknown News, April 25. <www.unknownnews.org>.

Wildman, Sarah. 2003. "Third Way Speaks to Europe's Young Muslims." *International Reporting Project,* Johns Hopkins School of Advanced International Studies (Spring). <www.journalismfellowships.org>.

Williams, Daniel. 2005. "Unveiling Islam: Author Challenges Orthodox Precepts." *Washington Post.* 9 September.

Willis, David K. 1984. "The Impact of Islam." *Christian Science Monitor,* weekly international edition. 18–24 August.

Wilson, Scott. 2005. "Shiites See an Opening in Saudi Arabia." *Washington Post.* 28 February.

"Women in National Parliaments, Situation as of 31 March 2011." Inter-Parliamentary Union. <www.ipu.org>.

"Women, Media and Politics in Lebanon." 2008. *Menassat.* 16 July. <www.menassat.com>.

"Women's Rights in Kuwait." 2011. Wikipedia.

"Women's Rights in the Middle East and North Africa: Citizenship and Justice, Palestine (Palestinian Authority and Israeli-Occupied Territories)." 2011. Freedom House. <www.freedomhouse.org>.

*World Urbanization Prospects, 2009 Revision.* 2011. U.N. Dept. of Economic and Social Affairs. 10 August. <http://esa.un.org>.

"Worldwide Suicide Rates." 2005. Suicide and Mental Health Association International. February. <www.suicideandmentalhealthassociationinternational.org>.

Worth, Robert F. 2009. "Preaching Moderate Islam and Becoming a TV Star." *New York Times.* 3 January.

Worth, Robert F. 2009. "Thirsty Plant Dries Out Yemen." *New York Times.* 1 November.

Wright, Robin. 2009. "Islam's Soft Revolution." *Time.* 30 March. 38.

Wright, Robin. 2011. "The Struggle Within Islam." *Smithsonian* (September). 104–114.

"Yemen." 2011. *The World Factbook.* Central Intelligence Agency. 17 May.

"Yemen Education." 2010. NationMaster. <www.nationmaster.com>.

"Young and Unmarried Yemeni Women More Likely to Pursue Career and Financial Independence." 2010. Newsdesk. Wowelle. 12 March. <http//wowelle.com>.

"Yemen Remittances Total $1.5 billion." 2011. Al-Shorfa. 8 January. <alshorfa.com>.

Zakaria, Fareed. 2010. "The Jihad Against the Jihadis." *Newsweek.* 22 February.

Ziad, Waleed. 2005. "Jihad's Fresh Face." *New York Times.* 16 September.

Zoepf, Katherine. 2008. "Deprogramming Jihadists." *New York Times,* 9 November.

Zogby, John. 2001. "American Muslim Poll, November-December 2001." Washington, D.C.: Zogby International. <www.amperspective.com>.

# INDEX

# ABOUT THE AUTHOR

Dr. Margaret Nydell is a widely respected scholar and professor of Modern Standard Arabic, Arabic dialectology, and many Arabic regional dialects. She was a visiting professor at Georgetown University and an Arabic linguist for the Foreign Service Institute and the U.S. Department of State, and has directed the latter's School of Advanced Arabic Training in Tunis, Tunisia. She has also headed several Arabic materials development projects and directed a summer Arabic program in Tangier, Morocco.

Dr. Nydell's publications include *Saudi Arabic Basic Course* (1975), *Arabic Dialect Identification Course* (1993), *Syrian Arabic Through Video* (1995), and a six-book series *From Modern Standard Arabic to the [regional Arabic] Dialect.* Dialects in the series include Levantine, Egyptian, Iraqi, Gulf, Moroccan, and Libyan. Many of Dr. Nydell's language books are in use as textbooks.

Dr. Nydell currently lectures on Arab cultural orientation for numerous government and private organizations. She holds a PhD in applied linguistics and a master's degree in Arabic, both from Georgetown University. She has lived and worked in Morocco, Saudi Arabia, and Tunisia, and Cairo.